BLOOD JUSTICE

BLOOD JUSTICE

The Lynching of
Mack Charles Parker

Howard Smead

OXFORD UNIVERSITY PRESS
New York   Oxford

Oxford University Press

Oxford New York Toronto
Delhi Bombay Calcutta Madras Karachi
Petaling Jaya Singapore Hong Kong Tokyo
Nairobi Dar es Salaam Cape Town
Melbourne Auckland

and associated companies in
Beirut Berlin Ibadan Nicosia

First published in 1986 by Oxford University Press, Inc.,
200 Madison Avenue, New York, New York 10016

First issued as an Oxford University Press paperback, 1988

Oxford is a registered trademark of Oxford University Press

Library of Congress Cataloging-in-Publication Data
Smead, Howard.
Blood justice.
Bibliography: p.   Includes index.
1. Parker, Mack Charles.   2. Lynching—Mississippi—Case studies.   I. Title.
HV6465.M7S64 1986   364.1′34   86-8720
ISBN-0-19-504121-6 (alk. paper)
ISBN-0-19-505429-6 (ppbk.)

9 8 7 6 5 4 3
Printed in the United States of America

For My Mother and Father

Contents

Illustrations follow page 106

Introduction

For well over a century white people lynched black people in this country with virtual impunity. The specter of the frenzied mob lashing a protesting black to a fence post and, after piling wood at his feet, meeting his pleas with curses and gasoline loomed large over black Americans. Nothing struck a sharper fear into the soul than the nauseating tale of bloodthirsty whites hanging a pregnant black woman from a nearby tree, cutting out her baby, and ripping it apart as its mother slowly twisted in the evening breeze; or the tale of a mob celebrating the lynching of a rapist by mutilating the body and saving the toes, fingers, and other appendages for souvenirs. The history of post-Civil War race relations is filled with such gruesome violence because after the demise of slavery, lynching became a vital underpinning of white supremacy. Whites erected the barriers of segregation behind the terrorism of the lynch mob, which forced freedmen to accommodate the emerging realities of Jim Crow or face the possibility of death. As for the public's conceptions, for too long lynching has been associated with the "Wild West," where the "good guys" lynched the "bad guys" because there was no court or legal system to enforce the law. This is extremely misleading.

Simply stated, lynching was extralegal punishment administered by a mob. And while lynching has long been synonymous with hanging, death by hanging was not at all necessary to a lynching. Many lynching victims were burned at the stake, dismembered, or shot to death. Nevertheless, all lynchings had several characteristics in common, and to varying degrees these features are what distinguish a post-Civil War lynching from a murder. A mob of at least three persons carried out the lynching. The mob acted without authority of law to punish its victim for some real or imagined legal, social, or racial transgression. The lynching resulted in the death or maiming of the victim. And those most often lynched were black men in the South.

Often the black victims of a lynching had not even been accused of a crime. The sad truth was that the mob usually wanted the lynching to carry a significance that transcended the specific act of punishment, turning the act into a symbolic rite in which the black victim became the representative of his race and, as such, was being disciplined for more than a single crime. Indeed, the guilt or innocence of the victim was always far less important than the act of lynching itself. The lynch mob, in its deadly act, was warning the black population not to challenge the supremacy of the white race.

Since Reconstruction several thousand blacks have been executed at the whim of white mobs in defiance of the law, because until this century white supremacy took precedence over the law. In fact, white supremacy was the unwritten law of the land. The results of a lynching, immediate and long-term, local and national, had consequences graver than the loss of one life. Whites had created a code of "justice" for blacks that often went under the rubric "Southern Justice." It wasn't until the 1934 lynching of Claude Neal that this began to change significantly.

The lynching of Claude Neal in Marianna, Florida, held special significance because of its effect on the national attitude toward lynching. That horrible affair outraged a previously indifferent white America, produced a shift in governmental policy, and led to the second and final major attempt to pass a federal anti-lynching law.* After the public spectacle of the Neal

---

* Claude Neal, a young black male, was lynched after having "confessed" to the murder of his young white neighbor, Lola Cannidy, with whom he had been having a love affair. The lynch mob, which grew into the thousands, pursued the sheriff and his deputies into Alabama in its attempt to seize Neal. Once Neal was taken from his cell in Brewton, Alabama, the mob subjected him to some ten hours of grievous torture involving castration and self-cannibalism before putting him to death. His death was followed by a race riot in the town of Marianna in which the white rioters attempted to drive all blacks out of the city limits. See James R. McGovern, *Anatomy of a Lynching: The Killing of Claude Neal* (Baton Rouge, 1982).

lynching, which made an utter mockery of law and order and equal justice under the law, national condemnation of the white mob and those who sought to explain away the practice of lynching by touting interracial rape as the prime cause was so widespread and uncompromising that local Southern leaders had to state openly their opposition to lynching to save face, if for no other reason. The more prominent Southern leaders had always publicly opposed lynching. Inflammatory statements by white supremacists like Theodore Bilbo, former governor and senator from Mississippi, or Cole Blease, former governor and senator from South Carolina—who in citing interracial rape as the justification for lynching said, "Whenever the Constitution comes between me and the virtue of the white women of South Carolina, I say 'to hell with the Constitution!' "—were usually reserved for local leaders and newspapers, people who operated away from the national eye. Like most prominent Southern leaders, the large city newspapers tended to oppose lynching.

After Claude Neal, *all* Southern leaders became more circumspect and even the Department of Justice, which had always remained aloof from lynching matters, began to instruct worried citizens who wrote to it how they might best seek help from the local and state authorities.[1] Although lynchings continued, they declined in number and the mobs became considerably more surreptitious. By the 1940s ritualized public executions were a thing of the past, and lynching practically disappeared altogether during the 1950s. The outrageous lynching of young Emmett Till in 1955 was the last reported lynching prior to that of Mack Charles Parker. The peculiar and gruesome nature of Till's lynching and the charade of a trial that followed embarrassed even the most determined Southern apologists.

The lynching of Mack Charles Parker in Poplarville, Mississippi, in 1959 was one of the last lynchings in America.* And even though it was not a direct throwback to the days of Claude Neal and earlier, it carried many of the notorious elements of past Southern lynchings: charges of interracial rape, a mob storming the jail, widespread and detailed knowledge of the lynching conspiracy before and after, and no punishment for the mob.

---

* In 1964, three civil rights workers were lynched in Philadelphia, Mississippi. In 1981 two men were lynched, one black, one white.

Because this lynching occurred so recently, it is still relatively accessible through interviews with contemporaries of the victim and members of the mob. Moreover, the increased federal involvement with civil rights and the full coverage by the national news media at the time enable us to look intimately into the dynamics of a lynch mob—who joined it, why they formed and carried out their crime, and, of equal importance, what effect the mob's act had on the community and the nation. An examination of the grisly details also sheds some light on why individual lynchings were so quickly purged from regional and national awareness.

It would be a mistake to assume that the study of one lynching ensures an adequate understanding of the subject, and certainly not everything learned from the account of this lynching can or should be applied universally. Nevertheless, much can be learned from a single, detailed analysis that contributes to the understanding of the process of lynching—its motivations and results. A look into the lynching in Poplarville offers a glimpse at the tidal forces at work in the South on the eve of the civil rights revolution. In this affair more than any other single event, the white South battled fiercely with tested methods to ward off inchoate post-World War II egalitarianism. In this case, in the pine barrens of Pearl River County and throughout the state of Mississippi, the extremists won. And their victory was neither short-lived nor Pyrrhic.

This lynching was just one of the countless, continual acts of violence perpetrated by whites against blacks in Mississippi during the 1950s. It was not isolated; it was part of an overall pattern of repression and retaliatory violence. Yet it *was* isolated in another sense. As a means of racial oppression it was passé. It involved the storming of a jail and the removal of a man from custody with the knowledge and cooperation of several local law-enforcement officers. Why did they feel compelled to assist the mob when the rural courtrooms of Mississippi were notoriously anti-black? What caused these seemingly desperate men to resort to such an anachronistic form of violence when they could have achieved the same end through slightly more subtle but equally effective means? Did the residents of Poplarville feel they were under siege? Or were there other, more personal reasons for the lynching?

In the past, outrage over a lynching often engendered hatred for the entire community where it occurred when only a small, or relatively small, number of people had been involved. There is a grave difference between the courtroom judgment and historical judgment, and in the end the historian is obligated to judge not only direct participants but also the society in which the events occurred. Yet it would be wrong to judge the white population of Poplarville with the same sort of monolithic attitude with which Southern whites, indeed almost all of white America, pre-judged blacks. Only the facts in this affair can determine the guilt or innocence of the people of Poplarville and Pearl River County. And the reader would do well to remember that this account is not an attempt to right past wrongs or to punish the guilty. It is an attempt to fill in a gap in our recent history, and with luck, to help us confront the *true* nature of racial discrimination.

The lynching of Mack Charles Parker was very much reminiscent of an era gone by, and as such represented a crude and erratic effort by whites to employ a once common means of safeguarding white supremacy. The lynching was not a spontaneous gathering but rather a planned and premeditated act of vigilante-style justice by men who felt that the federal judiciary meant to thwart the administration of justice on blacks accused of violent crimes against whites.

While most townspeople did not openly support the need for Parker's lynching before it occurred, they supported the reasons behind it. That support became an expression of local defiance against what they thought was a federal government basically hostile to their world. In this lynching, as with most other cases of racial violence in the South, especially after World War II, concern for justice was often a mask behind which lurked the misshapen face of white racism. The onslaught of adverse national and international publicity backed the town of Poplarville into a corner, making it appear unified in its defense of the lynching when in reality it was defending itself against hostile national and international criticism. It was not true, as Walter Prescott Webb said of Walter Van Tilburg Clark's fictional cowboy lynch mob in *The Ox-Bow Incident,* that "the mob is composed mainly of those who lack the physical or moral courage to oppose it or to refuse to be in it." In Poplarville those who lacked the courage to oppose the lynching stayed home or kept their heads down and their mouths shut.[2]

It has been the rule of recent history that few issues, events, or persons can easily withstand the tremendous, unblinking pressure of media scrutiny. And the people of Poplarville were no exception. Their overwhelming refusal to tolerate outside involvement in or examination of their affairs encouraged even harsher criticism than the town would have received had it been more receptive to outsiders. However, events during the aftermath of the lynching drove the people in Poplarville and throughout Mississippi to the reluctant conclusion that there were better ways to maintain white supremacy. As we learn about the lives of the members of the mob and their victims, we reach the painful conclusion that the lynching of Mack Charles Parker was not simply the story of the lynching of a black man, it was the story of a man caught in the turmoil of his times.[3]

BLOOD JUSTICE

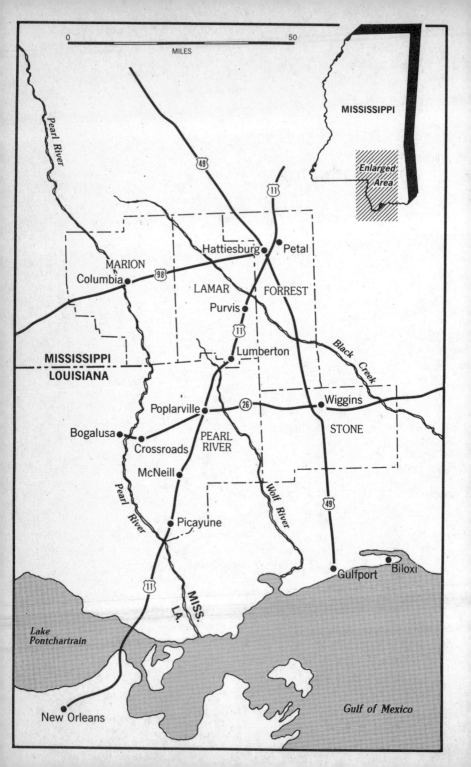

1

"Just Joe-Jacking Around"

The road from Poplarville to Lumberton wound through broad pine groves that covered the rolling hills of southern Mississippi with a thick green shroud. Interspersed among the miles of pines, tung trees thrived in the rich soil and helped make this section of the state one of the prettiest, and one of the more remote. Jimmy Walters, his wife, June, and their four-year-old daughter, Debbie Carol, were driving along an isolated stretch of Highway 11 toward their home in Petal outside of Hattiesburg on the evening of February 23, 1959. The night sky was dark; thick clouds obscured the moon; and the sharp wind whistling through the pines down onto the lonely road threatened to bring rain. The Walters had spent the evening at the Bogalusa home of Jimmy's brother Eddie, visiting Eddie's sick daughter. The evening ended sourly when Eddie refused to let Jimmy take his other daughter back to Hattiesburg to spend several days with her grandmother. Eddie protested he didn't feel like making the sixty-five-mile drive to pick her up, which angered Jimmy, and the two brothers had almost begun fighting. Besides that, Jimmy, who had picked up his family after work and come directly to Bogalusa, was tired from the long day and knew he had to be back at work early the next morning.[1]

As the wind began to drive sleet across the windshield of their car, Jimmy hunched over the wheel and pressed the pedal toward the floor. He wanted to be home by midnight and was determined not to be slowed by the weather. About 11:30 p.m., as they reached the top of the hill overlooking Little Black Creek, seven miles south of Lumberton and a mile south of the Lamar County line, their battered 1949 Dodge faltered and gave out a loud, metal-on-metal clank. Fearing the worst, Jimmy took the car out of gear and let it drift to the bottom of the hill, across a small concrete bridge before it rolled to a silent halt on a grassy shoulder so narrow that the left side of the car sat on the highway. A hasty check under the hood confirmed his fears: His car had thrown a main bearing and the engine had locked up. Jimmy tried pumping the gas and switching the ignition off and on just in case, but it was no use; the engine would not start. They were stranded. Little traffic passed along this way at such a late hour and the sheriff's patrols from Pearl River County rarely ventured so close to the county line unless trouble drew them there. It was a quiet Monday night and no one had reason to expect trouble, of any kind.[2]

Jimmy sat behind the wheel, staring out at the empty highway, unsure of just what he should do. He knew they would be unable to hitch a ride in the dark night and besides he couldn't for anything make his wife and little girl trudge into Lumberton in the rain and sleet. June was two months pregnant and Debbie was just about asleep anyway. No, there was no way around it; as tired as he was, he would have to walk alone into Lumberton to get help for his crippled car. To make matters worse, he was wearing only a lightweight jacket and low-cut shoes. He told June to stay with the car until he returned, "to roll the windows up tight, lock the doors and open them up for nobody," consoling her that he expected to be back in an hour with help. And there was always the chance a truck might come along and give him a lift. He kissed his wife goodbye and patted his daughter's head and, with a grim try at a reassuring smile, took off for Lumberton to call his stepfather. He walked as fast as he could on the right side of the road so he could hold his thumb out at every car and truck going north. When he had gone a hundred yards or so, he stopped and looked back at the car marooned at the side of the bleak road. Something inside him told him not to leave his family alone and unprotected, but he shrugged in resignation and turned back into the wind. As he reflected later, "That was the saddest mistake I'll ever live to make."[3]

Not fifteen minutes passed after Walters started for Lumberton before Mack Charles Parker and four of his friends spotted the Dodge sitting helplessly along the road. Parker, who was at the wheel of his brother's Chevy, slowed to a stop and jumped out, intending to see if the tires were worth stealing. Spotting the head of someone sitting alone in the darkness, he approached the car and shone his flashlight on the occupants: June huddled in fright on the passenger's side with her little girl asleep in her lap.[4] "When the first car stopped and shined their light into our car, I didn't know what to think." June said later, "I was surprised and kind of afraid because I couldn't tell if they were white or Negroes. Then they went away. It was quiet and I wondered if my husband was all right."[5]

As they headed off down the road, M. C., as he was known to his family and friends, turned to his companions and in the spirit of revelry said, "Why don't we stop and get some o' that white stuff?" The car fell quiet for a time, as each contemplated M. C.'s suggestion; then his brother-in-law, Curt Underwood, said, "Man, you're talkin' crazy!" From the back seat, Tommy Lee Grant told him emphatically, "Take us home, crazy man." Then the headlights picked up Jimmy Walters's slender form some distance down the road, his back against the driven sleet, his thumb out dejectedly. "Who's that sonofabitch?" the twenty-three-year-old Parker asked. "That's her man," Tommy Lee told him. "The man from the car."[6]

They sped on past Jimmy Walters, who tucked his hand back in his jacket and started walking again. M. C. watched him in the rear view mirror until Walters disappeared from sight. "What you know!" M. C. said, half laughing. "That sonofabitch better run faster or old M. C.'s gonna git back down there before he does. And when old M. C. gits off his nest, that white sonofabitch just ain't gonna recognize it." And with that, M. C. sped on into Lumberton.[7]

The five young men had spent the evening honky-tonking at several black bars on the other side of Poplarville, and as the twenty-year-old Curt Underwood phrased it, "just joe-jacking around."[8] Monday was payday in the pulp mills in and around Lumberton, and after cashing their checks at a local store, they headed out for a night of fun. Like the others, M. C. had changed from his work clothes into something more suitable for an evening's entertainment: white sweatshirt, dark Ivy League pants held up with a narrow black belt, and knee boots. As they had started out from Lumberton, M. C. had reached back and taken Tommy Lee's new cap off his head and placed it on his own, where it would stay for the rest of the evening. They stopped along the way for a half-gallon of "white lightning" and polished that off in rapid order. By the time the "shine" was gone, they had arrived at Bojack's, a black bar in Poplarville's colored section. Bojack's was closed, so they went over to Slim's, where they continued drinking while playing skin and tunk, a card game, with some of the other drinkers. As David Alfred and Norman "Rainbow" Malachy were being skinned of their pay, a sheriff's deputy on his nightly rounds came into Slim's. He complimented M. C. on his hat. Tommy Lee protested that it really belonged to him, but that he had lent it to M. C. The deputy warned the men not to drink too much. Mississippi was a dry state and he didn't want them getting into trouble.[9]

After the officer left, they decided to go to Purvis to see two whores known as the "Big Hams." But when they stopped for gas outside Poplarville and realized how late it was, they decided to forget about the Big Hams and call it a night. It was nearly midnight and they faced hangovers and hard work the next morning. On their way back to Lumberton, M. C. pulled over just south of Wolf Creek and they all got out to relieve themselves, all except Rainbow, who was passed out, dead drunk, in the back seat. They drove over the hill across the small concrete bridge at Little Black Creek and came upon the Walters car and farther down the road, Jimmy Walters heading toward Lumberton.[10]

After arriving at Lumberton's black district, M. C. dropped off Tommy Lee, Curt, and Rainbow. His own home was before David Alfred's, so he stopped there first. When questioned about his earlier threats, M. C. laughed at David's pleas, as he had laughed at his other friends' pleas not to return to the stranded car and the trouble that surely waited there. Reassuring David he had never really intended to go back anyway, Parker jumped from his car, leaving the lights on and the motor running, and ran inside to pick up his toy cap pistol. As he was leaving his house, he tripped and fell against the porch railing and cut his hand. Still woozy from all that he had drunk, M. C. began rummaging around the darkened porch for a cloth to bandage his hand. His banging around woke his mother, who came out in her nightgown to see what the fuss was about. Realizing that her son had been drinking and intended to go out again, and very much aware of the stiff state laws on drunken driving, especially as enforced against blacks, she pleaded with him to stay home. But M. C. refused. He wrapped an old washrag around his hand and was soon backing away, leaving his mother standing in the stark headlights, watching. He stopped next at David Alfred's home to let him off.[11]

When David went inside and prepared for bed, his mother questioned him anxiously. "Son, who was that who took off out there so fast?" "It was M. C. Parker," David responded, and proceeded to tell her what M. C. had been promising to do. "Thank God, you didn't go with him," said his mother. She awakened her husband, who was a minister in a local Baptist church, and told him about M. C. They considered going to the sheriff, but the clergyman decided to wait until morning, hoping for M. C.'s sake it had been only the whiskey talking.[12]

An hour and a half after Jimmy Walters left his wife and daughter, M. C. Parker drove up behind the stranded car and what appeared to June Walters to be a middle-aged black man of medium build came to the door to ask her if she needed help. The man had a cloth or bandage wrapped around his left hand and a gun in the other hand. "I didn't see him until he stopped his car behind ours," June said. "He came up to the window where I was sitting in the front seat and surprised me. The windows were closed and the doors were locked and I was holding the door on my side, so he couldn't get in. He asked me if I needed any help. I told him no thank you."[13]

"Open up and get out," M. C. said, pushing the gun against the window so she could see it clearly.[14]

Realizing he intended to do them harm, June told him that her husband had gone for help and would be returning any minute. "You mean that white sonofabitch that's walkin' up the street?" he snarled, and with the butt of his pistol and several blows, he smashed the vent window. June screamed and covered Debbie's eyes with her hand to shield them from the flying glass. Startled by her mother's screams, Debbie started to cry. A hand shot through the vent and reached down to unlock the door. "I am an escaped convict and have killed five people," Parker said in a gruff voice. "Two more won't make any difference." Pulling the door open, he pulled June's blue and white silk scarf from her head and looped it around her neck. "Please don't hurt my little girl," June cried. "You white trash bitch, I'm going to fuck you," he hissed. When she drew away he shouted, "Don't scream or I'll kill you and the little girl too."[15]

He took his cloth and hastily wiped the fingerprints from all the places he had touched and ordered June and her daughter to get out. When she refused, he pulled Debbie out and dragged June by her legs from the car onto the ground. Debbie started to cry harder and he told June to silence her. June tried but couldn't. Debbie only cried louder. To silence her, he hit her across the forehead with his pistol. Then, as June described later, "He made us get into his car. It was dirty. We both got in his car on his side and he made me sit in the middle. He started driving down the highway and I begged him not to kill us." He grabbed June in a headlock and pulled her close to him.[16] They drove down the highway on the left side of the road and turned onto Black Creek Ford Road, an old lumbering road just a few hundred feet inside the Pearl River County line, about a mile from the Walters car. They went half a mile down the sandstone road to a shallow dip canopied by trees. "When he turned off onto a narrow road just wide enough for one car, he told me he had to meet someone there. At first he told me he had to meet his father. I asked him if his father knew he had broken out of prison and he said, 'No.' Then he said he had to wait for a white man who was his partner. He told me not to be frightened. He kept pointing the gun at me and clicking it and he told me his arm was hurt and his hand was cut."[17]

"When he first came up and told us he had escaped from prison, I thought he was just going to use us as hostages or something. I never did think about him raping me, it never entered my mind. I was afraid he was going to kill us because he threatened to kill both of us if I didn't keep my little girl quiet." He stopped the car, switched off the lights, and got out so that Debbie could climb over her mother and get out. The door on the passenger side was broken, he explained. In nearly total darkness, he led Debbie by the arm to the back of the car and told her to stay there and be quiet. Returning to June, he stood over her, wrapping his gun in the cloth, "so he wouldn't leave any fingerprints on the gun," she thought. He tossed it onto the floor, but changed his mind and threw it into the back seat. "I'm pregnant!" June protested, worrying instinctively something might happen to her unborn child. "That don't matter," he said impatiently. "I've been told that before." He put his arms around June's neck and began kissing her and said, "If you don't do what I want you to I'll kill you right now." M. C. told her to lie down on the front seat. She did. He told her to pull up her dress. When she did, he tore her underpants off. Forcing his hand between her thighs, he told her to spread her legs. Fighting back tears she obeyed and rolled her head back and closed her eyes as the man lowered himself onto her. "When he started to rape me, I screamed and he jerked my scarf off my head again and gagged me with it. Then he began choking me with his hands. I kept trying to fight him off but it didn't do no good. He said, 'I've not been with a woman for a long time and I'm pretty hot.'" Debbie stood outside, in the rain and out of sight, crying the entire time. "He was dirty and his hands were greasy just like he had been working on a car. And he smelled bad. He had left grease marks on our car door when he broke in. He got grease on me and some on my underclothes and my legs where he had put his hands on them."[18]

"I kept begging him to stop and leave me alone. I told him that my husband had some wine that had not been opened in our car and that he could have that." After what seemed like forever, he withdrew to his haunches and told her to get out of his car and walk straight ahead and not to look back. "'If you or the kid looks back,' he said, 'I'll kill you both.'" June opened the car door and got out, and, taking Debbie's hand, headed into the woods. "I didn't look back until I got around a curve where he couldn't see me. When he flashed on his lights, my little girl looked back but nothing happened." After the sound of the car faded away entirely, leaving only the wind beating mournfully through the trees, they started toward the highway for help. "But we started out in the wrong direction. I was afraid he was going to come back." They walked for several hundred yards the wrong way, stumbling into mud holes in the darkness. "When we finally did get back to the highway it began to rain again and I was afraid no one was going to stop. I didn't break down until we got to the highway. I had to keep hold of myself for Debbie's sake."[19]

Once on the highway, they began walking north toward Lumberton. June was in a daze after her attack and little Debbie, with a small gash on her forehead, was bewildered and upset. Neither realized they were walking down the center of the highway, and when a Mack tractor-trailer came over the hill, the driver hit the brakes and skidded on the wet pavement to avoid them.[20] "I've been raped by a nigger," she told the driver when he opened his door and gazed apprehensively down on them. "Please help me to get to Lumberton to my husband."[21]

June held Debbie close to her during the ride and made only mumbled responses to the trucker's anxious questions. She repeated that she had been raped and that her husband was somewhere in Lumberton calling for help. As they pulled to a stop at Lumberton's only stoplight, June looked out the window and saw Jimmy talking on the phone in the all-night truck stop at the side of the road. "There he is!" she exclaimed. She began crying hysterically. The trucker helped Debbie and June down from the truck and the little girl raced across the lot to her father. "When I saw how greasy June was," Jimmy said, "I knew right off something horrible had happened." June collapsed in her husband's arms and he had to carry her back to the truck. It was from Debbie that Jimmy found out that his wife had been attacked. "We wandered around in the woods forever, Daddy," Debbie told him.[22]

The man on duty at the truck stop called the night patrolman, who called the highway patrol and Lamar County Sheriff C. H. Hickman. Jimmy, June, and Debbie waited in the truck for the officers to arrive. When Hickman came, he rushed June to the small hospital in Lumberton, where a doctor examined her and inoculated her against venereal disease. He also treated her for bruises on her arm, suffered when she was dragged from the car. The examination confirmed that sexual penetration had been complete, but the doctor reassured her that she was in no danger of losing her baby.[23]

While June was seeing the doctor, twenty sheriff's deputies and highway patrolmen arrived at the hospital and began questioning Jimmy and the truck driver. Lumberton City Marshal Ham Slade telephoned Pearl River County Sheriff W. Osborne Moody, who immediately came to Lumberton to begin an investigation. While at the hospital, Mrs. Walters gave her first description of the rapist. He was, she thought, a middle-aged black man, about thirty-nine to forty years old, weighing 160 to 170 pounds, approximately five feet, ten inches tall, and he wore a dirty and peculiarly shaped brimless cap. She also gave a detailed description of her assailant's dark car, its torn seat, its broken dome light, its broken horn ring, and the broken door on the passenger side. The police drove the Walters family back to the spot where the car was parked, and from there June directed them to the spot where she had been raped. Tire tracks stood out in the mud on the seldom-used road and officers even found footprints belonging to June and Debbie. It was a difficult time for June, telling and retelling her story, pointing out where exactly this happened or that took place. After answering police questions and making arrangements to have the car towed, the exhausted and distraught family finally returned to their home at 5:30 a.m.[24]

Sheriff Moody contacted the Mississippi and Louisiana state highway patrols, which quickly set up a dragnet in the lower bistate area and notified law enforcement officers in southern Mississippi and Louisiana to watch for a man fitting the description of the rapist. Mississippi highway patrolmen set up road blocks on all the roads around Lumberton and Poplarville, and police officers flooded into Lumberton. Sheriff Moody insisted from the outset that the crime had been the work of a local man because he seemed to know the roads well and had no trouble fading away afterward. The dragnet led to the apprehension of about thirty blacks that night, all of whom officers herded into Lumberton for a police lineup. Police roused many of these individuals from their homes and removed others from their cars at the various roadblocks. Any black male not old and feeble was subject to interrogation by sheriff's deputies or by the state highway patrol.[25]

In the morning two tips from vastly different sources sent Lamar County officers looking for Mack Charles Parker. Over in Pearl River County, where the crime had occurred, Poplarville Night Marshal Petey Carver remembered seeing a car fitting the description in Poplarville earlier that night with several black men in it. Marshal B. F. Orr began asking around and quickly learned the identity of two of the five men in the car. He relayed this information to Sheriff Moody and Ham Slade in Lumberton. But before officers could pick up Curt Underwood and Rainbow Malachy, David Alfred's father visited Sheriff Hickman. "M. C. Parker is your man," the Reverend Mr. Alfred told him. "The other boys got in about 12:30. My boy told us then he was afraid of it. I shoulda come to you then, but I didn't think he'd do it. M. C. got in after three."[26]

At 9:45 a.m. Ham Slade and several of his deputies went to Parker's home. Parker's mother answered the door and Slade and his deputies went inside and found Parker sleeping. He was so hung over that he had been unable to get up and go to work. They took him by the arms and dragged him out of the house and across the road to the woods. They hauled Parker back into the woods out of sight and began beating him.

Parker's screams could be heard several houses away. His mother stood at the front door crying for her son. After working Parker over, trying to wrest a confession from him—which they failed to get—Slade and his deputies put him in the squad car and drove away. At the Lumberton jail Slade charged Parker with drunken driving, improper car tags, and possession of an expired driver's permit.[27]

As soon as the sheriff hauled M. C. away, his terrified mother, Liza, sent a neighbor to Tommy Lee Grant's cabin to find out why. Tommy Grant came to Liza Parker with the sad news. "They've got him for rape," he told her. "For raping a white woman." Through her tears she said, "Let's pray for him." Liza Parker knew well what might happen to her son even if the charges proved completely false. She had no way of knowing yet that M. C. had not confessed to rape or abduction and that police were holding him on the lesser and seemingly insignificant charges—charges that scarcely warranted a severe beating—until they felt they could make the other charges stick.[28]

Marshal Slade called Jimmy Walters to tell him he had several suspects in custody and to ask him to bring June down to identify them. June was extremely reluctant to go, but Jimmy insisted she had to go if they were ever to bring her assailant to justice. Jimmy was worried about June's health. She had been extremely upset when they returned to Jimmy's mother's house in Hattiesburg and she seemed on the verge of hysteria as he and his mother tried to calm her. Finally, after talking it over with her own mother, June agreed to go.[29]

When they arrived at the small jail in Lumberton they were greeted by Bud Gray, of the Mississippi highway patrol, and one of his men, along with Ham Slade. Bud Gray led them to a back room, where through a small window that reminded Jimmy of an old-time bank teller's window they saw five black men lined up against a wall, waiting for June to view them. Jimmy was worried that June would break down as soon as she walked into the sheriff's office, but to his surprise she didn't appear nearly as nervous as he had expected. Bud Gray ordered each of the black men to repeat the words, "You white trash bitch, I'm going to fuck you." Each of the men repeated the line with no effect on June. Then they came to Mack Charles Parker, the last man in the lineup. His face was bruised and bloody from the beating he had taken a few hours earlier. Bud Gray ordered him to repeat the words. Parker started shaking all over—his head, his arms, his body twitched in fright. He looked at June wide-eyed and mumbled the words. "Louder," shouted Gray. At over two hundred pounds Gray was a commanding physical presence in any room. His voice echoed; Parker began shaking violently. Looking down at the floor, he repeated the words once again.[30]

"You're gonna say it loud, you're gonna say it clear!" Gray shouted at him. Parker raised his head slightly and repeated the words, less meekly this time. Sheriff Hickman, who was standing with the prisoners, drew his billy club and threatened to use it on Parker. Parker threw his head back and shouted, "You white trash bitch, I'm gonna fuck you!" When he did so, June looked at Parker in horror and her mouth dropped open. She collapsed against Jimmy. "That's him, that's him. That's . . . him."[31]

Thinking his wife was about to faint, Jimmy put his arms around her and held her against him. Bud Gray unsnapped his holster and drew his pistol. It was a .38 caliber six-shot revolver. Holding it by the barrel, he presented the butt end to Jimmy. "Son," he said, "you got a gun or do you want mine?" Jimmy looked at the pistol dumbfounded. In his anxious state, it looked more like a cannon. A strange, unreal feeling came over him. The man he believed had raped his wife was standing just a few feet away and he knew he could point the pistol at him and pull the trigger with impunity, but Jimmy lowered his head. "No," he told Gray. "I don't believe in violence. I want him to stand trial. So does my wife." Gray held his pistol out a moment longer before returning it to his holster and walking away. In spite of his strong conviction that Mack Charles Parker was indeed his wife's rapist, Walters did not want to see the man executed in such a fashion. And he certainly did not want to be the executioner. "I didn't want the man killed. I didn't want nobody killed," he later said. "I wanted him to be brought to trial where people could understand what things were—what we went through, what June went through, and the baby. Besides, I'm not a killer anyway. I coulda blown him in half." But, "I couldn'ta no more lifted that thing for nothin' in the world. I'm not a killer. I'm just not. You call me what you want to. You call me a coward or whatever you want to. I'm just not a killer."[32]

When asked to make a physical identification, June responded hesitantly, "He looks like the one." She refused to make a positive identification because she was not completely sure. The night had been dark and moonless. "I believe he's the one," she said, "but I can't be positive because I was scared to death and there wasn't much light. I believe he's the one."[33] She claimed that the slight Parker's physical appearance fit the rapist's general description, but that her attacker had been swearing and using abusive language, which gave her a lasting impression of his voice. Except for when he shouted the threat, Parker's voice was entirely different. She also told officials that she could not be sure her assailant's car was the same car that pulled up earlier, although she agreed Parker's car looked like the rapist's vehicle. A check of tire tracks indicated that the marks left by the rapist's car at the scene of the crime were similar to those of Parker's black 1950 Chevrolet. The light rain had washed away enough of the tracks to prevent positive identification. "It might be the car," said Sheriff Moody. "We have some other suspects and we are following them up but we feel this one is more like the one who did it." A check for fingerprints failed to reveal anything further incriminating Parker. Officials never located the pistol that June claimed he had brandished, even after a thorough search of the Parker residence. Their search did turn up a cap pistol similar to a .38 revolver, but the toy seemed much too fragile to break a car window.[34]

The police held Parker, impounded his car, and released the other men rounded up in the dragnet. Although they subsequently picked up his companions three times to question them about their activities on the night of the rape, officers had what they considered strong evidence that Parker had, in fact, raped June Walters. The mood in Lumberton quickly grew ugly, and the highway patrol escorted Parker to the jail at Jackson ostensibly to administer a lie detector test to him, but in reality to protect him. Late Tuesday, Sheriff Moody told reporters, "Feeling is very high about this thing. We're not saying where we have him now. We don't want any trouble, any violence. There was quite a crowd around when we left Lumberton. This thing could be a bombshell."[35]

Mack Charles Parker dénied outright that he had had anything to do with the rape of June Walters, a position he adhered to tenaciously throughout the events that followed. At the outset of his arrest, he admitted being in the area during the incidents, explaining over and over to police officials that he had been returning from Poplarville with several of his friends. Nevertheless, Sheriff Moody filed rape and abduction charges against Parker on Thursday. Moody chose not to indict as accessories Parker's four companions on that night: Curt Underwood, 20; David Al-

fred, 24; Tommy Lee Grant, 22; and Rainbow Malachy, 22. All
were questioned and released shortly after being apprehended.

On February 28, two Lamar County sheriff's deputies picked
up Malachy and tried to force a statement from him linking
Parker with the rape. They escorted Malachy out of the jail and
into a waiting squad car, where Malachy noticed a sawed-off
shotgun, an illegal police weapon, and a tape recorder. But
Malachy, who had been beaten by Sheriff Hickman the morning
after the rape, clung to the same story—that he had gotten
drunk and passed out in the back seat and did not remember
anything after they stopped for gas. He told them he got home
after midnight and Parker helped him into his house. Hickman
had earlier accused Malachy of lying and charged that Malachy
had seen the parked car with a woman and child in it and had
heard Parker say he intended to rape her. After repeating this
charge again and again, with no response from Malachy, the two
sheriff's deputies released Malachy and told him to go home. He
went first to get his shoes shined, and then to Eddie's Bar in
Lumberton, where he met Curt Underwood. Later that evening
as Malachy and Underwood were drinking beer and quietly discussing the events of the past several days, Sheriff Hickman
stormed into the bar and ordered everyone to leave, but Hickman stopped Malachy on his way out the door. Hickman
grabbed Malachy and shouted at him, "Nigger, I ought to whip
your black ass. You told me a lie." He handcuffed Malachy, the
first time the young man had ever been in handcuffs. Then he
punched him in the face. Malachy fell against the door, swearing
he had told the truth. He told Hickman he could kill him if he
wanted to, but he wasn't going to "lie on Parker." Hickman
struck Malachy several more times while he was handcuffed.
Then Hickman pushed Malachy through the door of Eddie's
Bar, striking him on the back of his head with his billy club as
they went out. Malachy collapsed onto the ground in front of the
bar. Hickman kicked his right leg, ordering him to get up. A girl
standing in the crowd of onlookers screamed at Malachy,
"You're going to die tonight." The sheriff wheeled around and
screamed at her, "Shut up." Sheriff Hickman and Sheriff Moody
drove Malachy to the Lumberton City Hall, where they questioned him again. The two men discussed whether to try to force
a statement from Malachy, but decided to question him again the
next day in the belief that he might change his mind after a
night in jail. The following morning Malachy gave them the

same statement. Malachy had known Parker ever since he was a kid. He said he'd never heard Parker boast about attacking white women and that to his knowledge Parker had never been involved in any sex crimes.[36]

Curt Underwood—who fled Eddie's Bar after Sheriff Hickman threw Malachy through the door and spent several days hiding in the swamps in terror—had first been questioned the morning after the rape and released still unaware of why officers had interrogated him. Upon his release he heard on the local radio station and then from friends in Lumberton what had happened, that authorities considered him, Parker, and the others suspects in the rape. Local law officers picked up Underwood two more times before the incident at Eddie's Bar and subjected him to intense questioning, threatening personal injury if he did not cooperate. It was during the third and last session with officials that he succumbed to the pressure and signed a statement incriminating Parker. "They made me say it," Underwood later complained. "They put those words in my mouth. Besides they were all threatening to whip me and beat me and throw me in jail." Law officers never actually beat Underwood to extract the statement from him. Fearing for his own life, he admitted seeing the Walters's car stranded along the highway and admitted that Parker stopped and shone his flashlight on its occupants. Underwood further related to police Parker's stated intention to return to the car to attack the woman. With prodding by police, he supplied more details, which Tommy Lee Grant and David Alfred, although reluctant to incriminate their friend, corroborated. Rainbow Malachy never changed his story.[37]

Following the statement by Underwood, Pearl River County Sheriff Osborne Moody, in whose county the rape had occurred, issued a statement of his own asserting that Parker's four friends had "blown the lid off" the Walters rape case. "We have our man," he claimed proudly. He said that M. C. Parker, charged with kidnapping and criminal assault, would remain at the Hinds County jail in Jackson until his trial in April.[38] While in Jackson, Parker underwent several lie detector tests. To the chagrin of police officers, the tests kept registering negatively or inconclusively. They insisted the frightened Parker repeat the tests until they confirmed what everyone already believed. Still, the results remained unfavorable to the state's case, so authorities refused to release the results. Officials never cited the tests as part of their "conclusive" proof of Parker's guilt. Moody felt he had enough evidence to file successful charges against Parker anyway, even without the use of the results from the lie detector tests.[39]

Meanwhile, with Parker up in Jackson languishing in the Hinds County jail, physically and emotionally exhausted after days of interrogation and mistreatment by police officers, whites in Hattiesburg, Lumberton, and Poplarville began grumbling that something ought to be done to prevent another "black fiend" from repeating what Mack Charles Parker had done. They were in no mood to quibble over so-called technicalities. For them Parker's admission that he had driven along the road between Poplarville and Lumberton the night of the rape, the similarity of the cars, and the statements by his friends pointed the finger of guilt at him.[40]

Parker's four companions refused to change their stories and tried hard to stay away from whites as much as possible. But other blacks, when well away from white ears, made it no secret they considered Parker to be innocent, that Underwood especially had lied to save himself from a beating. For blacks, Parker's troubles became just one more example of the oppression they lived under daily. They were sure Parker would not, could not, receive a fair trial before the notorious Sebe Dale, that whites had already decided M. C.'s guilt.[41]

At home in her three-room shack in Lumberton's poverty-stricken black section, Parker's forty-three-year-old mother, Liza, despaired for her son's life. Born and raised in nearby Angi, Louisiana, she was no stranger to Southern justice. Her son had always been a loyal family member. He began giving her part of his meager wages to help meet expenses when her husband had died three years earlier. She was sure M. C. was innocent and set out to find a way to secure him a fair trial, at which he could prove his innocence. Friends and relatives trickled into her ramshackle cabin off a muddy, rut-filled dirt road on the northern city limits of Lumberton, offering suggestions, sympathy, and in some cases financial assistance. Everyone agreed that unless her son received help from the black community, the white legal system would surely convict him. Friends advised the distraught woman to hire a white lawyer; since M. C. would be tried before white people, maybe that would help. At least it might improve his chances for a fair trial. The next day she approached every white attorney in Lumberton and Poplarville seeking legal representation for her son. No one was willing to take the case, and several of the lawyers told her they felt her son was guilty and they hoped he got the death sentence. A week after police took her son to Jackson, Mrs. Parker went to see a well-known black attorney named R. Jess Brown, in Vicksburg, whom she had heard of through his involvement in several Mississippi civil rights cases. She broke down and cried as she told him the ugly story of her son's arrest and now, she added, she was suffering the added indignity of not being allowed to visit him in jail. As moved as he was, Brown disliked working for free, even for a good cause. He told Mrs. Parker he would take the case for a $1500 fee, $500 of which she must give him as a retainer. The rest she could pay as she could. Like most blacks of the area, the Parkers lived in extreme poverty, and Liza was hard pressed to feed and clothe her children, let alone hire a lawyer. Nevertheless, she managed to scrape together about $180 by borrowing from friends and relatives, and hired Brown to defend her son. Brown took the case reluctantly and later enlisted the only other black attorney in Mississippi, Jack H. Young, Jr., to aid him.[42]

Finding a competent attorney was one thing, convincing people of her son's innocence was a different matter. Liza resented the picture the papers had painted of him, a picture considerably embellished by local wags, all of whom were white, all of whom found Parker to be an uppity smart aleck who talked back to white people.[43] "Mack was a good boy," she insisted. "He's never been in trouble before. I asked him, 'Did you do it?' and he said he didn't." Parker had no record of previous arrests in either Pearl River County, where the rape occurred, or in Lamar County, where he lived. He was born in Walthall County near Tylertown and moved at age five to Lumberton, about fifty miles away. He spent the typical childhood of a Southern black, attending the segregated elementary school and starting but never completing high school. He joined the army at age eighteen, and served for two years. On two occasions he went before a military court for "expropriating government property." His first trial, in 1956 at Camp Gordon, Georgia, during his basic training, resulted in a short stay in the guardhouse; the second, a year later at Fort Crowder, Missouri, led to a general discharge and an early exit from the military.[44]

After returning to Lumberton, Parker was idle for a time, then upon the death of his father got a job driving a truck for a local pulpwood cutter. Business often took him into Poplarville, but

he had limited contact with the people there. He had been working steadily for over two years and had acquired the reputation
of a hardworking young man who was loyal to his family and
avoided run-ins with the white law. He had begun seeing a
former childhood friend, Mattie Pearl Ott, when he returned to
Lumberton, and the two were married shortly after he started
working. But their marriage was doomed to failure, like that of
Parker's sixteen-year-old sister, Dolores, who had recently left
her husband, Curt Underwood, and returned home with her
baby son, Peanut. The pressures of building a marriage in the
already overcrowded cabin drove the two apart, and Mattie Pearl
eventually went back to her parents. With his brother Elmo away
in the service, it fell to Parker to support his mother and youngest brother, Charles, age four, plus Dolores and her child, a
grave responsibility to place on any twenty-three-year-old, especially one with a recently failed marriage. Parker felt the loss of
his young wife and had recently spoken to his mother about
marrying Ruth White, the daughter of Ruby Lee White, who
lived down the lane from the Parkers. Ruby Lee thought M. C.
"a decent sort. He's not a troublemaker. He did his work and
came home at night." In fact few people in the black community
spoke ill of Parker at all. Only one person in a position to know
had reservations about him. Curt Underwood's mother felt that
Parker, her son Curt, and their friends were "rough livers."
Ruth Underwood referred to them as a "hard-drinking crew of
youngsters that did what came to their mind."[45]

This was the description of Parker that found its way into the
white communities in southern Mississippi and made it difficult
for his attorneys to refute the circumstantial evidence that implicated Parker. They also had to contend with adverse public opinion. In addition, the fact that Parker was black and June Walters
was white distorted all other factors in the case and relegated
them to a secondary status. The case was virtually impossible to
win at trial. Brown concluded, quite understandably, that a defense based upon the merits of the case had little chance for
success. He felt that any who might be chosen to serve on the
jury had already made up their minds. And what was worse, the
trial judge, sixty-three-year-old Sebe Dale, was a disciple of the
late Theodore G. Bilbo and an active opponent of school integration and of the civil rights movement that had been percolat-
ing in the South. Like the well-known Bilbo, Dale was a virulent
racist. He belonged to the white Citizens Council and was a

charter member of the State Sovereignty Commission. He swore
to uphold the cause of white supremacy against the onslaught of
meddlesome outsiders, the NAACP, and Yankee liberals.[46]

The lean, bespectacled, popular jurist was born one of twelve
children in the tiny hamlet of Hathorn. His family first settled in
southern Missisippi in 1800 and his grandfather had been killed
at Gettysburg. Dale's love of the red-clay hills stemmed from his
family's long history in the area. He was well liked and highly
respected by his white constituents. He lived in nearby Columbia, where he shared law offices with his son. He combed his
gray hair straight back from his forehead and had a habit of
wearing a dark blue suit, a bright red tie with a matching pocket
handkerchief, and a tie clasp with the scales of justice on it—all
trademarks of his mentor, Bilbo. Dale's usual retort to questions
about his sartorial allegiance to "The Man" was that his dress did
not prove a thing. "The only thing it means is I'm getting old
enough to wear loud ties." Nevertheless, when Dale dressed in
the Bilbo manner, the meaning was lost on no one.*[47]

The razor-tongued judge had a perfect memory and often
quoted election results from previous years, particularly his own.
After World War I and a brief stint in the Texas oilfields, he
won election as district attorney in southern Mississippi. Later,
even though he lacked a formal legal education, he served two
terms as judge of the Fifteenth Circuit Court, representing five
counties including Pearl River. In 1955 his outspoken racism
and his inability to curtail his anti-federal tirades cost him the
lieutenant governorship under the comparatively moderate segregationist J. P. Coleman, who had favored Carroll Gartin for
the office. When Gartin won, Dale developed a grudge against
Coleman he never overcame. Greatly embittered by his foray
into state politics, he stood in 1958 for his second successful

---

* Dale had the dubious distinction of personally pulling the trap in the last hanging in
Mississippi. In 1940 as district attorney he had fought for and won the death sentence for
one of two black men who had ambushed and killed a law officer. Dale sought the death
penalty for both men, but one man turned state's evidence and received a life sentence as
a reward. On the gallows, just before the execution of the other man, Hilton Thornberry,
Dale said to him coldly, "You know that it's because of the government that your partner
got off and you're hanging." The crying man responded, "Yes, I know." It was such a
pitiful scene that the sheriff was unable to send him to his death. Dale impulsively
grabbed the lever and pulled the trap. The rope was too long. Thornberry kicked and
gurgled for eighteen minutes with his feet just scraping the ground until he died. His
death was so horrible that Mississippi afterward switched to the electric chair for capital
punishment.

reelection as circuit court judge. In the opinion of Southern whites, the county's case against Parker would be in sympathetic hands in Sebe Dale's courtroom.[48]

After taking on the case, R. Jess Brown telephoned Pearl River County attorney William Stewart to request a preliminary hearing on the charges against Parker. Stewart advised him against this because it would mean bringing Parker back to Poplarville in the midst of intense local feeling. Parker's safety, Stewart said, would be in jeopardy. Brown withdrew the request on March 17 explicitly because of Stewart's statements to him about the danger of bringing Parker into Pearl River County too early. An all-white Pearl River County grand jury indicted Parker on April 13 for rape and two counts of kidnapping after hearing evidence from police officials and testimony from all of Parker's friends except Rainbow Malachy. Said David Alfred after the hearing, "They don't want to talk to old drunk Rainbow." Two days later the highway patrol transferred Parker from Jackson to the Pearl River County Jail so he could appear before Judge Dale on Friday, April 17. M. C. showed youthful bravado as deputies led him from his cell in the courthouse to the crowded second-floor courtroom, where he stood by confidently as R. Jess Brown pleaded him not guilty to each charge. Parker's casual defiance and affected nonchalance, born of his age and not his race, promptly alienated Judge Dale and set the courtroom abuzz with indignation. Tension increased when Brown then moved that Dale drop the charges against Parker because the grand jury had excluded blacks. Dale took this motion under advisement, later rejecting it. Brown also entered a motion for a change of venue, stating that Parker's life was in danger, and filed another motion to dismiss the case on grounds that blacks were excluded from the trial jury list in Pearl River County. He argued that the absence of blacks from either jury deprived Parker of his right to a trial before a jury of his peers. Brown subpoenaed the voting records to support his claim of discriminatory jury selection procedures, arguing with ample justification that the absence of any black voters in a county with a 25 percent black population indicated a systematic exclusion of blacks from the voter rolls and jury lists.[49] Only fourteen blacks were registered to vote in Pearl River County and none of them had paid the poll tax. Consequently, they were not eligible to vote or to serve on the jury.

Brown raised the issue of blacks on the grand and petit juries because of a recent ruling by the U.S. Court of Appeals for the Fifth Circuit that reversed the decision of the all-white jury in Vaiden, Mississippi, that had convicted Robert Lee Goldsby of murdering a white woman. The federal appeals court voided the conviction because no blacks had been on the jury. The thirty-three-year-old St. Louis-born Robert Lee Goldsby was a school-teacher in Canton, Mississippi. In 1954 he was indicted, tried, and convicted of the shotgun slaying of a white woman in Vaiden in Carroll County. His second trial in front of another all-white jury in Vaiden led to a second death sentence. Goldsby won several stays of execution before a jury with one black sentenced him to life imprisonment in 1961. Contrary to what the people in Pearl River County claimed, Goldsby never spent one day out of custody after he was first arrested in 1954. The appeals court ruling reversed his first conviction in March 1959. Had Parker gone to trial and been convicted and Brown subsequently appealed, the same appeals court that heard Goldsby's case would have heard Parker's.

This case provided perfect legal precedent for Brown's tactic, and he knew full well that an appeals court would have to throw out Parker's conviction. Once raised by Brown, the *Goldsby* case became a major topic of conversation in Poplarville as Parker's trial date neared. The *Goldsby* case stirred up a tremendous amount of ill will among Southern whites, most particularly those living in southern Alabama and southern Mississippi near the location of the murder and subsequent trial.[50] Whites feared, and quite rightfully so, that Parker and any other black tried before an all-white jury could have a guilty verdict reversed because of the appeals court decision. Parker's alleged crime—the rape of a pregnant white woman—inflamed public opinion to a dangerous level. In the minds of many whites, interracial rape ranked above murder in severity because of its sociological implications. Drawing on the unquestioned tradition of white supremacy, local residents were also outraged at the double-edged insult of a black attorney interrogating a white woman on the witness stand in open court and the possibility, however remote, that Parker might go free because of her testimony and a federal court ruling. All this was too much for some proud Southern whites to tolerate.[51]

As might have been expected, Dale threw out an additional motion to quash the indictment for lack of positive evidence and, after interviewing witnesses, both white and black, concluded that Parker would indeed receive a fair trial in Poplarville. He granted Brown's request that a special jury list of one hundred people be drawn up, which was customary in capital cases. Dale set the trial date for Monday, April 27. His final act of business for this day in the *Parker* case was to deny Brown's motion for a change of venue because of the "high feeling" around Poplarsville.[52]

Around midnight that night as Parker, unable to sleep after his long day in court, was playing cards with his cellmate, C. J. Mondy, the jailer, Jewel Alford, brough a white prisoner in and placed him in the cell directly below Parker's. Several times after being left alone, the new prisoner yelled up for Parker and Mondy to be quiet. A few hours later, Jewel Alford and several men returned for the prisoner. They asked him how he had rested. "Not very well," he replied, "because those damn boys upstairs were making too much noise." One of the men with Alford asked, "Where is that boy at?" Up above, the prisoner responded.

"You should have went up there and cut his damn throat."

"I wish I could have."

One of the other men added, with Mondy and Parker listening, "What are we going to do about this? Hell, if we don't do something about this, we won't be able to hold up for Mississippi."[53]

2

Some Proud Southern Whites

In 1959 Poplarville seemed a storybook town—quiet and peaceful. It received its name from "Poplar" Jim Smith, who had moved into the area after the Civil War and opened a small general store near the railroad tracks. The New Orleans and Northeastern used his store as a depot and, knowing his nickname, called it Poplarville Station. The image and the name stuck. Every Sunday the town's Baptist and Methodist churches were filled with people who were by all accounts good, God-fearing Christians. Some of them worked in the small shops and garages in and around town. The main occupation for most was farming; many others worked for the Gaylord Pulpwood Company or Crown Zellerbach or the tung nut industry.* The extensive pine forests in the hills around the county made it one of the prime sources of pulpwood in the South, but the once-flourishing tung nut industry had begun to decline several years earlier.[1] Consumption of tung oil had been decreasing since World War II as manufacturers substituted the cheaper linseed oil.[2]

Poplarville, with 2,135 residents, lay 80 miles north of New Orleans along rough and tumble Highway 11 and 125 miles south of Jackson, the state capital and largest city. Pearl River

_____

* Tung nuts yield an oil used in paint, varnish, and turpentine.

24

County, of which Poplarville was the county seat, occupied the northwest corner of the southern edge of Mississippi, bordering the Pearl River. In size the county was one of the largest in the state, but fell far below Delta counties to the north in economic output and income. It never knew the prosperity of a plantation economy or the stability of a planter-dominated society. The rural economy had been stagnant for years; 44.5 percent of the people lived below the poverty line, and the population level hadn't changed significantly since 1915. Another 2,500 lived in outlying hamlets like Juniper Grove, Gumpond, McNeill, Derby, and White Sands. County residents tended to converge on the town to do their business, and on some days, especially Saturday, Main Street, which ran the length of town, dividing it in half, actually seemed crowded. Main Street was the only street to stretch farther than a few blocks, and Poplarville's one stoplight hung over the intersection of Main and West Pearl, down the street from the courthouse and in front of the Lone Star Movie House.[3]

The Poplarville *Democrat* described the town as "human, not passive, serene not chaotic, a town opposed to violence and wanting above all, justice. . . . small town, yes, but there are nine or ten cafés, two drug stores, eight churches (six Baptist and two Methodist), two car dealers, ten or eleven gas stations, seven or eight grocery stores, eight lawyers, no Snopes or Comptons [*sic*]—but as many types of characters as can be found in any place in the United States." Poplarville also boasted an active Chamber of Commerce, which built and maintained a softball diamond. In addition there were chapters of various men's service clubs, like the Rotary and Kiwanis. The town had a garden club, a women's club, a PTA, a Masonic Temple, and an Eastern Star. A small, eight-bed hospital attended by two physicians provided health care. In short, Poplarville was a rather average small town and, given the low standard of living characteristic of the rural South, there was nothing on the surface that made it any different from other small towns in America.[4]

Yet a traveler passing through from New Orleans had only to pause a while to discover that beneath the surface placidity lurked extremely strong and pervasive attitudes. In Mississippi since Reconstruction race had been the major factor, the all-encompassing issue of state politics. Whatever the social and economic conflicts among whites, and there were several, all whites stood foursquare and ten abreast for white supremacy.[5]

So strong were their beliefs that they had managed since the end of Reconstruction to lynch more blacks than any other state in the nation. Through the years Mississippi, followed by Georgia and Texas, lynched 539 blacks and 42 whites, but that wasn't all.[6] Even though the number of lynchings declined after World War II, racial violence did not. During the 1950s, especially after the Supreme Court's 1954 *Brown v. Board of Education* decision, racial violence actually increased in Mississippi. In 1955 the Reverend George Lee, the NAACP leader from Belzoni, died in an auto crash after "persons unknown" fired a shotgun into his face while he was driving. No one was ever indicted for that crime. Also in Belzoni, a white man gunned down Gus Courts, a friend of Lee's and an NAACP activist, while he was working in his grocery store. The FBI investigated the case and placed the blame on the white Citizens Council, but no one was ever indicted. These two attacks effectively put a stop to the black voter registration campaign in Belzoni. Similar racial murders occurred in other areas of the state.

Lynching was terrorism, and as such it was one of the white South's most effective weapons of repression. From the Civil War up to the 1950s, lynching was part of the oppressive routine of life.[7] It might occur at any time and in any place. At any given moment local whites might decide that a particular black had gotten uppity or that the community as a whole had gotten uppity, and lynching fever spread with the rapaciousness of the plague. Until the 1950s blacks generally responded by "going along to get along." This relatively timid response was a sign, not of black weakness, but of the power of the lynch mob. Change came after World War II, with a generation that had had enough. After the 1955 lynching of Emmett Till in Mississippi for wolf-whistling a white woman, his name became a rallying cry in the struggle to stop racial terrorism and to achieve equal rights under the law. These stirrings of change were sensed by the race-conscious whites of Pearl River County.

When whites faced the issue of race relations, they stood together against blacks, but a shared antipathy for blacks and determination to keep them in an inferior position did not eliminate the major political and socioeconomic divisions among whites in Mississippi—chiefly the split between the Delta planters and the so-called rednecks from the hills. These two strong factions had divided along sharp and antagonistic lines during the 1880s and 1890s. The planters ruled the state after Redemption until the election of James K. Vardaman to the governor's mansion in 1903, when the redneck faction came to power and stayed there. As a neo-populist, Vardaman was an anti-corporation, anti-planter, pro-common man white supremacist. He set the tone and the style for his ideological successor, Theodore G. Bilbo, who was born and raised on a farm in Juniper Grove, five miles outside Poplarville. Bilbo served as lieutenant governor, two terms as governor, and finally wound up in the United States Senate, where his thundering racism won the hearts of thousands of white Southerners, who admired him in spite of his scandal-ridden public career. Residents of Poplarville were proud to call Bilbo one of their own.[8] Although he died in 1947, throughout the 1950s his views on race enjoyed nearly unanimous support among whites. Any divisions that occurred among whites generally concerned style. Some whites preferred a more moderate approach to Bilbo's braggadocio and Bible-thumping tirades.

However, when race-baiting in Mississippi increased after the 1954 *Brown* decision, state leaders, forswearing integration at all costs, roused the fearful white population to action, then moved a step further in their extremism to avoid being accused of "moderation" by a new opponent. The abhorrent specter of racial equality underlay all other issues and led to a major effort to disenfranchise completely the blacks who had continued to vote over the decades in several scattered communities throughout the state. To that end, in 1954 the legislature adopted a literacy test that disenfranchised or otherwise circumscribed many of these voters, and federal protection was only a faint glimmer on the horizon. In Pearl River County no blacks had voted in decades. Few were permitted to register, and consequently few tried to vote. It was an unspoken rule that any black seeking to change the situation faced the possibility of retaliatory violence from whites.[9]

A single set of seldom-used tracks maintained by the Southern Railroad ran in front of the Pearl River Junior College and divided white from black. No blacks lived within the Poplarville city limits, even though blacks formed 23 percent of the county's population. All those living just outside of town lived on the east side of the tracks farther up Route 26 from the junior college. Their houses had no indoor plumbing, but most had a television antenna on the roof.[10]

Life in Pearl River County was largely defined by the regional poverty that blurred class lines among whites.[11] The county's 22,400 citizens lived contentedly in the piney woods isolated from the rest of the state and nation. Most of the residents had been born in the county or nearby. Few of them had traveled far from home or for very long. The movie theater showed only old movies, and all except the young men preferred them to traveling to New Orleans for a first-run film or other entertainment. Only in the past decade had television brought the outside world to this part of the country. For several generations, life had changed little. Families stayed, few people left, few moved in. Everyone knew everyone else, and everyone's affairs were subject to public scrutiny. Such insularity gave local citizens a sense of security and self-righteousness that reinforced their mistaken notion that they had to answer only to themselves for their actions. Since they cared little for what went on beyond the county line, why, they reasoned, should an outsider care what went on within the county? In Poplarville in 1959 class divisions were generally blurred, defined more along racial lines—not according to family heritage, wealth, or occupation. The largest landowners, the Moodys, hardly constituted a gentry unto themselves. The professions in town were so few as to be inconsequential. The underclass blacks kept to their tar paper shacks as much as possible. Whites often proudly referred to them as loyal people who knew their place. The political divisions within the town were manifestly non-doctrinal and had more to do with the remnants of Bilbo's coattails than anything else.[12]

One of the major occupations of the sheriff's department was the pursuit of whiskey runners passing through the county from further south. It was not unusual for police officers to administer their own brand of quick "justice" to captured bootleggers. As long as anyone could remember, people had been taking matters into their own hands. In racial and criminal matters, Southern law-enforcement officers on occasion followed tradition as they knew it and sometimes that tradition had included lynching. The last lynching in Pearl River County took place in 1932, when a mob lynched two white men for murdering a young white boy.[13]

As M. C. Parker's trial date approached, twin sentiments developed—that M. C. not escape punishment because of a ruling in another case and that Parker's two black attorneys not be permitted to affront the white community by cross-examining June Walters on the witness stand. Mississippians were well aware of the change that had come over the nation since *Brown v. Board of Education*, and although this ruling had not brought about anything tangible locally, it had signaled a new attitude of the federal government toward racial discrimination. Early stirrings of protest, a seemingly tougher stand by the federal government, and finger pointing by self-righteous Northerners frightened Mississippians, and in Poplarville this fear clouded every discussion about M. C. Parker. The immediate cause of concern remained his trial and punishment, but it was never far from anyone's mind that the Yankee-dominated United States Supreme Court had a lot to do with what they felt were the new and unfriendly aspects of race relations.

The sentiment against M. C. Parker was not restricted to Pearl River County. Sebe Dale reported that in Forrest County, where the Walters family lived, "some people there are pretty sore about this case," adding, as though to shift the focus elsewhere and ease worried minds, that he doubted "if ten people" in the Poplarville area knew either the rape victim or the man on trial for raping her. He was quite correct that few white people knew Parker and virtually no one knew June Walters, but Dale knew well the intensity of emotion in the community and outlying areas over the rape and especially the anticipated outcome of the trial. He himself succumbed to it. In denying R. Jess Brown's request for a change of venue, he closed his eyes to the obvious possibility that violence might erupt before or after the trial. There had even been talk of jumping Brown in court if he dared question Mrs. Walters.[14]

When Sheriff Moody received an anonymous telephone call reporting rumors that some people in Hattiesburg were upset about Parker's crime and upcoming trial, he quickly informed Dale. He had been hearing similar gossip around the courthouse ever since Parker was arrested and feared Parker might not be safe in the Pearl River County jail. The sheriff wanted Governor Coleman to send the National Guard to Parker's arraignment, but Dale demurred in spite of the visible unrest, counseling that the people would not molest Parker. Accordingly, Moody took no further action even though his better judgment told him trouble was in the wind. The rumors persisted. During the days that followed, Poplarville came alive with talk about lynching Parker. Publicly at least, Dale and Moody clung to their claims that Parker would not be harmed, ignoring the swirling pre-trial atmosphere.[15]

An infamous incident of racial violence had occurred just four years earlier in 1955 in LeFlore County, in Mississippi's Delta region, in a similar atmosphere of heightened emotions. White men had lynched Emmett Till, a fourteen-year-old Chicago youth, for whistling at a white girl. Till, who had been visiting relatives at the time, had no comprehension of the racial taboos of the deep South when, on a dare from friends, he committed what whites felt was a grave offense. The twenty-one-year-old woman at whom he directed his wolf-whistle, which resulted in part from a speech impediment, was working in the drugstore where Till had gone to buy some bubble gum. Later that night, at 2:00 a.m., two men, one married to the white woman, appeared at the door of the shack of Till's uncle and took Till away for "questioning." One of the men pointed a gun at Till's uncle in answer to his protests and his assurance that he would send his nephew back to Chicago early in the morning if only they would leave him alone. Two days later police found Till's body in the Tallahatchie River. He had a bullet hole over his right ear; his body had been bludgeoned, weighted down, and thrown into the water.

In spite of Till's mother's positive identification of his body, and the testimony of many witnesses, the jury deliberated for only one hour and found the two men innocent because of "the belief that there had been no identification of the dead body as that of Emmett Till." A grand jury had failed even to bring charges against the men who had joined in the lynch mob. During his final argument, the *prosecutor* said that Till should have been whipped, not murdered. When television reporters questioned the local sheriff about the outraged letters he had received, he pointed his finger straight into the camera and said, "Yes, I'm glad you asked me this. I just want to tell all of those people who've been sending me those threatening letters that if they ever come down here the same thing's gonna happen to them that happened to Emmett Till." The sheriff's message played to a national television audience.[16]

This act of racial murder, all the more brutal for its ridiculous pretext, took place in the wake of the *Brown* decision and the founding of the white Citizens Councils and the Mississippi State Sovereignty Commission. Whites intended both organizations to be instrumental in blocking desegregation. Their existence and the rhetoric that accompanied them made it easier for men to execute a young boy for an alleged racial offense. This lynching received widespread attention from news media and triggered national and international outrage of a degree never before seen in the deep South.

Throughout America, whites of all social and economic classes finally began to realize what black Americans had known for centuries—that the law was different for blacks and whites. Whites who normally didn't know and didn't care to know about racial oppression and violence in the rural South were appalled that mature white men would kill a naive boy for acting like a normal adolescent male. For blacks in the South, Emmett Till's death was a pivotal event in the mounting of the civil rights revolution. In that sense it was quite different from the Parker affair: Mack Charles Parker was neither naive nor especially tender of age. Nevertheless, white attitudes were again pointing out the double standard of justice in the South: one white, one black, and for blacks that meant the absence of standards altogether. When it came to racial matters, white Southerners showed contempt for the American values of justice and fair play they supposedly cherished. In the South, and throughout the country in fact, justice and fair play when it came to race were far from uniform. In Pearl River County, it was as though the Emmett Till lynching had never happened.

Even though Poplarville was involved in the *Parker* case only because it happened to be the county seat, many white residents of the county felt something should be done to ensure that Parker receive quick and severe justice.[17] People who felt this way were motivated primarily by a strong desire to prevent a black from avoiding justice rather than by the desire to avenge a specific grievance. They were far enough removed from the original crime that their call for action was not a spontaneous reaction to the crime itself but rather the result of a long-simmering suspicion that blacks would bend the court system to their own benefit. The man who headed the Mississippi State Sovereignty Commission at the time, Erle Johnston, editor of the Scott County *Times*, thought the lynching sentiment "was based upon previous experience that blacks would get off." He felt blacks knew they could use NAACP money and lawyers to beat the system of justice in the South. The social psychology of racial bias meant that when any individual black "got off," all blacks got off, whereas when a white got off, only an individual got off. "So," thought Johnston, "to prevent the possibility of trial and appeals, followed by more appeals," which might result in a reduced sentence or no sentence at all, the people decided to lynch Parker. The people felt at that time, "If we set back and wait for the government to prosecute and to punish Mack Parker, it would never happen. So we did it ourselves."[18]

The fear that the legal system would not convict and sentence blacks for any crimes was, ironically, the result of white control of the legal system. The Mississippi Plan, which the state had adopted in 1890, had, through the poll tax and literacy and understanding tests and other Jim Crow devices, disenfranchised thousands of black voters, and it eventually spread throughout the South. Names of those not allowed to register to vote did not appear on the jury rolls. Disenfranchisement, therefore, meant exclusion from the jury system as well. As a result—an intended result—white juries tried black criminals. Then came the *Goldsby* decision, which overturned the conviction of a black man because his trial jury had not included blacks. The *Goldsby* decision underscored the fact that the white South had crippled its own court system by rendering it incompetent to try black criminals. Unfortunately, the only alternative in many white minds was lynch law. Thus, the lynch mobs were not the result of black criminality or an unfriendly federal judiciary—these were red herrings. Lynch mobs, by 1959 at least, resulted from whites being ensnared by their own prejudice. Committed to seeing blacks punished for their offenses, whites now felt punishment was up to them rather than the legal system. They had already lynched the legal system.

One man in particular personified this self-righteousness. His name was J. P. Walker. Known as J. P. throughout the county, he served as deputy sheriff until 1956, when he lost the race for sheriff to Osborne Moody. In early 1959 he had already made it known he intended to run against Moody's chosen successor in the August primary. Walker was an active member of the Masonic Lodge and had discussed with some of his fellow Masons on several occasions his feelings that something should be done about Mack Parker.

When Parker first went before Sebe Dale, Walker had driven from his home in Picayune, where he ran an auto body shop, to see this young black man accused of raping a white woman. Seated well back in the courtroom, he watched Parker intently while listening to R. Jess Brown's careful legal maneuvers. Something about Parker—his demeanor, the nature of his crime, the possibility he might go free—provoked him. He left the court-

room convinced it was up to him to ensure Parker got the punishment he deserved. Talk of Walker's often drunken tirades
against M. C. Parker traveled quickly throughout the close-knit,
rural white society, enhanced by his reputation as a fearless lawman. Residents of like mind began to wonder aloud what would
happen if Parker, whom they already had convicted in their
hearts and minds, won an acquittal.

On Wednesday night, April 22, 1959, Walker decided the time
was right to do a little politicking in Gumpond, a tiny hamlet six
miles east of Poplarville. On Wednesday nights the Pearl River
County Baptist congregations attended prayer meetings at their
respective churches. Walker drove to Gumpond knowing he
could catch a large group of potential voters at the service presided over by Preacher Lee. Though it was only April, several
months before the election, Walker had an issue he hoped would
put him in the sheriff's office for the next four years. After
Preacher Lee's racial invective-filled sermon, several men gathered outside the small one-room church under one of the large
oak trees. It was the custom for friends to get together for half an
hour of socializing before returning to their homes. Walker
joined some of his friends from the local Masonic hall: Preacher
Lee, his son Jeff, local farmer L. C. Davis, and Francis Barker,
who worked at the county Health Department vaccinating dogs.
Walker had no need to prove his tough reputation, but he did not
miss the opportunity to point out that he was the right man to
prevent Parker from getting off in court. He made his usual promises of "keeping the niggers down" if he became sheriff and
argued that attorneys Brown and Young should be prevented
from questioning June Walters in court on the following Monday.
The burly ex-deputy told the men that he had been in court when
Parker had been indicted and found Parker to be surly and overconfident as he slouched in his seat, smirking at Judge Dale and
the prosecutors. Parker's attitude was so brazen, Walker told
them, that he even provoked Dale into lashing out at him from
the bench. Dale had warned Parker he was asking for trouble.
Even though, Walker admitted with a chuckle, "the only thing
June Walters had going for her was that she was white," Parker
had no business acting the way he did in court, and self-respecting
whites should not permit it. Walker's slighting comment about
June Walters was a sign that whites were slowly beginning to turn
against her because she did not support their violent intentions.
The crime committed against her was becoming secondary to the

issue of race. Walker articulated the widely shared belief that it would be unhealthy for race relations if two black lawyers questioned June on the witness stand in open court. It would set a bad precedent and for that reason should not take place.[19]

Walker also related to his friends his first encounter with Parker's attorneys. As Walker stood outside the courtroom, he proclaimed loudly and defiantly that if either Brown or Young attempted to drink from the water fountain down the hall from him, he would personally knock one or both of them down on the spot. Between them Brown and Young had many years of experience contending with resentful whites in the rural courtrooms in Mississippi, and the two men never considered using the water fountain or the small, dirty first-floor restroom shared by whites of both sexes.[20]

J. P. Walker, age forty, was six feet, one inch tall, weighed over 230 pounds, had a tattoo on his left forearm and a reputation along with others in the large Lee clan of Gumpond of being among the toughest and least law-abiding men in the county. Local attorneys often scoffed at the idea of his becoming sheriff, because they considered him, unlike his father, Buford, who had been sheriff in the 1940s, to be a habitué of bars and poolrooms. As a deputy sheriff he had earned the reputation of being tough on prisoners, especially blacks, and more than once he was accused of mistreating men while escorting them to jail. His fellow law officers also accused him of sexually abusing women prisoners. Yet his reputation seemed to help his election chances; he was expected to win in August. The pastor of the largest Baptist church in Mississippi, located in Picayune, said of Walker, "I've never known a finer man than J. P. He will be our next sheriff." The state representative of Pearl River County commented, "We aren't political allies, but I'd have to say J. P. is a solid citizen, one of the best."[21]

J. P. Walker's past revealed other qualities. According to his military personnel record, he entered the United States Army on June 26, 1936, only to desert two years later on February 1, 1938, from Fort Benning, Georgia. During his first enlistment, a military court convicted him of neglecting proper prophylaxis after illicit sexual intercourse and sentenced him to one month's hard labor and fined him twelve dollars. After deserting, he returned home to Picayune, where military police eventually apprehended him. After a short trial the army issued him a general discharge on April 10, 1941, at the rank of private. Yet it wasn't a simple matter of his unwillingness to remain in the military. During the time he was AWOL from Fort Benning, Walker re-enlisted in the army at New Orleans under an assumed name. He had been home on leave from his second enlistment when military police caught up with him. Following an investigation Walker was medically discharged as a private from his second enlistment on June 22, 1943, for a cyst on his tailbone that was progressive enough to incapacitate him for further service. In truth, the army had found him psychologically unfit to serve. At the time of his second discharge, army doctors diagnosed him as being in a "constitutional psychopathic state" with an "inadequate personality." Twice during his second enlistment military courts convicted him of drunk and disorderly charges.[22]

Walker returned to Picayune, where he worked as a mechanic until the Korean conflict drew him back to the military. In 1950 he enlisted in the Mississippi National Guard and later served in Korea until he received an honorable discharge in 1951 because of family hardship. When he came home to Picayune, he started Walker's Auto Body Shop and served as deputy sheriff for four years. Of the primary conspirators Walker was the only one who had ever spent any length of time away from home and the only one to serve in the armed forces.[23]

Walker's attitudes were persuasive, and the prayer meeting broke up after the men agreed that Friday night April 24, would be the best time to remove Parker from jail. They decided to meet first at L. C. Davis's farm to lay plans. At Preacher Lee's suggestion, his son Jeff agreed to drive to Petal on Friday to ask Jimmy Walters and his brother if they wanted to participate. The men believed that Jimmy ought to have the opportunity to get even with M. C. Parker. The men also agreed to invite others they felt could be trusted to participate. Walker suggested his buddy Crip Reyer might want to help out; he had a car with a large back seat that might prove useful. Walker asked Francis Barker to stop by Crip's barbershop to ask him to come out to the Davis farm.[24]

Although some residents of Pearl River County considered the itinerant Baptist preacher James Floren Lee to be in effect a co-leader of the conspiracy, he played a somewhat lesser role, not because of a lack of will to act, but because of J. P. Walker's higher visibility. Walker possessed near legendary bravado, which was another reason he was much better known throughout the county. If Walker made the mob a cohesive unit with himself at the center, Lee gave it inspiration with his Biblical invective, chapter-and-verse references to the black man's innate inferiority, and wrathful tirades against Parker. Where Walker was calm and calculating in his determination to dispose of Parker, Lee was the wild-eyed fanatic, ranting in the style of Theodore Bilbo for the lynching of M. C. Parker. The presence of a preacher in the conspiracy was not at all unusual. Erle Johnston insisted that "some of the greatest preachers in the South were for segregation" and "would back up their beliefs with action." They were men given to extreme violence who invoked the Bible to justify black subordination.[25]

Preacher Lee came from the large Lee clan of several families that had long ago spread out from Lee's Mill (sometimes called Leetown) located twenty miles south of Picayune. Lee's Mill was one of the earliest settlements in southern Mississippi and received its name from the family who founded it and for decades provided its leadership. Lee hailed from a long line of preachers, the one fixed vocation of male family members. Lee and his eight sons, most of whom lived in the impoverished Gumpond area, fervently believed God had intended blacks to be servants to whites and thus found the rape itself and the prospective acquittal of the rapist intolerable. The elder Lee felt Parker's crime, more than the chance he might go free or that Brown might question June Walters, merited the lynching. A scraggly, toothless backwoods country preacher who always wore bib overalls and a hat to cover his bald head, even when inside, Lee, whom people described as a "Bible-thumping, Holy Roller-type," freely admitted he knew some people in the county considered him a "crank," but it failed to discourage him from championing his cause. He stated unequivocally, "God's word set forth that the negro is a servant." He later charged that the NAACP and the communists were responsible for the abduction of Parker and that they were fast bringing to a climax the racial situation, which would erupt in all-out war within the country.[26]

One of the peculiar factors in the conspiracy stemmed from the rather sharp political division within the county. The Republican party was nonexistent, and the opposing Democratic factions had existed since the turn of the century, appearing first in response to the 1909 state legislature's censure of Theodore Bilbo. Although the details of the issue faded long ago, people remembered that Bilbo caused the original factionalization. In 1959 the Moody family, members of which had been partisan supporters of Bilbo, owned the largest chunk of property in the county, picking up much of it for a dollar an acre during the Depression. Historically, the Moodys lived along the Pearl River but their holdings extended inland. George Moody had owned the largest sheep herd east of the Mississippi and took advantage of the open range laws to expand his flock. George's brother Solomon ruled the county with an iron hand for nearly ten years as chairman of the county board of supervisors. His eldest son, Jim, who preceded Osborne as sheriff, owned and operated the only bank in the county. Many families were allied against the Moodys simply because they were one of the more established families in the county.[27]

Osborne was only a cousin to the powerful Moody clan; nevertheless, he inherited its allies as well as its enemies. The Moodys cooperated closely with the Morse and the Williams families to maintain their position in the county. Osborne Moody, his son and deputy, George Vaught Moody, who also taught mathematics at the junior high school during the day, his cousin and deputy sheriff, Will Estes Moody, and his son-in-law and deputy-jailer, Jewel Alford, ran on one ticket backed by the Chamber of Commerce. Men such as J. P. Walker, Petey Carver, B. F. Orr, District Attorney Vernon Broome, County Prosecutor Bill Stewart, and Mayor Pat Hyde opposed them. The ill will created by this political rivalry grew so intense that opposing members rarely went on police patrols with one another or cooperated in law enforcement. In 1959 there were in effect two law-enforcement factions operating simultaneously within the county. Only on special occasions did Sheriff Moody allow his son or his cousin to patrol with Orr or Carver, and only then when the county was helping the Mississippi highway patrol to intercept bootleggers on their way from Kiln, in Hancock County, through Pearl River County into Louisiana. The growing conspiracy took full advantage of this rift. Ironically, although the Moody faction in the county was Bilbo's political offspring, Sheriff Moody's political rivals were Bilbo's ideological offspring.[28]

The distinction between the two factions is important. It was highly doubtful that the Moodys would have led the conspiracy had they been seeking to replace Walker. That did not mean the Moodys disagreed with the racial motivations behind the lynching; only that Sheriff Moody and his relatives and allies were less likely to lead it. Indeed, they put as much distance as possible between themselves and the spreading fever. The Moodys and their allies did not hold more enlightened views on race relations; rather the Moodys and those who called themselves moderates in the hushed privacy of their homes only hoped their mild approach would be matched by blacks. They argued that blacks would keep in their place if only whites would be a little kinder to them. In this way, the split between the Moody and the Walker factions mimicked the statewide split between the "moderates" led by Governor J. P. Coleman and more outspoken white racists like Ross Barnett. This division, on local and state levels, intensified whenever a crisis underscored the two possible approaches to resolving the problems of the South.

To the gathering storm a local newspaper editor added another gust. On Thursday, April 23, in his last issue before the trial, the editor of the Picayune *Item* wrote an inflammatory editorial blasting the NAACP for sending in black attorneys. Chance Cole had no grounds whatsoever for his accusation because the NAACP had absolutely nothing to do with Brown's involvement and had rebuffed Liza Parker's pleas for help back in February. Cole summoned his deepest wrath when he wrote, knowing the volatile mood of his fellow whites, "The vicious, violent treatment meted out to this white, Forrest County housewife, helpless as she was to defend herself, is enough to make any American's blood boil. We have never believed in mob violence, but if M. C. Parker is found guilty of this crime no treatment is too bad for him or those who would attempt to get him out of it." No one could fail to see the direction toward which Cole pointed.[29]

In accordance with the plans set after the prayer meeting at Gumpond, Jeff Lee and his friend Tullie Lee Dunn drove to Hattiesburg on Friday morning ostensibly to apply for jobs at the Southern Shipping Company. Lee knew slightly a man named William Lowell Mooney, who worked for Gulf Oil there. Jeff Lee and Tullie Dunn stopped first for gas at the Site Service Station outside Poplarville, where the attendant C. M. Douglas, who had heard of the meeting at the Davis farm, asked about what would follow the meeting. They told him that they along with some others were going into town to have some fun at the Poplarville jail later on that night. The jail keys, he assured Douglas, would not be hard to find; arrangements had already been made.[30]

When they arrived at Mooney's home and asked Mooney where Jim Walters was, Mooney said he didn't know but offered to show them where he worked. After stopping for some fishing worms, Mooney took them to the Komp Equipment Company. Mooney went inside. When Walters appeared from the storage area behind the counter, Mooney bought some supplies from him before saying, "Jimmy, I've got a proposition for you, son." Jimmy, who was aware of the now widespread conspiracy, responded, "What can I do for you?" Mooney told him there were two men outside waiting to speak to him. Walters obediently followed him outside. He had never met either Dunn or Lee before, and offered neither his name nor any sort of greeting. One of them said to Walters as Jimmy leaned in the window, "We have something to talk to you about." "What is it?" Walters asked, although he had known exactly what they wanted from the minute Mooney came in and asked for him. This man, who Walters thought was "a rough looking person," said, "We was driving by to see if you wanted to get in on something." When Walters asked him what it was, the man responded, "We are going down there and drag that nigger out of jail."[31]

Mooney stood behind Walters, embarrassed at being unable to introduce Walters to either Lee or his friend. He interrupted the conversation to tell Walters that he had to go to work. As he started to walk away he overheard them telling Walters about the meeting that night on the road to Wiggins. They called to Mooney, "If you want to attend the meeting, come down." Mooney told them he would come sometime after dark if he could, but he was supposed to go fishing. Walters told them he didn't believe in violence and added, "You guys ought not to go down there and do that either," because June was not sure Parker had been the one who raped her. "We are," they said angrily, "and we are going down there to get him. We got the right nigger." Then they added somewhat uncertainly, "We were passing by and wanted to see if you wanted any part of it." Tullie Dunn told him it had been fixed so that they could get into the jail. Walters said again he wanted no part of a lynching party. "I don't believe in that kind of crap," he insisted. They conferred briefly and said to Walters, "OK, we'll see you later." As they drove away they shouted out the window that they would see him that night in Pearl River County.[32]

Walters bowed his head and walked back inside. "What was that all about?" he was asked. "Aw, nothing," Jimmy replied, but he was in turmoil. Since his brother had been approached by a neighbor, Jimmy had been in considerable agony. The neighbor, who had been an active member of the Hattiesburg Ku Klux Klan during the twenties, had tried to convince Eddie Walters to ride down to Poplarville for the meeting at the Davis farm. He told Eddie it was his duty, and Eddie tended to agree. But Jimmy was different. He abhorred violence and wanted only to spend the rest of his life in peace. He wanted nothing more to do with M. C. Parker, and he certainly wanted nothing to do with ex-Klan members who wanted him to go to Poplarville. These were men he feared and mistrusted.[33]

The twenty-two-year-old Walters was a quiet, mild youth with a crew cut. He was born in Oklahoma and extremely proud of his Indian heritage. The third of five brothers, slightly built and weighing 140 pounds, he was not a beer-drinking rowdy like his brother Eddie, and he had never fired a gun in his life. He felt no need to prove his manhood through violence, especially since an older brother had been killed in France during World War II. His real passion in life was music. He was a talented musician who could play a variety of musical instruments: guitar, bass, pedal steel guitar, drums, and even a little tenor sax. Usually, he played pedal steel in Jimmy Swann's Blue Sky Playboys and appeared every Thursday night on Hattiesburg television. The band had been on the Grand Ole Opry several times. Jimmy had had his name inscribed across the front of his instrument so everyone would know who he was. It had been the high point of his life. He and his wife both came from broken homes. June was born in Watertown, New York, and after her army sergeant father deserted the family, she had lived until age ten in a foster home. The following year, she moved to Hattiesburg with her mother. She met Jimmy in high school. They both quit in the eleventh grade to get married. He was eighteen, she was seventeen. Like her husband, June was small, five feet, two inches tall, and weighed only one hundred pounds. Several months before she was raped, their marriage had become seriously strained by Jimmy's inability to hold down a job. They had separated several times; on each occasion Jimmy stayed with his mother on Roby Street in Hattiesburg until he and June made up. Both hoped the new baby's arrival would save their marriage, which had barely survived the rape. Neither Jimmy nor June had any violence in his or her past, and neither one wanted any violence in the future. Still, the pressure was there.[34]

Some of his fellow Blue Sky Playboys began riding Jimmy when he insisted he wanted nothing to do with the lynch mob. A prominent Hattiesburg businessman had personally approached Jimmy about going to Poplarville. Jimmy flatly refused, and the criticism he received because of it cost him dearly. Even Jimmy Swann, a Klan member and erstwhile candidate for governor, considered that he lacked the character of a typical man he kept in his band for not wanting to get even with M. C. Parker. His brother Eddie was more forthright about it: he called Jimmy a coward to his face. In Poplarville, Jimmy and June became the butt of cruel jokes for their rejection of violence. Jimmy began drinking in the aftermath of the rape, and this continued to be a problem.[35]

At noon on Friday, while Jeff Lee and his companion were seeing Jimmy Walters in Petal, Francis Barker stopped by Crip Reyer's barbershop in McNeill, just north of Picayune. Barker, who was suffering from heart disease, walked in and sat down in the barber's chair and, as Crip shaved him, told him about the meeting at the Davis farm out on the road to Wiggins. He asked Reyer if he wanted to go. The forty-five-year-old former prize-fighter told Barker he didn't "particularly care" about going but would think it over. Christopher Columbus Reyer had a small farm north of McNeill on the road to Poplarville. He maintained his barbershop to supplement his income and to keep up with local gossip and goings-on. Crip, as he was known, was as gregarious as he was garrulous and was given to practical jokes and idle boasting, boasting that would cost him dearly in the days to come. While not as large as the Lee family, the Reyer family was spread throughout the county. Crip's forebears had settled there during the dispossessed days of Reconstruction.[36]

Later that day, when his nephew Arthur Smith stopped by with the news of the meeting, Crip agreed to attend just to see what would come of it. The thirty-two-year-old Smith, who had only a fourth-grade education and was a functional illiterate, lived less than a mile away from Reyer and he supported his wife and child as a tractor driver and part-time stump hauler for his brother, who owned a large farm nearby. He also helped his Uncle Crip brand pigs every year. Smith's car had broken down, so Reyer offered to give him a ride to the meeting. Reyer told Smith that Francis Barker had asked him, if he came, to be sure and drive his own car.[37]

About 7:30 that night, Arthur Smith returned to Crip Reyer's barbershop to ride with him to Wiggins to set the plans "to move that nigger." They stopped at the Star Cafe in Poplarville, and

Reyer went inside and was observed talking to Petey Carver. The subject of their conversation is unknown. Smith waited in the car while the two men talked and then he and Crip drove out toward Wiggins. The meeting at the Davis farm included men from Gumpond, Petal, Hattiesburg, McNeill, Picayune, Poplarville, and Lumberton, including Lumberton's marshal, Ham Slade. As a full moon rose over the countryside, thirty determined men parked their cars along the side of the road and hurried back along the lane to the barren frontyard. They quickly fell quiet as J. P. Walker and Preacher Lee began to discuss the best way to remove Parker from the jail.[38]

As a former deputy whose commitment to law enforcement caused him to spend hours each week at the courthouse, Walker claimed he had complete familiarity with both the old brick building and the jail attached to it. He suggested they break in by using the acetylene torch he had brought with him from his body shop. A few men in the crowd worried that this would take too long and that the bright light might attract attention. Preacher Lee suggested they get someone to let them into the courthouse, as he and Walker had previously discussed. But Walker enjoyed feats of derring-do and favored storming the jail. He tried to convince Lee to support him, but others in the crowd supported Lee. Walker bowed to their wishes. Someone mentioned two of the Amacker brothers, who served as janitors. They seemed likely candidates because of their intimate knowledge of the courthouse. Surely one of them knew where the keys were kept. No, argued Walker, they were both unreliable, and besides their older brother was a town constable. It might be unwise to involve another officer unnecessarily. That left only the jailer, Jewel Alford, who had earlier refused to help, Petey Carver, and B. F. Orr. Alford was a kindly man who had married Osborne Moody's sister after moving into the county after World War II. He had been the logical choice to approach because he lacked the extensive family ties of the Moodys. Furthermore, Alford did not possess a tremendous amount of courage and was not the type to carry on a vendetta. Walker thought that Alford suspected he might be approached for the keys because lately he had been cautious about keeping them.[39]

Walker had already spoken to Herman Schulz, an auto mechanic in his early thirties who ran a body shop out of Jewel Alford's tin garage up on the hill behind the Alford house, about approaching Jewel for the keys. Mrs. Alford considered Schulz a rambler with no permanent roots in the town. Shortly after authorities transferred Parker from Jackson to the Poplarville jail, Jewel Alford had begun burying the jail keys at night in his backyard to prevent anyone from stealing them. After spending two or three uncomfortable nights, he asked Sheriff Moody if he could discontinue this practice and return the keys at the end of each day to their regular place in the top drawer of the filing cabinet in the sheriff's office. Like Moody, Alford had heard the gossip about Parker and was increasingly apprehensive with the keys in his possession, especially since he knew it was no secret what he had been doing with them since Parker's arrival. Like many others, Alford had heard J. P. Walker threaten Parker's attorneys against drinking at the water fountain, and as talk spread he feared for the safety of his family. Moody consulted Sebe Dale about Alford's request, and Dale instructed the sheriff to tell Alford to leave the keys in the cabinet at the end of each day. Dale doubted there would be any trouble, but he added that in the event someone should try to snatch Parker from his cell, no action should be taken that might endanger any law officers or any of the white prisoners.[40]

Jewel made it clear he didn't want to have anything to do with the lynching. He also let it be known he no longer took the keys home with him, returning them instead to Moody's office each night when he left. Alford did agree, however, to allow Schulz to accompany him into the cell area at mealtimes. Since Schulz had done this in the past, Alford saw nothing untoward in allowing him to do it again. On the first day Schulz accompanied Alford, Parker had been complaining of headaches, and when he asked Alford who the man staring at him was, Alford joked that Schulz was a doctor. Parker's cell mate, C. J. Mondy, suspected something was afoot, but he didn't know what and kept his suspicions to himself. With Schulz at his side, Alford also took trusty Dwight Ladner aside and told him that if anybody came for Parker, he should point him out and make sure they got the right man. So strong an impression did Alford's warning, repeated on Friday, make on Ladner that the thirty-four-year-old trusty remarked to his fellow white prisoners, as evening approached, that they would have "a party tonight."[41]

The problem of getting into the jail was all that remained to be worked out before the mob headed for town. No one had been able to sway Alford, and the only logical remaining alternative was to jimmy the window to the sheriff's office to get the keys.

As the other men stayed at the Davis farm talking and drinking, Crip Reyer, Arthur Smith, and L. C. Davis drove back to town to the Star Cafe. They met Carver as he pulled his cruiser up to the curb.[42]

Harold Pierre Carver, age forty-one—Petey as he was known to everyone—became night marshal in 1956, when he defeated Jewel Alford. In his official capacity he made nightly rounds of the Poplarville area. Although it was a violence-prone area, there were few crimes against property in the dark of night. Police officers dealt most often with personal squabbles out in the county and the usual number of troublesome drunks. The nightly patrols had long ago become a nuisance to Carver, who often took two of his friends along with him to break the monotony. Several nights each week R. J. Wheat, an auto mechanics instructor at the junior college, and T. G. Stringfellow, blacksmith and junior college janitor, rode with Carver after Stringfellow got off work. Neither man had any police powers and merely accompanied Petey for amusement.[43]

At 9:00 p.m., after Wheat and Stringfellow had helped him put out a fire, Petey checked in at the Star Cafe, which he used as his unofficial headquarters, where messages could be left for him. He had coffee with Walker, Barker, Wheat, Stringfellow, and Houston Amacker, the janitor at the jail. Upon leaving to take Wheat and Stringfellow back to the junior college, where a dance was in progress, Petey told J. M. Howard, the cafe's eighty-one-year-old owner, that he would be around that night as usual in case anyone should need him. As was his custom, he promised to stop back from time to time to see if anyone had called for him.

About an hour later Carver returned as several men drove up in a black Oldsmobile. Carver saw Crip at the wheel and in the back seat L. C. Davis, who asked him to get in and talk for a while. Carver slid in the back seat and saw that in addition to Reyer and Davis, Arthur Smith was in the car. Reyer remarked that someone was liable to get killed Monday with "them nigger lawyers" being in the courtroom. Reyer asked him if he knew about the meeting about Parker and added that several men had been thinking about "getting the nigger out of jail tonight." Carver told them he knew nothing about any such plans and immediately got out of the car. Reyer, Smith, and Davis returned to the Davis farm.[44]

At the farm, Walker began transferring the chains he brought from his pickup to Reyer's Oldsmobile. Seven men decided to accompany Walker to the jail, and each made sure he had a scarf or bandanna to hide his identity from the other prisoners and gloves to avoid leaving fingerprints. Walker picked the men he wanted to accompany him to the jail. He turned first to Eddie Walters as the man who had more reason for going than anyone else—he had a score to settle. Walters made disparaging remarks about his fainthearted brother. Many of the men at the Davis farm agreed to serve as lookouts. Crip Reyer agreed to drive Barker's car into town due to Barker's poor health—he was too weak to drive his own car. After they decided which cars to take and who would drive, the men fell silent; the atmosphere in the dark night air became solemn and serious as though these men were about to embark on a mission of honor rather than a gang murder. The meeting broke up after 11:00, and the lynch mob headed into town. J. P. Walker, Preacher Lee, and others left in Crip Reyer's Oldsmobile, followed by Reyer driving Barker's car. Several other cars followed them.[45]

3

A Quiet Friday Evening

The three-story yellow brick Pearl River County Courthouse sat back on a large lawn on which citizens had erected a small monument to Theodore Bilbo in 1947. Beyond the lush, trusty-tended lawn lay Main Street, the street that divided Poplarville. No traffic passed through the front entrance of the courthouse; unused desks and chairs blocked it from the inside. The south entrance, on West Pearl Street, served as the main entrance, although the north exit on West Willie Street was open for use. The jail annex, attached to the rear of the courthouse, opened onto the second floor just outside the courtroom where Parker had been arraigned and indicted. Although the jail was three stories high, the actual cell block was only two stories. From the second floor of the courthouse a half-flight of iron stairs led down into the lower four cells of two beds each. The second level, a half-flight up from the second floor of the courthouse, contained a bullpen and two additional cells, which housed the black inmates. The windows in the cells afforded a view of South Julia Street, behind the courthouse; the parking lot directly across Julia; and the Pearl River County Hospital, a small, one-story building that looked more like a family residence than a hospital. The parking lot served the hospital, the courthouse, and the one-room county Health Department, where Francis Barker worked.

In the darkness of the evening of April 24, 1959, a Friday, several cars pulled up across the street from the Health Department in front of the south entrance to the courthouse. L. C. Davis got out of one of the cars; Crip Reyer emerged from Barker's car. Two lone figures crossed the lawn and headed around to the front of the courthouse. Reyer followed Davis onto the front porch, where Davis put the heels of his hands on the window of Sheriff Moody's office and pushed. The window didn't budge. The rangy forty-five-year-old Davis was no weakling; he leaned into the window with all his might. The window refused to give. "It's stuck," Davis whispered over his shoulder in disgust. The window had never been unlocked. The two men returned to the waiting automobiles and informed J. P. Walker. Walker decided on the spot they had to go for Jewel Alford. They didn't want to have to break into the courthouse to get the keys.[1]

Sometime after 11:30 p.m., as Jewel Alford and his wife sat in the living room of their small, clapboard home watching television, someone knocked on the front door. Jewel had been the last man to leave the jail that night. Houston Amacker had been late bringing the food from the C and A Cafe for the prisoners, and when he had finally locked up the courthouse, Alford had seen no sign of trouble. Yet he had known as he stared fitfully at the late night television show that it was only a matter of time before trouble struck. He got up to answer the door, inwardly relieved that the keys to the cells were no longer buried in his backyard. Opening the door, he saw Francis Barker standing in his frontyard about fifteen feet from the door.* Barker said to him in his high nasal voice, "Jewel, come out. My wife wants to see you." Alford reached backed inside for his shirt and told his wife not to worry, there was no trouble. He closed the door behind him and approached the men in Reyer's Olds parked in front of the house on the wrong side of the street. Barker stepped aside and motioned for Alford to speak to the people inside. When Alford leaned in the open left rear door, he heard

---

* There is some doubt that Francis Barker was the man who knocked on Alford's door. Other evidence indicates it may have been Preacher Lee, who was in the Oldsmobile with L. C. Davis and J. P. Walker. The FBI had a degree of doubt about Barker's presence at Alford's home, because later, when Jewel Alford described to the FBI the encounter in front of his house, Francis Barker had died and Alford had two times previously denied that anyone came to his house. See Justice Department memorandum, Joseph Ryan to W. Wilson White, July 7, 1959.

someone in the front say, "Get in." Barker shoved Alford into the back seat and followed him in, forcing Alford to sit between himself and L. C. Davis. None of the men wore masks. Alford recognized the driver as J. P. Walker. The other man in the front seat beside Walker was Preacher Lee, who sat nervously quiet, staring out at the street ahead.[2]

After Barker closed the door, one of the men said, "We've come after the nigger and we want the keys." Another added, "Jewel, we don't want any trouble, we just want the keys. We don't want to tear up the courthouse or destroy any of the property." This visit did not come as a surprise to the jailer, and he had his response ready. "I'll get the keys for you," Alford said slowly, recalling Judge Dale's cryptic instructions to avoid trouble, "but I'm not going with you to get the nigger." "We just want the keys," they responded.[3] When Alford insisted he be allowed to drive unaccompanied to the courthouse, the men told him four or five more cars were probably already parked there. Alford promised to leave the keys on Sheriff Moody's desk only if there was no one waiting outside. The men in the car agreed to go on ahead and disperse the other cars so Alford might enter the courthouse alone and unseen. Having agreed to this plan of action, Alford got out and watched the men drive away. When he went back inside, he told his anxious wife that he had to go to the courthouse to release a man named Green because someone had paid his bond. As Jewel left his house and started across the lawn toward his driveway, the Oldsmobile rounded the corner and passed his house again, the men inside checking to make sure he honored his part of the bargain. The streets around the courthouse, which was only a few blocks from Alford's house, were deserted when Alford arrived, except for Reyer's Oldsmobile, which was parked in front of the south entrance. Alford pulled his Nash Rambler into the lot behind the courthouse and went inside. He walked down the long, dark corridor to the sheriff's office at the end of the hall, took the keys from the filing cabinet, and threw them on the desk. Before leaving he opened the bathroom window and unlocked and raised the front window to make it appear as though the mob had entered through the windows. He closed the door to the hall behind him, locked it, and headed back down the hall to the waiting men.[4]

While Alford was still inside, other cars crept onto the courthouse street from several directions. Two cars parked in the lot behind the courthouse. One car pulled up behind Walker and two other cars parked further down West Pearl Street. They turned their lights out and waited to see if anyone was walking nearby. Each man in the two cars in front of the courthouse donned his bandanna or scarf and slipped on the white cotton gloves purchased from the local hardware store. Then J. P. Walker, wearing a red bandanna, got out and stood alone on the street beside the car. He glanced around one last time before signaling to those in his own car to get out. Eight men walked straight up the sidewalk and climbed the four concrete steps.[5]

The mob huddled nervously by the doorway, waiting for Jewel to appear from the darkness of the hallway. When he opened the door, the lynch mob stepped into the quiet of the court-house. Upon entering, J. P. Walker turned to the other men and put his finger to his lips. He then turned abruptly and headed down the hall, past the county clerk's office and the records room, toward the steps to the second floor and the jail. Jewel Alford had not agreed to anything more than getting the keys, but with the mob inside the courthouse and heading toward the cells and M. C. Parker, Alford changed his mind and returned to Sheriff Moody's office for the keys.* The other men followed Walker nervously, single file, with one man staying behind to take one last look at the street to make sure Petey Carver had not returned to the courthouse unexpectedly. To his relief he saw only familiar faces at various vantage points—behind shrubs, be-hind cars, or beside the building. On this quiet night nothing yet disturbed the peaceful side streets beside the courthouse. The dance at the junior college had just ended and cars were working their way into town. The lookout scurried after the other men. Wearing a borrowed black silk scarf with eye slits, held in place by his rumpled gray felt hat and white cotton work gloves, Alford tried two keys unsuccessfully in the dark hallway before unlocking the door to the jail.

The noise of fitting the keys into the lock and shoving the wooden door open awakened all the white prisoners on the first level and C. J. Mondy up in Parker's cell. The trusty Dwight Ladner was resting on his cot in the hallway outside the white cells. It was after midnight, Saturday morning. "While I was lying awake on my bunk, I heard keys rattling in the door lead-

---

* Jewel Alford admitted to the FBI getting the keys for Walker and the others, leaving his house after 11:30 and returning shortly thereafter. He steadfastly denied going into M. C. Parker's cell and forcibly removing him from the jail. He did, however, name in an interview with the author the other men in the mob inside the courthouse.

ing from the cell block to the courtroom. Since I had been told several times by Jewel Alford, the jailer, that if anybody came up there for Parker . . . . I should point Parker out . . . . to them and to make sure they got the right Negro, I immediately assumed that the keys rattling at the door indicated that somebody had come for Parker. My bunk being at the south end of the bullpen, I got up and walked over by the steps leading up to the door." A light was burning over the landing in the upper tier of cells and one in the lower. As he came to the steps, Francis Barker shoved open the door and headed down the steps to the lower tier to unscrew the light bulb. After Barker, J. P. Walker entered, with Preacher Lee and Jewel Alford close on his heels. Ladner recognized the masked Walker and Preacher Lee and was surprised to see Alford beneath the black scarf. He recognized Alford's .38 caliber blue steel revolver with a bolt holding the bone handles to the grip. He also recognized Alford's light tan, low-quarter dress shoes, which he frequently polished. Alford was wearing his blue chambray work shirt and blue dungarees, the same clothes he had worn to work that day. Through the scarf Ladner also saw Jewel's black-rimmed glasses. As though to confirm Ladner's surprise, Alford leaned over to Ladner immediately upon entering and said, "Be quiet, boy." It was Jewel Alford all right, Ladner realized; his voice was a dead giveaway. Alford saw Barker, Walker, and Lee going the wrong way and called out to them in a hoarse whisper, "No, it's this way." The men turned abruptly and came back. Walker, Lee, and then Alford marched up the steps toward Parker's cell. The other men waited on the landing or crowded outside the doorway, straining for a better view.[6]

Before they started up the steps, Mondy called to Parker, who was just beginning to awaken, "Better get up, M. C., I bet they're coming for you."[7] At the top of the steps, Walker, his face hidden behind his bandanna, shouted to another black prisoner. "Boy, where is M. C. Parker at? We want him." "He's over there!" the prisoner shouted excitedly and pointed in the dim light toward the other cell. Walker unlocked the door at the head of the stairway and the three men walked into the cell area. Then Walker shouted, "How do you get in this door?" He held out the keys. Seeing them for the first time and certain they would be able to get him, Parker jumped down from the upper bunk and danced into his pants. From behind, Alford told Walker he had to unlock the control in the center of the second-tier box and then simply pull the levers. He did and the door drifted open.[8] Then Parker's cell mate "saw one man with a pistol and some of them had sticks in their hands. The one with the pistol went in Parker's cell first and Parker started hollering for help."[9]

The terrified Parker ran into the toilet area as the three men swarmed in after him, each brandishing a stick or club. Walker stuffed his police billy club in his belt and held only his pistol. As the mob closed in, Parker yelled to Mondy, "Help me, don't let them run over me this way!" Then Parker "went to hollering for help," shouting three or four times very loudly for assistance from anyone.[10]

When they cornered him by the toilet, Preacher Lee cried out to Walker to shoot him on the spot, but Walker stuffed his pistol into his pocket instead. In desperation, Parker, now screaming wildly, picked up the scrub bucket from beneath the sink and threw water over Walker and Alford. Walker backed up a step or two. Lee yelled, "Let's tie him up." He pulled a rope from his belt. The three men jumped Parker and began beating him with their clubs. Parker managed to grab Preacher Lee's club and cracked him across the head with it. Before he could use it further, the other men throttled him until he relinquished the club. Alford picked up the broom used by Parker and Mondy to sweep out their cell and beat the struggling Parker with it until the handle snapped in two. Furious at having been hit with his own stick, Preacher Lee began beating Parker while Alford grabbed the smaller piece of the broom handle and returned to the melee once again. Parker fought wildly to prevent the mob from tying his hands. Alford ran into the bullpen and returned with the garbage can. He emptied its contents onto the floor and smashed the can over Parker's head until Parker fell back against the sink.[11]

When Parker showed signs of giving up, Preacher Lee backed out of the cell, holding his throbbing head. Meanwhile, Parker, woozy and with his face and arms bloody, made one last attempt to flee. He dashed straight at the men, slipping through Walker's grasp, and ran toward Mondy, who was sitting on the lower bunk with his feet against his chest, trying to stay out of the way. Parker got close enough to Mondy to splatter blood on the front of Mondy's shirt before the men seized him and pulled him out of the cell by his heels. Parker grabbed the bars and Alford had to kick at his hands several times to make him let go. Parker screamed, "At least let me walk!" Walker replied curtly, "Hell no, you won't walk." In the ensuing confusion, as they dragged Parker out of the second-floor cell area, someone yelled to him, "Why did you do it?" "I didn't do it. I swear I didn't do it," the desperate Parker replied. "Who did then?" Parker looked up from the floor toward Mondy. "He did," he shouted and tried to point at his cell mate, still cowering on his bunk. Walker held Parker by his right leg while Preacher Lee grabbed the left. Jewel Alford followed closely behind. As they pulled him toward the steps, Alford began beating the flailing Parker with the broom handle. Before leaving, Alford reentered the cell and said to Mondy, "Don't say anything, there's more of us outside." Parker was still calling for help, but his strength was waning. "Don't let them take me out! Mondy, Mondy, don't let them kill me!"[12]

When they began dragging Parker down the steps toward the exit, Ladner, who had been standing by the landing, ran over to Helen Van Ness, the only female prisoner, and told her to put her head down on her bunk so she couldn't see anything. It was too late. The frightened woman had already recognized Herman Schulz and possibly Alford and Walker. Ladner thought he noticed through the open door six men standing around the courtroom in the eerie half-light cast by the single bare bulb on the second floor.[13] Only three men—J. P. Walker, Preacher Lee, and Jewel Alford—had actually entered Parker's cell. The rest stayed by the door and retreated into the hall as the mob hauled Parker down the steps. Parker continued to protest his innocence, said Mondy, repeating that it had been Mondy who "bothered the lady and this one and that one, everyone but himself." Down the iron steps Parker went, "his head banging like the chime on a clock."[14] Up in his cell his boots remained neatly arranged by the bunks, undisturbed by the life-and-death struggle in the cell, a reminder of Parker's fate to all who entered later. Still he grasped at the railing. At the botton of the steps he latched onto a rail again and Alford kicked at his hands once more until he let go.[15]

By the time they reached the landing with Parker in tow, he was bleeding profusely and still shouting for help. The furious mob had beaten much of the fight out of him, though. His resistance was so weak that it took only Walker and Lee to pull him down past the courtroom. Blood spurted from gashes on his head and face, and his upper arms bore large red welts from the beating. Just before going out the door, Walker turned to the prisoners and repeated Jewel Alford's earlier warning to C. J. Mondy. "Keep your damn mouths shut." "There are 200 or 300 men outside." He slammed the door behind him. In the hall Parker tried to yell again, and other members of the mob closed in to silence him.[16]

The commotion in the jail had been so loud that across the street at the hospital the two night nurses, Dimple Burge and Mrs. Odell Loveless, heard the noise from the struggle and someone yelling, "Help, help, help!" Dimple Burge, who had recently moved to Poplarville, immediately telephoned Sheriff Moody. In her haste she accidentally called Moody's son, George Vaught. "I called the first one's name I saw" on the list by the phone, she said. "I didn't know who it was or what it was." Panic-stricken, she told the gentle voice at the other end of the phone "that something terrible was going on over at the jail, that there was a desperate cry for help and to come quick."[17] George Vaught Moody, who had just returned home from chaperoning the dance at the Pearl River Junior College, called his father and told him one of the nurses had just reported trouble at the jail. There was little question in either man's mind about the nature of the trouble. The question was what they would encounter at the courthouse. The sheriff instructed his son to wait at home until he was called for. Moody wanted to arrive alone. Dimple Burge also telephoned the Star Cafe and left a message with the owner for Petey Carver to come to the jail immediately.[18]

The mob dragged Parker down the main flight of steps, then down the corridor to the door. Parker grabbed vainly at the plaster walls on the staircase, leaving bloody handprints with the fingers splayed, grotesquely clawing at the smooth surface. Small pools of blood formed at various points along the route where he struggled and received more beatings from his abductors as a consequence. The other inmates gathered at the cell windows, from which they saw people crowded on the front porch of the hospital, among them the night nurses in their starched white uniforms. From among them someone yelled at a group of men who stood like schoolboys by the large shrubs at the corner across from the hospital that the sheriff was on his way. Hearing this, they broke and ran for their cars. The mob emerged dragging Parker. On the top step, realizing he was away from the relative safety of the jail, Parker began screaming again, even louder than before, and managed to kick a leg free. The mob closed in on him again and beat him nearly unconscious. They pulled him down the concrete walk to the waiting Oldsmobile. As a last thought, Walker handed the keys to Jewel Alford, who tossed them onto the top step into a puddle of blood. Alford then ran to his car and drove home. He had been away from his worried wife for less than fifteen minutes. Jewel decided not to tell her what had happened for fear "it would kill her right then. She had been having problems with her nerves."[19]

Just before putting Parker into the back seat, Preacher Lee clubbed Parker two more times, causing him to cry out in pain. Then they stuffed him into the car. With Walker and the elder Lee in front, the dark car sped away in a harsh squeal of rubber. As it drove under the street light at the corner of West Pearl Street by the Poplarville Furniture Company, Ladner saw from the jail window several persons struggling in the back seat of the car. During the brief melee outside the courthouse, Crip's cousin, John Reyer, a crusty old truck farmer who had just taken his brother's wife to the hospital, rounded the south side of the courthouse and stumbled onto the mob. "I saw them throw him in the back of the car and then they jumped into the car and it took off fast. They drove east on the road that dead ends two blocks from the courthouse," Reyer said. "I didn't see which way they turned."[20] Five other cars also pulled away from the courthouse after the Oldsmobile and followed it for several blocks. The other men who had entered the jail followed in a car closely behind Walker. They turned right on Pine Street two blocks behind the courthouse and followed Walker's car for two more blocks to North Street, careening around corners in a mad dash to get out of town. They turned left onto Highway 26, which led past the junior college to the Pearl River and eventually to Bogalusa, Louisiana. The other cars followed for only a few blocks. Near the railroad tracks Alvin Gipson, owner of the Magnolia Court, the town's only motel, encountered the escaping cars. Gipson had held an organizational meeting of the local Barnett-for-Governor Committee at his motel and was driving some of the guests home. Walker drove so fast and so recklessly that he ran Gipson completely off the road up onto the grass, where Gipson and his friends watched the lynch mob roar by. Gipson himself recognized J. P. Walker and Preacher Lee in the first car. He could identify only Arthur Smith in the second and no one in the remaining cars, but the sight of the well-known Gipson, who also ran a prosperous construction business in the county, prompted the driver of every car behind Smith to turn off and head home.

The car containing Parker and the one following it had to thread their way through a knot of cars in front of the junior college, where the dance was still letting out, before resuming their flight out of town.[21] Once past the junior college they sped down the two-lane, blacktop highway toward the river. The night sky was clear and the moon provided enough light for them to see into the surrounding countryside. With his hands tied behind his back and his head pushed down onto the transmission hump, Parker bled onto the floor mats. He had grown too weak to put up much resistance in the crowded car. They continued to the Bogalusa Bridge, where Walker stopped and began to get out. As Walker opened the back door, a car rounded the bend on the Louisiana side of the river and headed across the bridge toward them. Seeing the oncoming lights, Walker hastily slammed the rear door, jumped back in, and continued across the river into Louisiana. The other car, which had followed Walker closely from the jail until he reached the bridge, remained at the side of the road about fifty yards down the highway from the home of T. G. Stringfellow. The Oldsmobile with Parker still inside continued down Highway 26, now in the state of Louisiana, and, after traveling several miles, pulled into a cattle-loading station. By this time it was after 12:30 a.m. and the road was virtually deserted. After a brief wait to make sure the road was completely free of traffic, Walker drove back to the Pearl River and crossed to the Mississippi side of the bridge. The second car drove onto the bridge, nose to nose with the Olds, and cut the engine.[22]

Again Walker opened the rear door to pull Parker out. When Parker realized that this was the end of the trip for him, he summoned every bit of his remaining strength and made a final attempt to escape. He kicked out wildly and tried to run away across the bridge. But he was much too unsteady to get far. J. P. Walker grabbed him by the shoulders and spun him around. Parker sagged to one knee. Walker knocked him to the ground with a blow to his chin, and the bound and beaten black man lay flat on his back beneath him. Others yanked him up and propped him on the edge of the concrete railing. From there two rounds from a .38 caliber revolver were fired from a distance of six inches directly into Parker's chest. The first shot pierced Parker's heart and he died within seconds.[23]

The original plan had been to castrate Parker and hang him from the metal superstructure of the bridge. Simple concrete retaining walls bordered most of the bridge, but at the center of the river the bridge was covered by a metal superstructure which in the moonlight resembled a rusty spider's web, with numerous joints on which to tie a rope for hanging Parker. But Parker was already dead. The men present decided to dispense with the morbid act of castrating a dead man. Seeing him executed at close range had had a dampening effect on even the most hardened of them. They cut the rope around Parker's hands, weighted him down with chains, lifted him up, and tossed him over the chest-high concrete railing into the river, swollen and muddy from the spring rains. The body landed with a smack and sank straight down. After watching for a minute or two, the grim men returned to their cars and headed out. Walker drove Reyer's car to a previously designated spot at Crossroads, Mississippi, where he turned over the car to Reyer. Reyer and Smith left immediately for McNeill. The other mob members went their separate ways, fading away into the night.[24]

During the lynching Poplarville's night marshal, Petey Carver, was absent from the town. Carver had returned for his two friends at 11:30, when the dance was scheduled to end. They drove north on Highway 11 to the Amoco station and cafe owned by George Rester, Jr., well outside of town and away from the meeting that was just breaking up to the east of Route 26, and had a cup of coffee. When they returned to town several minutes later, they noticed two men walking on the street behind the Star Cafe. They also saw a two-toned Chevrolet on Main Street near the courthouse. The car had no license plates, and three men were sitting in it, as though they were waiting for someone on an errand inside the courthouse. With R. J. Wheat sitting silently beside him and Stringfellow in the back seat, Carver drove not to the courthouse to investigate but over to B. F. Orr's house to awaken him. Carver and Orr had an agreement that whenever Petey suspected trouble, which was seldom, he would immediately alert Orr. He had not awakened him at night for about seven years previous to this night. On the way to Orr's house, they noticed two women standing on the corner of Cumberland Street, about three blocks from the courthouse. Petey had seen these two an hour earlier standing in front of the Star Cafe, talking with its owner. He thought it unusual that they would be walking the normally quiet streets at such a late hour, but because they had been talking to someone he knew, he gave it no significance. Before going to Orr's house, Carver drove around several blocks and all the way out Main Street, looking for anyone else out at that late hour. Finding no one, he continued through the railroad underpass into town to Orr's, where he arrived shortly after 11:30.[25]

Carver left Stringfellow and Wheat in the car and walked through the garage to a back window, where he awakened Orr. The wily Orr had a reputation of being a crafty lawman who often outwitted his adversaries. Those who knew him often joked that Orr was such a good marshal because he had the mind of a first-rate criminal. Ten minutes later Orr joined them in the car. After listening patiently to Carver's reasons for awakening him, the marshal suggested that they drive to the Amoco station for a quick cup of coffee, even though Carver had just come from there. The fastest route there went straight through town past the courthouse. Instead of this, they took the circuitous back road out of Poplarville to Route 11 and then backtracked to the Amoco station. There they saw Junior Rester, a number of teen-age boys, and several men. Carver and Orr maintained to the FBI that their car had stalled at the station. They later admitted to the FBI that they had lied about this. The four men remained at Junior Rester's for twenty-five minutes drinking coffee—when for years prior to this Carver and Orr always had coffee at the Star Cafe. After spending over half an hour out of town, they reentered Poplarville and drove down Main Street. Although the mob had just left with Parker, the two marshals and their two companions claimed they noticed no unusual activity at the courthouse. Two blocks past the courthouse, Bessie Davis, a waitress at the Star Cafe, flagged them down to tell them that Nurse Burge had called from the hospital and asked that Carver be sent to jail immediately—there was a disturbance among the prisoners. Carver circled the block and returned to the courthouse, driving to the south entrance, where he saw a small group of people standing around talking excitedly.[26]

When they pulled up to the south entrance, Orr told Wheat to get out and see what the men were doing there. As Wheat approached the crowd, someone volunteered, "They got the nigger out of jail." "What nigger?" Carver yelled from his car. "The nigger in jail." From someone else they learned that Sheriff Moody was on his way. John Reyer approached the car and told Carver about the men dragging Parker into the back seat of a car. Reyer described the car as blue and gray, while someone else remembered it as blue and white. Dimple Burge told the marshal there had actually been four or five cars; all left hurriedly and "went every which way" when the car carrying Parker departed. After examining the spot where John Reyer and others claimed the car carrying Parker had been parked, Carver and Orr found five marks indicating a sudden acceleration. Meanwhile, across the street at the hospital, Dimple Burge and Nurse Odell Loveless talked to anyone who would listen about what they had seen. The more Dimple talked, the more confusion she created, until Orr walked over and asked her to be quiet.[27]

4

The Morning After
the Night Before

On Friday night Sheriff Moody went to his son's home just before midnight to pick up his wife, who had been baby-sitting for their two-month-old grandson while George Vaught and his wife chaperoned the dance at the junior college. Shortly after the sheriff and his wife returned home, their son, George Vaught, telephoned to say that Dimple Burge had just called him about a commotion at the jail. Sheriff Moody told his wife he felt sure someone had come for Parker, and he feared some of his political opponents might be responsible.[1]

Sheriff Moody had mixed emotions about Parker and about the people he felt might be involved in the trouble at the jail. Coming from a deeply religious family, the respected Moody resisted the stereotypical image of the flamboyant Southern sheriff who regularly and with impunity practiced his own brand of individualized justice. Moody wanted to see Parker punished for his crime and felt no remorse that Parker might be dead and out of the way, but the thought of a lynching troubled him deeply. He suspected all along something might happen to prevent Parker from standing trial, although he had only vague notions of what it might be. The greatest danger, he felt, was that someone might try something in court during the trial. In any case, Moody had been unwilling to differ with Sebe Dale and unilaterally post guards at the courthouse or request National Guard assistance. As for the trouble at the jail, Petey Carver's late arrival troubled him simply because he should have been there the minute trouble started. Moody and his wife lived outside of town on the Bogalusa road, the same road the mob took to the Pearl River. A very brief time elapsed between the time the mob left the courthouse and Moody left his home. He arrived at the courthouse at 1:00 a.m., where the normally officious Petey Carver and B. F. Orr were waiting in their car with Wheat and Stringfellow. Others stood around outside. Moody knew something serious had happened because Orr never left his house at night. When he called the marshal over to his car, Orr told him, "They got the nigger."[2]

Moody drove behind the courthouse and parked in the space reserved for him. The door to the courthouse stood wide open. All the lights were out. He returned to his car for his flashlight. Coming back up the walk, he played his light across the puddles of blood on the steps and a bloody hand print on the top step before going inside—followed at a discreet distance by the men in Carver's car and some of the others. The inside of the courthouse looked like a Roman amphitheater. There was a large smear of blood by the door and long streaks of blood down the hall nearly two feet wide. In some places the blood was steady for seven or eight feet. The path of blood continued up the steps to the jail. The light in Moody's office was off and the door locked. His one standing order since becoming sheriff was to leave a light on in his office and keep the hall door unlocked in case someone had to get the cell keys in a hurry or needed access to documents. Entering his office he noticed the open windows. It was the custom to close and latch them each night. The key to the filing cabinet was still in the lock and the top left-hand desk drawer, where the key should have been, was partially opened. The keys to the jail were missing. Taking care to leave everything undisturbed, Moody hastened upstairs. At the passage into the jail, located just outside the door to the courtroom, he encountered Marshal Orr. Orr handed him the keys. When asked where they had been, Orr replied he found them on the outside steps.[3]

Moody asked him what had happened. Orr said only that Petey Carver stopped for him shortly before midnight and they had come down to the jail. That was obvious, Moody thought. Inside the jail Dwight Ladner cowered behind the door, listening. When the men unlocked the door and came in to question the prisoners, Ladner was so frightened for his own safety he reported only that a group of men "got that boy." Moody asked which one. "Parker," Ladner answered. As Wheat joined him, Moody walked part way up the steps to the second tier. He looked around the tier and over toward Parker's cell, asking the black prisoners, "Did they get the right one?" Mondy spoke for them all, "Yes, suh, I guess so—they got Parker," adding that all the men in the mob had worn white gloves. The sheriff asked how the mob got the keys and none of the men knew. He tried the door to the tier and found it locked. Feeling regret at his possible complicity, Mondy volunteered he had helped one man open the cell door because he had brandished a pistol. The prisoners agreed there had been seven or eight men in the mob, and Helen Van Ness, on the verge of hysteria, explained to Moody that some of the men had waited in the courtroom while the others went up to Parker's cell. None of the prisoners would identify any of the mob members.[4]

Sheriff Moody returned to his office and called a Mississippi highway patrolman who lived in Poplarville. Moody told him what had happened and asked him to alert the highway patrol. He gave him a description of Parker to distribute. He next called the FBI agent in Gulfport, but his line was busy. After that he telephoned District Attorney Vernon Broome—who was to have prosecuted Parker—and Sebe Dale. A short time later, the head of the southern branch of the highway patrol called Moody to tell him to call the governor. J. P. Coleman had addressed a high school group in Newton, Mississippi, about sixty miles from Jackson that night. He had just returned to the Governor's Mansion and gone to bed when the highway patrol reported the lynching. Within minutes Moody telephoned, and Coleman instructed him to contact the FBI in Gulfport, which Moody said he had already tried to do. Half an hour later Coleman called Moody to make sure he had reached the FBI.

At 4:00 a.m. the FBI contacted Joseph Ryan, second to W. Wilson White in the newly created Civil Rights Division, to get Justice Department authorization to enter the case.* Ryan felt the nature of the case merited immediate federal involvement under the Lindbergh law—even though that statute fell under

---

* The Civil Rights Act of 1957 expanded the Civil Rights Section in the Justice Department to a full division.

the purview of the Criminal Division—and the civil rights statutes, which were the responsibility of his own division. Within
hours after Parker had been lynched, all the town officials, the
state highway patrol, the governor, and in Washington the FBI,
the Justice Department, and the White House had been notified.
The news quickly reached both wire services.[5]

During the early morning hours countless people began showing up at the sheriff's already crowded office, where some of
them exuded an air of tense excitement tempered by the unspoken fear that the mob had not made a clean getaway. The
situation lapsed into such confusion that people only knew one
thing for sure—the rapist was dead. But then, could they really
trust these early rumors? Maybe Parker was not dead. After
Moody talked for the second time to Governor Coleman, he
called his wife to let her know he was all right and would be
home later. As they talked, John Reyer came into the office and
sat down beside the desk. Others in the room—Orr, Carver,
Wheat, Stringfellow, Will Estes Moody, and several of the lookouts who had brazenly returned to the courthouse—crowded
around the crusty old farmer to hear his story.

Reyer told Moody he had been standing on the porch of the
hospital, where he had taken his brother's wife, and had crossed
the street when he heard the commotion at the south entrance.
He came fairly close to the mob, he claimed, but explained
quickly that everyone had worn masks, making it impossible to
identify any of them. He knew they were white because two of
them had covered the lower portion of their faces with handker-
chiefs, which left much of their face exposed. Reyer repeated
that he had never seen these two men before. As for the others,
no one looked familiar. Moody telephoned his son and Jewel
Alford to come to the jail to help with the search. About that
time County Attorney Bill Stewart arrived and began taking
Polaroid pictures of the blood on the front steps, the bloody
stairs, Parker's jail cell, and other parts of the courthouse
thought to be involved in the abduction.[6]

In spite of John Reyer's graphic description, the gruesome
nature of the crime was of less concern to Moody than the possible implications. Clearly, several law enforcement officers should
have been in a position to prevent the lynching, yet they had
been nowhere near the courthouse at the time. This alone made
it appear that not only had the conspiracy been widespread but
some law officers had purposely kept Moody in the dark. The

sheriff may have suspected a lynching might occur, but he had no reason to anticipate that the men involved in it would receive cooperation from any local law-enforcement officer.[7]

After Orr had given Moody the keys, he and Carver left the courthouse for the marshal's office at the Poplarville City Hall to call Sheriff Hickman in Purvis and Marshal Ham Slade in Lumberton. When Hickman arrived, he and Orr conducted a search of the area where the rape had taken place, checking numerous side roads around Poplarville but found nothing.[8]

Carver, Wheat, and Stringfellow also decided to inspect the roads around Poplarville. After checking with Moody, Carver and his friends spent an hour riding along Highway 26 east toward the Wolf River Bridge. Carver and his two friends assumed the mob had killed Parker, but where, they wanted to know, had it disposed of the body? No one entertained a serious thought that Parker might still be alive. It seemed most likely that the mob had dumped Parker's body into one of the nearby rivers. The Wolf River ran east of Poplarville toward the Gulf of Mexico, but its waters were shallow in spite of the spring runoff. Only the swollen waters of the Pearl River were deep enough to conceal a body. In spite of the fact that names of potential mob leaders had been circulating in town prior to the lynching, these three men suggested a connection between the two women and the two men they saw, neglecting to mention the unlicensed Chevrolet. Carver said he thought the women were lookouts for a burglary.[9]

Sheriff Moody also made a personal search of the roads around Poplarville with a highway patrolman. They too went to the spot where June Walters had been raped but found no evidence indicating the mob had taken Parker there. Throughout the night the highway patrol and other law officers conducted random searches of the county. Sheriff Moody, waiting for the arrival of the FBI, neither conducted nor authorized an organized, extensive search for Parker. The scattered, independent patrols turned up nothing to indicate what might have happened to Parker. In the confusion and heightened emotions at the sheriff's office, officers did not rush to the homes of any of the more outspoken critics of the trial. At 6:00 a.m. Jewel Alford told Houston Amacker and his brother Jeppie that Sheriff Moody wanted them to clean up the blood before the office workers arrived. Houston grumbled about the sickening mess, but complied. He soon became nauseated and left for the doctor's office.[10]

After his brief search of the site of the rape, Moody remained at his office throughout the night and into the morning. During these long hours people strayed in and out of his office, some connected with the investigation, others merely onlookers and curiosity seekers. It was customary in Pearl River County for people to drop by the sheriff's office in times of trouble. No one considered it unprofessional that Wheat and Stringfellow accompanied Carver on his nightly rounds. Friends often idled away the hours at the courthouse, a tradition in small-town America, conversing with the people researching deeds in the clerk's office, sharing a bit of gossip, or running errands for the sheriff. It made official business something less than privileged information and, in this case, helped make the lynching and knowledge of it a community affair. At Moody's request Wheat tried to telephone a reporter at the Jackson *Daily News* but was unable to reach him. Wheat tried radio station WFOR in Hattiesburg and informed newsman Ed Jenkins of the lynching. Jenkins rushed to Poplarville and became the first out-of-town newsman on the scene.[11]

Other members of the police force contacted the New Orleans *Times-Picayune* and the Picayune *Item*, papers they thought would be friendly to Poplarville. As a result, well before 8:00 a.m. on Saturday morning, members of the regional press began arriving in Poplarville. These were known to local citizens and a few, such as Bill Minor, the head of the *Times-Picayune*'s Jackson office, had over the years become close personal friends of Sebe Dale's and several town officials. Once the story reached AP and UPI, reporters arrived from as far away as New York City. The prompt arrival of journalists from the outside frightened the citizens of Poplarville, who had failed to anticipate the tremendous amount of attention that the media would give to the lynching. Initially, the townspeople made light of the lynching, not so much to cover their concern as to conceal their fear of potentially critical outsiders. The story the first reporters received was simply this: A group of eight to ten men, who were probably not from Poplarville, entered the courthouse and, possibly with the assistance of "someone" in Poplarville, located the keys and entered the jail, where they beat M. C. Parker semiconscious and dragged him out of the south entrance. They sped away, followed by four or five other cars that disappeared in various directions. The abductors probably took Parker to the Pearl River, the Wolf River, or a neighboring bayou and drowned him. From coast to coast the reports did not vary; the press accepted for the time being that Poplarville itself was as much a victim as M. C. Parker. Reporters dutifully filed stories that local residents had no idea who had been in the lynch mob but were absolutely certain none of its members came from their quiet little town.[12]

This soon began to change. By midmorning shouting, craning reporters crowded the sheriff's office, pestering the sheriff for every little extra fact and detail, asking probing questions about the origins of the lynch mob and the results of its work. Where was Mack Charles Parker? "I'm certain he's either been removed from the area or dumped in some water," Moody replied, telling them also that there had been no witnesses to the abduction. He patiently explained and re-explained that he had conducted a search of the area fifteen miles around Poplarville to no avail.[13] The highway patrolmen from Jackson and Gulfport who arrived during the early morning hours also had to contend with busy reporters trying to glean extra tidbits of information about the sensational story. The noisy scene contrasted sharply with a normal Saturday in Poplarville. In a quiet moment to themselves Moody remarked to his son and Jewel Alford, who remained with him at his office during the long night and into the morning, that certain factions might have conducted the lynching in such a way as to embarrass him. Jewel Alford, who was only beginning to feel the burden that would fall on him in the days to come, kept silent about his part in the lynching. Although Moody wondered from the very beginning how the lynchers could have gotten to Parker so easily, he was reluctant to focus his suspicions. The sheriff, his son, Alford, and Will Estes Moody found themselves in a tightly besieged circle as the press began to point the finger of blame at them, hinting that the sheriff had been lax in his duties, that he should have called in the National Guard or at least the highway patrol, that perhaps Parker should have been removed from the jail entirely to prevent such a thing from happening. Any factional squabbling resulting from this was short-lived because as the investigation developed and was reported in the papers, the entire town found itself saddled with blame. By noon, with policemen, FBI agents, and reporters from out of state pouring into tiny Poplarville, an air of anxiety began to replace the initial celebration over Parker's death. The FBI questioned those present in the courthouse about a conspiracy to "set Moody up." From the outset agents doubted official claims of innocence. The lynching appeared to them to conform to the old rule that every major crime is to some extent an inside job. Sheriff Moody consistently denied such accusations, but the circumstances indicated otherwise. Almost at once, however, George Vaught Moody suspected J. P. Walker had planned the lynching partly as an act of racial prejudice and partly as an election ploy.[14]

While Poplarville reeled from the shock of its instant celebrity, several miles away, back in the quiet of a country lane, Crip Reyer and Arthur Smith scrubbed furiously at the interior of Crip's Oldsmobile, trying to remove the blood from the rear floor. It was especially thick on the rear hump. They worked for hours cleaning blood from the car until it looked cleaner than it ever had, suspiciously so, but, they hoped, clean enough to fool any nosy FBI men. They had already heard that the governor would soon call in the FBI, if he hadn't already done so.

At his home in Bogalusa, Eddie Walters was the first to learn how quickly the FBI could move. He became the first person to receive a visit from federal agents, even before most people in Poplarville knew definitely that the FBI had entered the case. Upon rising and listening to the news on the radio, he had left for his home. Shortly after he arrived, Roy K. Moore, the local FBI agent, drove up in front of his house and knocked on his door. Moore asked Walters about his activities the night before while his men made a plaster cast of his tire tread. When Moore left, Eddie got on the phone to warn some of the others. Jimmy Walters had already headed out the door for work when June came running after him with tears in her eyes. Hearing the news, he shrugged his shoulders and told her he had to go, he'd be late for work. He wondered, though, how many of the mob members he knew.[15]

About the time the FBI was questioning Eddie Walters, Sebe Dale donned his blue suit and red tie, stuffed a bright red bandanna into his breast pocket, and hastened to Poplarville from his home in Columbia. Reflecting the prevailing attitude in Pearl River County, he too felt Parker got what was coming to him. Never possessing a strong intellect, the Southern jurist had shown a notable lack of concern over his own words and deeds prior to the lynching. Only now did he begin to worry about his own pre-trial role. Of greatest concern to him were possible accusations that he should have authorized Moody to call in the National Guard when the sheriff first suggested it. Dale feared in light of what had happened that the public at large would not readily believe he had not expected any violence. Dale found himself caught in a potentially embarrassing dilemma: If he used FBI involvement in the lynching investigation to score political points against his foe, J. P. Coleman, he risked being embarrassed by his own bland assertions about Parker's safety in an unguarded jail. On the other hand, since he had blasted Parker in open court, to oppose the FBI would invite the nation to conclude he favored the lynching. The consequences were frightening. Dale followed his sentiments, counseling Moody to maintain that there had been no threat or indication of trouble in the days preceding the lynching and that the mob had not originated in the town. He feared the damage that might be done to Poplarville should the FBI apprehend some or all of the mob members and their places of residence become public knowledge. The judge was concerned about the effect the lynching would have on the civil rights bill pending in Congress. He knew State Attorney General Joe Patterson had already testified against the bill and that Governor Coleman was planning to travel to Washington to testify against it as well. Dale worried this lynching might have an adverse effect on the senators who had not yet decided their position.[16]

When reporters began to ask Dale to explain how he failed to anticipate some degree of violence when officers in Lumberton and Jackson had expressed concern that trouble might develop, Dale told them, "I didn't hear a grumble in Pearl River County. No one in Pearl River County seemed to want anything other than Parker be given a legal trial." Asked why he had denied defense attorney R. Jess Brown's motion for a change of venue, he replied that June Walters was from Forrest County and although he knew some people there were upset about the case, he doubted that anyone in the Poplarville area cared about the rape victim or the man on trial.[17]

Dale was initially less than forthright with the press, but as attitudes about the lynching began to change and more people attacked the FBI and the media, he gave the lie to his early claims of not suspecting violence. "I saw Parker in court before he was taken," he said. "I never saw anybody so smug in a courtroom. It was like he was sitting there getting an award." Dale blamed Brown for instilling in his client the belief that he would win on appeal. "Looking at him, I gave thanks to God that it didn't happen in my family. I'm scared to death I might have taken the law in my own hands right there in court." This is indeed what J. P. Walker had talked of doing. And yet after admitting to harboring such intense animosity for Parker, the outspoken judge never reconsidered his position that Parker would have received a fair trial in his court.[18]

On Saturday morning, from his office in Jackson, far north of Poplarville, a chagrined Governor Coleman made it official that he had requested aid from the FBI to speed apprehension of the mob. Weary from his night-long vigil, the governor said he called in the FBI immediately because it would have entered the case in twenty-four hours anyway since federal law assumed any kidnapping unsolved after twenty-four hours to have involved interstate flight. Echoing Moody's public views, Coleman said, "The men possibly were not from Pearl River County, but we don't know where they are from." The violence "came as a complete surprise," he said, because neither Parker's attorney nor any Pearl River County official had notified him of any "high feeling. But it was evident," he continued, "that neither of them [Moody or Dale] had any hint this was going to happen." Coleman had predicted that his four years as governor would end in January without racial violence. Noted for his persuasive personality, the popular Coleman was severely shaken by the lynching and sought to put it into perspective by reminding the public that it was the first such incident since the 1939 Duck Hill lynching. He vowed that "every possible effort" would be made to apprehend the members of the mob. Speaking in a hushed voice that emphasized his anguish, he promised, "The violators will be prosecuted according to law."

Although an ardent segregationist, Coleman had acquired a reputation for being a racial moderate. The term *moderate,* however, is misleading. J. P. Coleman did not espouse racial terrorism, but he *did* espouse Massive Resistance; perhaps more than most whites, he exemplified it. He knew what would have to be done to block the trends of recent history and he understood implicitly what would have to be done to thwart the *Brown* decision. When Senator Eastland called for his state to form a State Sovereignty Commission as a means for preventing change in the state, Governor Coleman became its head, declaring in his initial speech in 1956, "After all, integration came about because people gave up. We will not give up." The commission was founded to "do and perform any and all acts and things deemed necessary and proper to protect the sovereignty of the state of Mississippi and her sister states from encroachment thereon by the Federal government or any branch, department, or agency thereof." This expressed in moderate terms the extreme philosophy of Theodore Bilbo.[19] Coleman's lieutenant governor, Carroll Gartin, and his attorney general, Joe Patterson, and other leading state politicians were also founding members of the state-funded commission. It had an original appropriation of $250,000 and an investigatory unit headed by the former head of the highway patrol, utilizing paid informers and secret investigators "to save the white race from amalgamation, mongrelization and destruction." As a candidate for governor, Coleman had said that he was "thoroughly ready for anything those who wish to destroy segregation may wish to come up with."[20] Anything but racial violence, because he was one of the few Southern whites intelligent enough to understand that violence would eventually have the reverse effect: it would raise before the public the question of the character of the people in power in the South.[21]

Along with the white Citizens Councils, the state-sanctioned commission localized, regionalized, and legitimized the white stand against integration.[22] Resistance as fundamental and widespread as this could only be undercut by intemperate acts from within. Coleman's outrage at the lynching thus was a genuine expression of his feelings, not feigned as was Dale's. "Any killing in premeditation is murder in Mississippi under any circumstances," he said angrily, "and we will prosecute one as such. I never expected to live to see the day anything like this would happen in Mississippi again."[23] The governor's outrage clearly had more to do with other factors than the death of a black man. As newsmen crowded around him and Joe Patterson, Coleman expressed deep concern over the effect of the lynching on the civil rights bill. Never one to remain on the defensive, he attacked the bill and M. C. Parker. "This violence comes at a bad time. I had considered antilynching laws as necessary as one against racing a buggy on a highway. Every citizen will be looking for the men. We would use the National Guard if we thought that would contribute anything. As far as I know this is the first incident of this kind in 20 years. It is the first since I've been governor and I doubly regret it for that reason. The proof of this man's guilt was conclusive. There was no question he would have been convicted. This made the action all the more unnecessary. The people of Mississippi as a whole do not approve of taking the law into their own hands. I trust the overwhelming majority of Mississippians won't be punished by Civil Rights leg-

islation for what a handful have done in violation of the law."
This was the first public mention by a Mississippi state official of
the connection between the lynching and civil rights legislation
as well as the first public discussion of the rape case against
Parker. Coleman's pre-trial assertion of Parker's guilt, which any
appeals court would surely have considered prejudicial, indicated that the governor too, reflecting his knowledge of Mississippi lynch mobs in the past, believed Parker already dead.[24]

Coleman also defended the absence of a guard in the jail the
previous night. "A vast number of Mississippi jails are locked up
without night jailers," usually because they have "too few prisoners to warrant a night jailer," he claimed, citing his hometown
of Ackerman as an example. He ended by reiterating he had no
way of knowing of Brown's motion for a change of venue except
through newspapers, and none had reported it. After the governor had spoken, Joe Patterson told newsmen, "It is to be regret-
ted that a small number of men have seen fit to attempt to take
the law into their own hands and thwart the administration of
justice in this case. I know the good law-abiding people of Pearl
River County, as good law-abiding people of the State of Mississippi as a whole, regret this unfortunate incident." Like Coleman, Patterson later attempted to alter the focus of his public
statements when accusations echoed across the state that Coleman had betrayed Mississippi by needlessly summoning the
FBI.[25]

By late morning the posse of some forty men, including the
highway patrol, sheriff's deputies, and Poplarville marshals and
constables, had initiated a search. They fanned out over a radius
of fifteen miles. Although Moody said publicly he thought the
mob had taken Parker from the area, he concentrated the search
on the bodies of water deep enough to hide a body. Never well
organized, the search floundered as the weary sheriff contended
with the ever-growing number of reporters and curiosity seekers
wandering into his office. At one point in the morning J. P.
Walker joined the crowd of hangers-on at the courthouse, trying
to learn as much as he could about the investigation without
appearing too interested or too blasé. Late in the morning the
first contingent of FBI agents from the regional headquarters in
New Orleans arrived. The branch chief, the stern Ralph W.
Bachman, immediately assumed command of the investigation.
After briefing the agents and assisting them in securing temporary office space, Moody returned to his home for some much-

needed sleep. "If I knew this was going to happen," he explained to the grim-faced Bachman, "I would have moved him to another jail or put on several guards. I think I could have stopped it all if I had gotten there in time," he offered. "At least, I would have done my best to stop it."[26]

When Bachman approached Bill Stewart for his view of the situation, the county attorney openly applauded the lynching, and assured him the jury would have convicted Parker by noon of the trial day and the state would have carried the case all the way to the Supreme Court if a federal judge reversed the local verdict. If the Supreme Court had released Parker, the outspoken Stewart proclaimed, he personally would have been one of the first to do something about it. In that case the lynching would have been the fault of the federal judge, not the sovereign state of Mississippi, he said. It would have been fine with him if the mob "cut off the goddam nigger's balls and mailed them to the judge" with a note saying, "We did all we could. This is your fault." Stewart added, "We weren't going to make any further effort to try him, but we would turn him loose from the jail some dark night, about the same time this lynching occurred." Interestingly enough, reporters in Poplarville found the outspoken Stewart to be the friendliest Poplarville official. "He was the fun loving type," thought reporter Claude Sitton, who noted with amusement that Stewart also served as "the town's unofficial publicity agent" during the investigation.[27]

5

A Small Town in Mississippi

Had anyone in Poplarville, including Petey Carver and his cousin B. F. Orr,[1] chosen to speak up against the lynching before it occurred or to stop the mob from entering the jail, Parker would have lived and the townspeople would not have been faced with a painful dilemma in the days that followed. People with knowledge of the lynching tried to adhere to the tradition of silence in an effort to stay out of the investigation. But the spectacular nature of the crime and the strong federal involvement meant that a mere shrug of the shoulders would not settle the matter. This state of affairs alone underscored the anachronistic nature of the lynching. The younger elements of the community had had a limited hand in the crime. Older elements with a stronger affinity for the tactics of the past designed, planned, and carried out the lynching. In that respect the members of the lynch mob represented the vestiges of the old tradition of vigilante-enforced racial oppression.[2]

Fear played an important role in keeping people quiet. As events during the week after the lynching proved, even whites felt they were not safe from mob members, who having struck once might with provocation strike again. Although the wife of the mayor feared black retaliation against innocent whites, she

demonstrated an even greater fear of the mob. Such fear prevented whites who opposed the lynching from speaking out. The
arrival of newsmen and the FBI further suppressed any opposition to the lynching. Whites put aside their factional disputes
and came together to defend their town. As much as the mayor's
wife, Mrs. Pat Hyde, disliked J. P. Walker, she disliked the press
and the FBI even more. Whatever the sentiments of the townspeople, whether they agreed that Parker got what he deserved
or that the law was inviolate and should have been allowed to
take its course (so long as Parker was eventually punished), immediately after the lynching most people carefully avoided asking questions or naming names, and went about their business as
though nothing at all had happened.[3]

While generally making light of the lynching to reporters with
jokes and buffoonery, local residents were developing considerable although masked animosity toward the FBI and the
press. This plus adverse presidential and congressional criticism
spawned a defiance that observers came to construe as wholesale
support for the lynching. This did not mean that left to their
own devices the citizenry would have eventually spoken out
against the lynching, it meant that national hostility caused them
to unify as a measure of self-defense. This unity directly benefited the most ardent extremists. On a state level, the lynching
fractured already divided political loyalties and in the end resulted in a ten-year setback for Coleman-style racial moderation.
Although the clash in state politics was ostensibly between Sebe
Dale, along with other followers of Theodore Bilbo, and Coleman and his fellow moderates, who eschewed Bilbo-inspired invective, the real subject of debate became Coleman himself.*
According to Lieutenant Governor Carroll Gartin, "He almost

---

* At the time of the lynching, Dale and Coleman were on strained terms. Coleman had
backed Carroll Gartin over Dale for lieutenant governor in 1955, and Dale never forgave
him. In the 1959 state gubernatorial race, Dale backed Ross Barnett. Dale and Coleman
had exchanged angry letters in March over Dale's handling of a case involving a black
man accused of manslaughter. In 1956 Lydus Bass, a retarded epileptic, pleaded guilty to
the charge and placed himself at the mercy of the court, saying he could not afford an
attorney. Dale sentenced him to twenty years without even taking a token recess to review
the case. Bass's father and several whites brought the matter to Coleman's attention, who,
after reviewing the facts, suspended the sentence. In an angry letter to Dale, Coleman
observed, "From an examination of the record in this case, I am convinced that if the
prisoner had had counsel and had gone to trial he would have been acquitted. I do not
know why the trial judge assessed a penalty of twenty years when the subject pleaded
guilty and threw himself on the mercy of the court." Dale responded that

radiates confidence, his opponents can't help but wonder if he isn't right after all." The governor's overpowering personality created an undercurrent of resentment. Mississippi politicians either loved him or hated him. Racial extremists left no one in doubt about how they felt.[4]

Coleman did not escape criticism from Parker's attorney either. The governor committed a serious legal blunder by declaring "conclusive" the evidence that Parker had raped June Walters. Brown called public attention to it and added cryptically, "Parker's guilt could have at best only been deemed conclusive after the defense had presented its side. Mr. Coleman, himself a lawyer, knows that." Brown felt, quite justifiably, that Parker had every chance to win an acquittal and offered to defend him *in absentia* if it was possible under state law to do so. But the damage had already been done. The issue of Parker's guilt or innocence had become one of official speculation. The citizens of Poplarville seized upon the governor's remarks as support for their claims.[5]

More serious problems for Governor Coleman accompanied the FBI into the case. When Coleman so swiftly called in the FBI, he was acting at least in part on the conversation he had had with Sheriff Moody in which Moody expressed virtual certainty that the known witnesses could identify some or all of the mob members. The governor wanted to show the nation a desire by the people of his state to bring the guilty parties to immediate justice. Unlike most Southern segregationist governors, James Plemon Coleman (Plemon to many of his close friends) had toned down his rhetoric when addressing a national audience, and he was considerably more aware of Mississippi's position in the nation than were his rivals. But the governor seriously underestimated the reaction of white Mississippians to Parker's crime as well as the support they would give to advocates of the more violent forms of

---

"a bit of personal motivation could have been a motivating factor in your caustic remarks about the judge when the records don't warrant such."

The Bass incident exacerbated another festering disagreement between Coleman and Dale. Lately Coleman had stepped up efforts to halt the bootlegging in southern Mississippi, particularly the interstate trade with Louisiana. Mississippi had adopted a curious black market tax on illegal liquor, and Coleman permitted the state tax collector to make known the names of those who paid their tax so that Louisiana wholesalers might deal only with these parties. Dale, who had been working with the police to clean up or at least regulate whiskey running, accused Coleman of conspiring to violate the state prohibition laws. Jackson *Clarion-Ledger*, March 7, 9, 1959; New Orleans *Times-Picayune*, November 7, 1959.

racism. White citizens began to denounce the once popular governor for calling in the FBI so precipitously.[6]

FBI director J. Edgar Hoover dispatched a large squad of agents to Poplarville and announced that Attorney General William Rogers would keep "the White House fully informed of developments of this case." The political demands of an election year forced the Eisenhower administration to show a degree of concern in this investigation it had not demonstrated in past incidents of racial violence, with the possible exception of the 1957 Little Rock school crisis. Beginning Saturday, after the lynching, the Justice Department began making regular reports to the White House on the case. The affair was quickly becoming a national scandal. Speaking for the administration, Hoover reassured the country that "every possible lead will be expeditiously covered," and the "full facilities of the FBI, including laboratory and identification divisions, will be exerted to determine the complete facts."[7]

Within twenty-hours after the lynch mob pulled Mack Charles Parker from the Poplarville jail, the FBI entered the case in force. The squad, which ultimately grew to sixty agents, quickly organized an extensive, well-coordinated search of the surrounding countryside. The highway patrol gave the FBI its complete cooperation. Working in tandem the FBI and the highway patrol crossed the Pearl River into Louisiana in an effort to track down clues. The FBI began its investigation with the approval of the sheriff's department and with the cooperation of other law enforcement agencies, and it appeared to Ralph Bachman and local officials that such a massive joint effort would produce quick, positive results.[8]

Voicing support from Washington, Mississippi's Fifth District congressman, William M. "Buddy" Colmer, who represented Pearl River County, reflected Moody's sentiments with one slight qualification. "Along with all Mississippians I greatly deplore this [lynching] as well as other aspects of violence, including the one this man was charged with committing."[9] At the time a subcommittee of the House Judiciary Committee was considering several versions of a new civil rights bill and a member on that panel declared the lynching undermined Southern arguments that no federal legislation was needed to guarantee blacks their rights. Southern response was quick and predictable. Congressman Frank E. Smith from central Mississippi deeply deplored the lynching but felt more civil rights legislation was unnecessary and would not have prevented the incident. In that at least he was probably correct. James O. Eastland, the senior senator from Mississippi, in an attempt to shift the focus of national attention, drew attention to the recent mob killing of a black child in Boston. The 1957 killing in Boston occurred, he said, when "a colored boy" sought to defend a white girl he was with from the insults of a group of white youths. In the past the South had made repeated references to incidents of racial violence in the North as proof that Northern legislators intentionally made a scapegoat of the South. Even Southern liberals supported this argument. Mississippi's other senator, John Stennis, made a similar reference to the incident in Boston, and as for the Parker lynching, he was "sure that the governor, sheriff and other authorities are doing everything to apprehend those responsible and see that justice is done." Testifying before the subcommittee of the House Judiciary Committee before the lynching occurred, Joe Patterson had argued that Mississippi's laws "provided stiffer penalties for lynching than those proposed in the federal anti-lynching bills." He added, "We haven't had a lynching in Mississippi to the best of my knowledge in more than twenty years." Southern law enforcement officers, he strenuously maintained, could handle their own law enforcement without federal interference.[10] The *Clarion-Ledger* later mourned: "The emphatic and well documented statement by Attorney General Joe Patterson and the biting, convicting speech by Congressman John Bell Williams [against] the proposed civil rights legislation at Washington were flushed down the drain Saturday morning by the Poplarville lynching."[11]

The attorney general erred when he argued that there hadn't been a lynching in the state in twenty years. He had overlooked the lynching of Emmett Till, who had been denied even the early procedural due process that whites had begrudgingly given Parker. Perhaps Patterson realized the rallying cry that the Till lynching had become and was trying in some way to gloss over the braggadocio that had overwhelmed the white community following the Till lynching. Most probably, however, Patterson was exhibiting the standard white self-deception over the Till incident. White leaders never could bring themselves to admit publicly that the murder of Emmett Till was in fact a lynching.

Poplarville's mayor Pat Hyde repeatedly disassociated his town from the mob and its deed. "The people here are not concerned with this case. I doubt if ten people in town, outside of the law enforcement people, knew anything about that Negro or that white woman." He reported that he drove through the black section on his way to church on Sunday and found to his delight that the blacks "waved . . . just like they would any other Sunday." He claimed, "We have the best race relations of any town in the United States and I challenge anyone to prove me wrong on that statement. I think the town is getting the brunt end of the publicity."[12] The mayor's claim notwithstanding, during that first weekend townspeople bought all the out-of-town newspapers and clogged the halls of the courthouse, trying to get into the sheriff's office to hear news of the investigation. Many pasted on their windshields newspaper photos of the raided jail, with a white X superimposed on Parker's cell, and rode through Poplarville's narrow streets, blowing their horns in celebration. Of what? Well, no one was exactly sure.[13]

To the blacks living in Pearl River County, Mack Parker's death confirmed their worst fears. Few black men or women had a bad word to say about Parker. Most reiterated the by-now-familiar story of how young Parker helped support his mother and family. If they considered this seriously at all, whites dismissed it as weak-kneed sentimentality and gossip given to outsiders. Fearing further violence, blacks tried outwardly to continue their daily routines as though nothing had happened, hoping that nothing more would happen. Up in Lamar County friends and neighbors flocked to the Parkers' three-room cabin in Lumberton with condolences and advice. There was talk of revenge against the mob members, the names of some of whom had already surfaced, but in Pearl River County such threats were only idle boasts. Pearl River County blacks were too terrorized by the lynching to challenge the white opinion that they were content with their lot. A retired gardener and the deacon of the black community's Triumph Baptist Church put it most succinctly, "We're under them whites and we've got to accept it." His people were frightened, he said, but of Governor Coleman, "I'll have to compliment my Governor for not wanting such a thing to happen." Parker's mother, Liza, bedridden with grief all day Saturday and Sunday, afraid to go out and confront white reaction, moaned, "Jesus, Jesus, Jesus, why didn't they give him a fair trial."[14] She told lawyer R. Jess Brown she feared something like this might happen.[15]

"If they don't find my brother, what's going to happen then?" wondered Dolores Parker. Blacks in both Poplarville and Lumberton openly feared Parker's death might bring further racial strife to their counties. This fear even touched black reporters. A reporter for the Chicago *Defender* wrote, "Negroes here are suspicious and cringing with fright at the sight of a stranger, regardless of his race. A vicious cloud of ironhand rule has beaten them into submission, a submission so effective that they have surrendered to it as the southern way of life. 'Hare yah a FBI man? Hare yah a NAACP investigator?' they will ask you, and then after asking these questions they will sigh and say: 'I don't know nothing anyway.' What is their opinion regarding the Mack C. Parker abduction? 'Well, I don't know anything about it,' they will tell you. But their faces show disgust and contempt for this latest racial development in Mississippi and their eyes shine with fear—for tomorrow it could be them."[16] As one black journalist observed when he entered the area a few days after the lynching, blacks were simply "scared to death."[17]

Local whites insisted "their" blacks actually liked their lives of oppression. Commented one white resident after the lynching, "Now you take most of the niggers around here. They wouldn't have it any other way than the way it is here. They like to live right close together, just like Indians. They like to live day by day, you see. They like to spend all their money and let the white people take care of them." Blacks scoffed at this attitude, but they also accepted it for what it was—blind racism, strong enough to produce a bloodthirsty lynch mob if they acted out any role other than that of a happy, shuffling, mischievous Sambo.[18]

Many whites not connected with the lynching feared retaliation by local blacks, who, they surmised, might receive aid from such organizations as the NAACP or the Communist party. As ludicrous as this fear was, it was quite real. Most whites thought NAACP aid was tantamount to supplying arms and legal counsel to blacks should they desire to commit acts of violence. The wife of the mayor kept a loaded gun by her bed because, as she put it, "We was scared of them damn niggers more than what the reporters might turn up, to tell you the truth."[19] Both races had drawn back in fear, and while they tried to put up a front of good will and unconcern for what had happened, they feared each other more than ever. As fate would have it, the one faction in Pearl River County that benefited most from increased white anxiety was that advocating a more violent and assertive stance against civil rights and "uppity" blacks. Partially to ease this fear, partially to shift the blame, when pressed, residents said the mob came from Petal and Hattiesburg, where the Walters family lived. As with most lynchings in the past, residents would not admit that local citizens had anything to do with it. "I don't think the people that did it came from Pearl River County," said County Prosecutor Bill Stewart. "I'd be willing to bet my right arm that nobody from Poplarville is involved." A student at the University of Mississippi home for the weekend to attend the dance at the junior college worried about the effect the lynching would have on the town's reputation. "Well, we got on the map," he said, "but I hope people in the North realize that we don't condone this use of violence. I don't believe this is representative of the sentiments of Mississippians."[20]

Pearl River County whites were convinced that Parker raped June Walters, so no one expressed any sympathy for him or his family, or any regret over the denial of justice. On Saturday afternoon June Walters herself gave a veiled blessing to the mob. "They got the right one," she said. When her remark circulated, it confirmed what everyone believed. A local businessman repeated the standard formula, "We hate what happened yesterday but we hate what caused it to happen more than anything else."[21] During the next several days Mississippi newspapers repeated this familiar theme as they cited Parker's crime to justify his lynching. For the majority of whites in Pearl River County the lynching, apart from the carefully concealed fears it generated, was a cause for celebration, a reason to be proud. A Southern town had been tested and had reacted with a strength that matched its outrage. People declaimed loudly after Sunday morning church services that they would have participated in the lynching had they known about it. Yet their loud celebration had a hollow ring. While the lynching itself prompted backslapping and self-congratulation, the identity of those participating was becoming a worrisome secret. When asked if J. P. Walker or Preacher Lee or Jeff Lee, or even Jewel Alford or anyone else had been involved, residents responded with stony silence or a quick "I don't know nuthin' about it!"[22] Ironically, the brutalizing atmosphere of terror and violence that always accompanied a lynching affected whites as well, frightening those few who may have protested into joining

the growing conspiracy of silence.[23] Even those who claimed to
have no firsthand information of the lynching usually had one or
two obscure facts at their command. The topic was well discussed,
but even if people were known or suspected, they were never
mentioned in public conversation lest those not directly involved
run the risk of alienating the lynch mob.

"This thing is a cancer in the vitals of the community," one
man complained. "Until all the facts come out, and all the names
of those who did it are known, the cancer will keep spreading
and corroding the life of every individual here." When asked if
he would give his name, the man demurred. "If you quoted me
by name, no matter what I said they'd tear down my place."
"Who are they?" he was asked. "I don't know."[24] Open resentment against the lynch mob remained uncommon. Those who
complained about the lynching did so in more general terms,
like the wife of the owner of the Star Cafe, who said, "I wish it
hadn't happened in Mississippi. You know, they say we're so bad
with the niggers. But that's not true." The prospect of mob retaliation caused the white people of Pearl River County to develop
a Janus-faced personality about the lynching: one proud that the
white South had asserted itself, the other terrified that the mob
might punish people for talking too much. Everyone knew J. P.
Walker had driven the car, and most people had a good idea of
who else had been with him, although they debated whether J. P.
Walker or Preacher Lee actually led the mob. It was becoming
common knowledge that Francis Barker and Jeff Lee were involved. The best-kept secret, perhaps because of his kinship to
Sheriff Moody, was Jewel Alford's role of reluctant accomplice.
But even that did not remain secret for long. In a matter of days,
names and details began floating around town. No one knew
anything and everyone knew too much.[25]

One citizen, Royce Malley, typified the surface attitude that
the lynching amounted to nothing more than an event akin to a
county fair. Malley came to town Monday morning amid the
scores of press people and lawmen, "all starched up with bow tie,
etc. just as if he was going to be in *Life* magazine. He must have
been kidded plenty," joked Poplarville's newspaper, "for later in
the day, he had on his regular working clothes." Royce Malley
was just one of the many citizens who dressed for the occasion or
cut out the picture of the jail and pasted it on the windshield of
the family car. Local papers joined the public reaction to the
lynching just as they had helped stir up pro-lynching sentiments

before Parker's trial. "Rumors indicate that the abduction was so well planned," the Poplarville *Democrat* snickered, "that if Parker is dead it will be difficult to locate the body. If he is alive he will probably be like an ambassador without a portfolio." It added with almost intentional self-parody, "It is hard to believe that either the abductors or those engaged in the campaign of hate [against Poplarville] are possessed with any degree of the love of God in their hearts. No people in the world are doing more than the state of Mississippi in furthering the cause of the colored race." The wife of the editor wrote, "One thing for sure, Poplarville pushed Castro aside in the headlines for a few days. When one citizen visited Chicago and people asked him where he was from," she reported, "they didn't meet his response with 'where's that?' They all knew!" To her column she appended a "Note to the visiting newsmen, FBI'ers, TV men, and others: had we known you were coming, we'd planned a party. According to a beloved former 'Belle of the Ball,' we could have had a big dance at the Community Center and for once in the history of Poplarville, there would have been enough good looking men to go around."[26] The paper's bland irresponsibility mocked Mayor Hyde's candid assessment of his town. "Not one person out of 100 realizes the national implications of the case and not one out of 1,000 would care anyway."[27]

On Sunday it was religion as usual in Poplarville's churches. None of the seven ministers who preached sermons that morning mentioned the lynching from the pulpit. The ministers of the town's two largest congregations, the Reverend Frank H. Thomas of the Poplarville Baptist Church and the Reverend I. H. Sells of the First Methodist Church, both claimed they had written their sermons previously and did not wish to change them at so late a date. Explained an indignant Mr. Thomas, "I have faith enough in my people to believe that none of them were involved in the forcible removal of M. C. Parker from his cell. I did not feel that I should subject my congregation, who were already shocked and distressed by the action, to any further indignities. It is not always the mission of the church and its ministers to denounce. It is many times the mission of the church and its ministers to comfort and to instruct. And I am thankful that I do not have to answer to any man as to my conduct from the pulpit of the church which has been given to my charge. No man can tell me what I must preach or what I must not preach. I am responsible only to my Lord in that respect."[28] Later, a local minister commented that "not a single member" of his congregation had mentioned the lynching to him and he had not mentioned it to them.

Acutely aware of the upheaval in other Southern towns caused by racial strife, residents and town leaders alike were determined not to allow it to happen in Poplarville. To reporters covering the investigation in a town where any gathering of five people was cause for comment, they exuded friendliness and cooperation. Many reporters found lodging in local homes or in Alvin Gipson's Magnolia Court Motel, where Ralph Bachman and other FBI agents were staying.[29] But most experienced journalists were not deceived. Cliff Sessions from UPI in Jackson, who stayed in Poplarville the entire summer, found the people friendly and "buddy-buddy on the surface, but they had no intention of cooperating with reporters." Claude Sitton, representing the New York *Times,* encountered the same joking, but it was "disguised hostility" and "no cooperation." Some black residents agreed to talk to reporters, but only a few of them. Bill Minor of the New Orleans *Times-Picayune,* who was friendly with many of the local leaders, spoke fondly of how Sebe Dale would always acknowledge him from the bench when he entered the courtroom, but even for him "the town clammed up." They were "hostile to Coleman for inviting the FBI" and treated the reporters as though it were all a big joke. Still, Minor recalled, "No TV reporter had the nerve to do a stand-up story there."[30]

The local barber said of his home town, "It's the best place on earth." Could he be quoted on that? "Hell yes," he laughed. Yet other emotions lurked beneath the "good old boy" façade. "Listen, mister," a red-faced farmer snapped, "ain't nobody gonna talk to you. May as well go home. We're sick and tired of this stuff."[31] A Poplarville attorney who later represented several of the mob members counseled: "The people in this town don't talk about the lynching and don't even think about it. We think about football and quail hunting, but not about that thing. No, we don't even talk about it to our own wives."[32] "It was shocking," lamented a Southern newspaperman, "to find that the reaction of intelligent leaders in town was not one of surprise and outrage. Instead, there was an air of inevitability—that the lynching was bound to happen. What was most heart-sickening to one who has long-time friends in the county was to hear supposedly level-headed persons remark, 'Well, I'm glad it happened. This

will show them we mean business.' The attitude of support for
the lynching was far more general in those critical early hours
than most of the local leaders were willing to admit. If the
people had risen up and demanded that the lynchers be found
and punished, there would have been no difficulty in quickly
solving the crime."[33]

While the townspeople went to Sunday morning church services and gossiped afterwards, the FBI continued its search for
the body. Eight more agents joined the sixteen already present,
and additional law enforcement officers from Mississippi and
Pearl River County met in the FBI's temporary headquarters
across from the courthouse, above the offices of the *Democrat*.
Ralph W. Bachman divided his agents into two teams, each with
a complement of highway patrolmen. After studying a large map
pinned to the wall, they drove away in cars equipped with newly
installed two-way radios. Their hunt eventually spread over 600
square miles, from the Pearl River swamps along the Louisiana
border into neighboring Forrest County. The search extended as
far away as Lamar County, thirty-five miles from Poplarville, but
concentrated in Pearl River County. The brash, mocking Bill
Stewart told reporters he personally "wouldn't be surprised" if
the mob had come from Forrest County, still insisting local residents had nothing to do with Parker's abduction.[34] Sheriff
Moody, who had gone home Saturday after the appearance of
the FBI agents, returned to his office Sunday morning to join in
the search.[35]

Later that morning a fisherman discovered a bundle of blood-
stained clothes near Brooklyn, Mississippi, in Forrest County
about twenty miles northeast of Poplarville, along the road to
Petal. The items of clothing included a boy's shirt, a jacket, and a
pair of blue jeans. The FBI sent the clothing to its laboratory in
Washington, but it never linked those items to Parker. Their discovery created a frenzy in Poplarville, for it seemed to indicate
that the mob had dropped them off on their way back to Petal
after the lynching. In the afternoon, the governor dispatched 25
percent of the men in the highway patrol to aid in the search,
swelling the number to more than sixty law-enforcement officers.
At the FBI's request, Moody assigned his deputies to a twenty-
four-hour watch on the jail to guard against efforts to intimidate
the prisoners who witnessed the abduction.[36]

That afternoon reporters tracked down an eyewitness to the
lynching, who at first appeared unafraid to speak to them about

what he had seen, even if he was careful about what he said. The man was John Reyer. Amid the activity around the courthouse and across the street at FBI headquarters, reporters spotted Reyer sitting in the back seat of an FBI car, talking with one of the agents. When the agent drove Reyer home, reporters followed and found the farmer willing to make a public statement about what he had seen. On the front lawn of his home north of town, Reyer, a short man of sixty-three missing most of his front teeth, stepped somewhat shyly up to the microphone before the whirring camera from television station WTTV in New Orleans and began answering questions. Reyer said he had taken his brother and sister-in-law to the hospital after she had suffered a heart attack. When they pulled up in front of the hospital, they heard noises inside the jail. Once his sister-in-law was inside the hospital, Reyer decided to have coffee at the Star Cafe and cut across the street toward the south side of the courthouse. "I could see they were masked and dragging something." It was possible, he felt, they failed to see him as they threw Parker in the back seat of a late model car. Reyer claimed to have been frozen with fear when he realized what was happening and was therefore unable to make any identification of the men or the automobile. "There could have been other cars," he claimed, "but I couldn't see them. I didn't look for them when the car drove past me," because "I realized I was in the wrong place when I saw them, and I didn't want to get involved. Where they all went, I don't know, and I don't want to know."[37]

None of the lynchers spoke to him, he claimed. "I didn't hear none of them say anything. It happened so fast, I really didn't see much. This bunch of men came running from the jail dragging this other man. I thought they were carrying a drunk. All of the men were hooded." As reporters, starved for information, pressed him further, Reyer grew defensive. Finally he insisted he had given them everything he had given the FBI. "I'm afraid I couldn't help those fellows much," he added. As he launched into another recitation of the facts, his wife charged out the front door of the house and yelled at her husband, "John Reyer, have you lost your mind? Come in this house right away. You don't know anything those newspaper people want to know. All you are going to do is get your name and picture in the paper." Reyer grimaced at the reporters and continued the interview. When the reporters finally left, it was the last time an eyewitness spoke publicly about the lynching. The most immediate result of

Reyer's disclosures was that Sheriff Moody, who on Saturday had asserted there had been no witnesses to the abduction, now admitted that there had been witnesses after all.[38]

On Monday morning, the day Mack Charles Parker was to have been tried for the rape of June Walters, Sebe Dale drove from his home in Columbia to Poplarville's Pearl River County Circuit Court to preside over a jammed courtroom. People crowded into the usually lightly attended court to await Dale's pronouncements on the lynching. Over the weekend the judge's earthy demeanor had been anything but judicial. He had treated the entire affair glibly. As the seriousness of the lynching began to sink in, he became rueful and reflective. It was widely known throughout the county that the locally popular judge disagreed vehemently with what he considered Governor Coleman's fawning invitation to the FBI. In addition to a clarification of his position, people hoped for some new facts about the investigation. How would it all end? White people were afraid to hazard a guess. They found themselves increasingly distressed at the endless stream of people coming to their town, many of whom, they felt, had come solely to discredit the good people of Poplarville and Pearl River County. Residents naturally looked to Dale for guidance.[39]

Three blacks sat in the balcony; reporters and lawmen took the remaining seats there and on the first floor. After I. H. Sells gave a short prayer opening the session, Sebe Dale, dressed in a blue suit with a red handkerchief, a red tie, and suspenders, strutted into the courtroom and mounted the bench. The session was to be short and very painful. After granting a motion from County Prosecutor Stewart that the trial of M. C. Parker be continued for lack of a defendant, Dale dismissed the special sixty-man jury list and postponed the trial indefinitely, stating there would be no trial that day even if Parker were found. Dale "wanted to see the function of the court carried out like it should be to show the world we would proceed according to the law regardless of race, creed or color. A fair trial has been denied this man." Reading from a prepared statement, he continued piously, without hint of irony, "I believe had he been tried, the record would have brought a kinder feeling toward the people of Mississippi. I do not know what to expect, what laws will be passed against us. I am convinced that what has happened was not at the instigation of the people of this county. I believe someone would have told me if they were planning anything like this." But, he said sadly, "It has opened up the floodgates of hate and hell upon us. The people of Mississippi have been sinned against. They do not deserve it." Then after a brief conference with Stewart and District Attorney Vernon Broome, Dale concluded, because of the tense atmosphere, "Perhaps we had better not dispose of any criminal matters by jury trial this week. None of the other black defendants or the state could receive fair treatment." He continued all criminal cases until November and with a rap of the gavel ended the last week of the spring session.[40]

Later in his chambers, Dale told reporters he thought "the testimony of the three Negro witnesses was enough to hang Parker." He acknowledged that people had freely speculated that Parker would have won an appeal on the grounds blacks were excluded from the jury in Pearl River County and that townspeople referred to this expectation when discussing the case, but Dale disagreed with that belief. "I think [a conviction] would have been affirmed in the federal courts," he said, adding that the *Goldsby* case would not have applied. In Carroll County, Dale pointed out, there were no blacks registered. "But in Pearl River County there are forty registered. . . . The only reason they are not qualified is because they did not pay their poll taxes like everybody else." Dale suggested that to avoid this problem Mississippi should follow Louisiana by stipulating that jurors did not have to be qualified voters. "Otherwise all a Negro has to do to keep from being tried for a crime against a white person is not to pay his poll taxes."[41]

The question of Parker's guilt or innocence was never resolved with absolute certainty. He never confessed and there were no eyewitnesses other than the rape victim and her daughter. Medical authorities who examined June Walters on the night of the rape confirmed only that she had had sexual intercourse. She claimed she had been raped—by a black man. Her statements, those of her husband and her mother, and her appearance at the truck stop in Lumberton, hysterical and disheveled, left little doubt the rape occurred. The rape itself was not the problem. The problem was whether it was committed by Mack Charles Parker. As with most cases of alleged interracial rape resulting in a lynching, there were two stories—one white, one black. Historically, the white story carried more weight. In Parker's case, white society was virtually unanimous in its agreement over his guilt. If anyone doubted his guilt, he or she *never* spoke up. The black community remained split over this question. Some people felt him an innocent victim of a white frame-up. Other blacks, including some who knew Parker, considered him guilty at the time—said so in conversation with other blacks—and never wavered in that conviction. Yet in light of June Walters's uncertain identification of Parker, no conclusive proof will ever be forthcoming.

It is possible that someone spotted Parker and his companions riding around the night of the rape and concluded that one of them was the rapist. After all, by Curt Underwood's own admission they covered a lot of territory that evening. Underwood changed his story about sighting the Walters car several times. He claimed first they had seen the car, then they had not, then he changed his mind again and said they did, and concluded by saying, "I don't want to deal with it." R. Jess Brown told the FBI that Underwood told him they *had* seen the car. He also stated Tommy Lee Grant had supported this claim. It was entirely likely, given the time and similarities, that they had in fact spotted the car. But that still does not prove that Parker was the rapist. That evidence will always be largely circumstantial. Local law-enforcement officials reported no prison breaks in the area as far south as New Orleans any time prior to the rape. The stretch of road was lightly traveled at night and the possibility of someone happening by at random was remote. The rapist knew where to take his victim for maximum privacy. Parker knew the area and had consumed more than enough alcohol during the evening to erase any inhibitions. In the end, though, his own words pointed toward his guilt. Others within the black community were sufficiently convinced of his guilt to report him, which was not something a black man did lightly in the South in the 1950s, considering what the consequences had often been in the past. Beyond that, Parker's cut hand, the matching tire tracks, matching shards of glass, similarities of the hunting cap and trousers, and internal similarities between his car and the rapist's all implicated him or at least indicated he was at the rape scene with June Walters. In assessing the evidence the FBI appeared to agree with R. Jess Brown's conclusions that although the evidence was damning, the crux of the state's case rested on June Walters's uncertain testimony.

R. Jess Brown never publicly affirmed Parker's innocence. He claimed several times he felt his client would have been found not guilty, but given the opportunity in subsequent years to state unequivocally that M. C. Parker was innocent, he said only, "We pleaded him not guilty and expected to win the case." He felt his best strategy was to attack along procedural grounds. June Walters's uncertainty greatly diminished the state's case, he felt, except for the fact that she was white. The testimony of Parker's friends would have been damaging, but June Walters was the key to the case. He would have pressed her for positive identification in court, hoping she would have continued faltering. Brown "had no information" about Parker's owning a pistol, real or toy, even though local police recovered three toy pistols from Parker's house. If the law had been allowed to take its course and race had not been a factor, the case would have depended on how the prosecution and the defense handled June Walters on the stand. The race factor meant Parker would more than likely have been convicted, but he would very likely have won on appeal on procedural grounds. Whether or not he would ever have gone free is another matter entirely.[42]

6

"The Floodgates
of Hate and Hell"

As the FBI began to concentrate its investigation on several likely suspects, it appeared to local white citizens that Sebe Dale's fears about the "floodgates of hate and hell" had indeed come to pass. To their dismay, residents learned firsthand about the tremendous power of the federal government and the freedom with which its agents often operated. Ironically, those who acted extralegally against Parker and others who supported those actions began to complain about the FBI doing the same thing to them. Many began to feel that events had conspired to subject Poplarville, Pearl River County, the state of Mississippi, and the South to unwarranted and harsh scrutiny.

No one was exempt from the criticism. Mayor Hyde and Sheriff Moody received about forty letters, most of them condemning the abduction and slaying of Parker, only two praising it. Writers labeled them cowards. One lady told them, "You are a disgrace to walk the earth with decent people." From Palo Alto, California, came the message, "Get out of the union, we don't want you." Sebe Dale also received hate mail, and although the letters aroused his curiosity, he quickly wearied of subjecting himself to such easily avoidable calumny. Like the mayor and the sheriff, he stuffed the letters in a drawer and forgot about them. "I don't want them," he said. "When I see what they're like, I quit reading them." The letters prompted a long response by the editor of the town's newspaper, in which he protested that Pearl River County was being vilified for a crime perpetrated by "outsiders." Extolling the friendship between black and white in his town, he added, "This friendship is linked with the way of life called segregation, and underlying it is an understanding that the Negro knows, and keeps—his place." The angry Picayune *Item* acknowledged that "just about everybody in this section has received at least one piece of fan mail regarding the Parker case." It echoed its sister paper when it said, "The bad publicity was bound to come, because if it wasn't bad enough, some reporters have a way of making it bad particularly if the South is involved. . . . It's a shame, but it's also true." And while the *Item* received nothing that compared with the long-distance call Mayor Hyde received from a curious London newspaper, the *Item* "almost daily received letters from all over the nation. . . . Some bad, some good," most portraying locals as a "kind of cross between Uncle Remus and Tobacco Road."[1]

As the grim search for Parker continued, two pieces of information contributed significantly to the increasing anxiety in Poplarville. Bill Stewart made it known the FBI suspected the lynching had been an inside job and was proceeding under that assumption. According to Stewart, the mob had too highly detailed a knowledge of the courthouse and the jail annex for some or all of the mob members not to have been familiar with it to a certain extent. Rumors began to circulate that the mob beat up Sheriff Moody to get the jail keys. Moody had no trouble convincing the FBI this was untrue (agents never considered it a possibility), but the rumor cast a poor light on Moody's earlier claims that so many people came and went in the courthouse that virtually anyone could have inspected the building before a lynching. Such an explanation did not explain how the mob had so easily obtained the keys, why no officers had been nearby, and why no one got a good look at the mob members and yet everyone was so sure they came from outside Poplarville. Jewel Alford, to a large extent shielded by his close relationship with the sheriff, kept quiet about his role and at first did not come under suspicion. His earliest statements to the FBI were the statements of an officer of the law reporting to fellow officers on what he knew.[2]

The other information disturbing to the people of Poplarville came from Governor Coleman on Monday. The saddened governor predicted the mob would be apprehended soon and made it clear that the crime, which he termed premeditated murder, would be prosecuted accordingly. This meant that any of the convicted members of the mob could receive the death sentence. As if that weren't enough, Coleman admitted he was willing to turn mob members over to the federal government for prosecution, although, he explained, "[I] would still like to see them tried in Pearl River County because I believe the people of that county would want to see justice done." This provided small comfort to residents who had no sympathy for Parker and could not understand why the men who murdered him should be tried in a federal court. Beyond that, they considered the death penalty excessive punishment for people who had given the black rapist of a pregnant white woman his comeuppance. If Coleman's early summoning of the FBI strained his relations with Pearl River County, his pronouncements on the possible fate of the mob members created a considerable disturbance and a great deal of resentment. This turn of events marked the beginning of a long process of alienation of Coleman from many citizens of the state over the lynching. In Poplarville, upon hearing of the governor's decree, an irate Bill Stewart paraded Parker's guilt around for anyone interested, asserting that Parker's companions agreed unanimously in their statements to police that Parker had threatened to return to the stranded automobile and rape the woman locked inside it. In addition, the FBI had uncovered "technical evidence" implicating Parker, Stewart claimed. These facts, offered as a defense of the mob, added to the growing feeling that however wrong the men may have been, they did not deserve severe punishment. And they certainly did not deserve a trial before outsiders in federal court.[3]

From her home in Petal, June Walters added to the growing controversy when she decided to speak out against the "terrible lynching." She denied she had said "They got the right one" the day after the lynching, and insisted that the picture of Parker in the newspapers only *looked* like the man who had raped her. To the further discomfort of county authorities, she added, "When I saw the man [in the lineup] I told the police that I wasn't positive, but it looked like him." County officials had been stating since February that June Walters had made positive identification of Parker in the lineup. The woman scoffed at the idea that the mob lynched Parker to prevent her from being cross-examined by black attorneys: "I would have rather they had gone through with the trial." She had no objection to being questioned by black attorneys. "I wouldn't have minded. I would have gone right through with it—all the way through with it." As she talked, her little daughter, who had been with her in the car the night of the rape, gazed at the picture of Parker in the papers spread before her and, pointing to them, said, "That's him, that's the one."[4]

On Tuesday Governor Coleman inexplicably authorized the release of C. J. Mondy on $350 bond. Both Sheriff Moody and D. A. Vernon Broome approved the release even though Mondy, who provided FBI agents with their first and best account of the fight in the jail, was to stand trial for murder on Wednesday. Mondy also told the FBI that J. P. Walker had visited him in his cell and told him if he ever gave any information to the agents he had better not return to his home in Picayune.[5] Mondy had also spoken to two black reporters, giving them a detailed account of Parker's abduction. County Prosecutor Stewart told reporters of Mondy's impending release only as a way to avoid their questions: Earlier in the day he had mentioned matter-of-factly to Cliff Sessions of UPI that two of the mob members lived in Poplarville, and now the embarrassed Stewart was going to considerable lengths to deny it. "I have no reason to believe any of the men were from Poplarville," he replied to repeated requests that he elaborate. His self-serving denials notwithstanding, his remarks created a flurry equal in intensity to news of the FBI's theory that the lynch mob may have received help from a local law-enforcement officer.[6]

As Stewart attempted to recover from his intemperate remark, Sheriff Moody drove to the Parker home, where he joined Sheriff Hickman of Lamar County in offering official condolences to Liza Parker. Still weak from the shock of her son's abduction, she asked if M. C. had any chance of being alive. Moody told her he personally doubted it because of the nature of his crime, but he tried to comfort her by saying that they would not give up until they had located her son, or his remains.[7]

Though Bill Stewart and Sheriff Moody exhibited some willingness to speak to the ever-present reporters, the FBI agents, especially Ralph Bachman, remained tight-lipped. FBI press releases on the investigation came from Washington via the White House and the Justice Department. The Bureau's reticence failed to slow the press, which began to create as much anxiety among the local citizens as the official investigation. Press activity grew so intense, according to the wife of the mayor, that "You couldn't stoop, bend or squat without a cameraman or a reporter pushing a microphone under your nose" and firing questions. Townspeople were unaccustomed to the new phenomenon of a "media blitz." They had no idea that such behavior by hungry journalists was becoming part of American life. For white residents of Poplarville it seemed an unwarranted invasion of their peace and quiet, their privacy, and all because of "that nigger, M. C. Parker."[8]

The FBI, meanwhile, methodically pursued its investigation. Agents questioned the students attending the dance at Pearl River Junior College to see if anyone could identify any of the mob members when their cars wove through the cars driven by the people leaving the dance. But none of the ten students questioned claimed to have noticed anything unusual that night. The interrogation of the students succeeded only in further arousing the citizens of Poplarville, adding another log to the growing fire of discontent. The influx of twenty-four additional agents on Sunday forced fifteen of them to go to Bogalusa, twenty-one miles away in Louisiana, to find lodging. The agents took most of the rooms of a motel, turning the place into a second office. Some of the most grueling hours of investigation occurred there, away from the probing eyes of reporters and other citizens. The first suspect brought there was Jimmy Walters. Agents held him for five hours, grilling him about his whereabouts on Friday night. His friends considered him a weakling who would never have resorted to violence on his own. FBI agents sensed this, but they still pressed him relentlessly while other agents went to Petal to question June, who told them she was "taking pills for her nerves" as a result of the lynching.

The pressure had begun to take its toll. Local whites had started disparaging the Walters couple almost as soon as the rape had occurred. The sexual taboos of the South meant that any white rape victim faced ostracism from white society. If the violator was a black man, the humiliation was intensified to an unimaginable extent. Both June and Jimmy were much too naive and preoccupied to grasp the immediate social implications of the rape. They were having serious trouble keeping their marriage on an even keel. From Jimmy's point of view, the major obstacle to his marriage had long been June's mother, who had opposed the marriage and continued to criticize Jimmy whenever she could. After the lynching she criticized her son-in-law even more openly than before, making him the brunt of cruel jokes. June had suffered for years from her domineering mother. Now, torn between her mother and her husband, she began slowly to succumb to her mother's arguments against Jimmy. She gradually lost respect for her husband until she began to laugh at him—at first with considerable embarrassment—behind his back for being weak and passive. Family tensions bristled so much that Jimmy began to avoid his mother-in-law as often as possible, finding excuses to be away from home when she was there—which was often—and not speaking to her when they were together.[9]

The Walters were gentle to the point of vulnerability; they only wanted to forget and be forgotten. Jimmy internalized his frustration and bitterness and turned to alcohol. June began to foist hers onto Jimmy. June had not wanted him to participate in the lynching and upon reflection her mind didn't change, but her opinion of her husband began to drop nevertheless. Perhaps it was inevitable. News of Parker's death had hit them both hard, dredging up all the emotions they had tried to repress. The lives of the young couple came to bear an ironic similarity to the lives of Parker's family. The horror and degradation of the lynching would eventually drive M. C.'s mother and sisters from the area. While still married and living just outside Hattiesburg, the Walters found themselves driven by forces beyond their comprehension deeper into the world of poor whites.

June confirmed to FBI agents that her husband was home the entire evening watching the Don Jordan–Virgil Atkins championship fight on television. She also gave her interrogators a description of her life that made them wonder why so many people referred to her as an outsider. Even though she was born in New York, she moved as a child to the South and had been there ever since. Still, she had not lost—and never could lose—her Northern origins. That would make her suspect to born Southerners. For his part Jimmy Walters—when taken to the FBI offices—admitted only to being approached by two men on the morning of the lynching. The two people most tightly linked to the original motivation of the lynching had the least to offer to the FBI.[10]

Of the one hundred FBI agents and highway patrolmen in Poplarville, more than half left headquarters each morning dressed in work clothes as the extensive search of the bayous interlacing the swamps and flatlands of the county continued into its third day without uncovering any new evidence. These men combed the banks of the muddy Pearl River in a fruitless foot-by-foot search. Elsewhere, as other agents groped toward a clearer picture of who had been involved, weary police officers plodded through moss-draped swamps and rough pine thickets, each new area presenting countless potential hiding places for a body. By Monday evening almost everyone in the investigation agreed that the abductors had slain Parker and hidden his body so well that it might never be found. Governor Coleman reasserted that he wanted the mob "apprehended and vigorously prosecuted" and expressed certainty there would be a break in the case. The governor was to leave soon for Washington to testify against the civil rights bill and saw a quick resolution of the case as his only hope for success before a hostile Senate committee. That same day, however, Senator Wayne Morse, a proponent of stronger civil rights measures, commented that the lynching demonstrated the need for further legislation to restore the measures that had been stripped by a coalition of Southerners and conservative Republicans from the 1957 Civil Rights Act, a bill that provided a measure of federal election supervision. Senator Jacob Javits's prediction that the communists would be certain to exploit the incident provoked a public response from several Poplarville officials stating their belief that the NAACP and the Communist party conducted the lynching to reflect badly on the South during the hearings in Washington. NAACP head Roy Wilkins blamed Parker's abduction on Southern politicians and sent duplicate telegrams to the House and Senate Judiciary committees, urging prompt action "on legislation which would enable the federal government to enter in such murderous breakdowns of law enforcement as that in Poplarville." He called the lynching "the natural consequences of an organized campaign of law defiance by governors of states, members of the U. S. Senate and House of Representatives and state and local politicians." The telegrams captured national headlines.[11]

By Tuesday, the number of suspects had grown from eight to twenty-five—in direct proportion, it seemed in Poplarville, to the ever-growing number of FBI agents. The town was beginning to feel the brunt of adverse publicity from a nation that was astonished that such a crime could occur in 1959 and wondered about its effect on international relations. In Jackson, Governor Coleman, realizing he needed justification from the national government for his actions now more than ever, made public a telegram President Eisenhower had sent him late on Monday in response to his telegram requesting that the FBI "be allowed to pursue their investigation until the guilty persons have been apprehended." Ike reminded Coleman of the damage done to American prestige abroad and informed him further, "It is my earnest hope that there will be swift apprehension of the guilty persons. These agents will, of course, continue to provide full facilities to help in any way in this matter."[12]

Speaking in Washington, Attorney General William Rogers said the nation's conscience was "revolted and stunned" by the abduction. Rogers acknowledged that the lynching provided a propaganda windfall for the Soviets. "This reprehensible act brings into sharp focus the vital part that the rule of law plays in the free world and emphasizes the tragedy and shame that takes place when a few men do not live by that precept." With the cold war still lingering, every controversial domestic event prompted a worried acknowledgment that the Soviets might turn it to their own advantage. So acutely conscious of damage to the national reputation was the American Legion that at the behest of its national commander the all-white tenth and eleventh districts of the Mississippi American Legion met jointly at Vicksburg to vote formal protests against the abduction and to urge speedy apprehension of those involved.[13]

While several of Mississippi's large, influential newspapers remained silent on their editorial pages, the relatively liberal New Orleans *Times-Picayune* spoke out against the lynching. The precedent of an all-white jury overturning the conviction of a black man in the *Goldsby* case was "not the slightest justification for the apparently criminal act in Poplarville," the newspaper stated. The Jackson *State-Times* agreed: "The perpetrators of the Friday night offense not only committed a crime against society in violation of Mississippi law, they also committed a grave disservice to the people of our state and the South. Disciples of hate," it added, "will warp the truth of this tragedy in Poplarville." The Memphis *Commercial Appeal* urged a speedy resolution: "The surest way for Mississippi to counteract the injury now done is to make certain that the Poplarville lynchers are brought to the justice they defiled."[14]

Urban Southern newspapers almost universally condemned the lynching, but in their condemnation lurked noticeable fear of Northern-sponsored congressional retribution. "Once again the ugly word lynching is heard in the South and being heard here, is echoed practically everywhere in the civilized world," said the Atlanta *Journal*. "The entire South is condemned for the sorry act of a few in its midst. As it well knows, this happening will generate or harden in many the world over an abstract hate for the South and its people." The Selma *Times-Journal* encouraged its fellow Southerners to repudiate the lynching to "convince the nation that [the South] really does not hate Negroes, but that it only is trying to preserve its basic civilization." The Tuscaloosa *Times* reminded its readers that "disregard for the law and order and the due process of our judicial system reflects on the entire region."[15]

With national journals expressing fears that the lynching might seriously damage America's international relations and decrying Coleman's undue concern for the passage of the civil rights bill, even a Klan leader from North Carolina was moved to condemn the lynching for its violence, not for its intent, claiming, "The Ku Klux Klan does not advocate violence. Mob action is ugly." It seemed to southern Mississippi that all the world was taking out its anger on Poplarville.[16] In response to this barrage of criticism and aware that the unsolved lynching was generating headlines as far away as Paris and Manila, Governor Coleman announced on Tuesday he had "excellent reason" to expect a break in the case. On the other hand, the chief of the highway patrol said that from his perspective the investigation had reached a "standstill," only five days after it started, because the extensive search had failed to locate Parker's body.[17]

In Poplarville residents sensed trouble. Speculation circulated that the FBI had uncovered much more than anyone knew, that it had a clear idea of what had happened. On the day Governor Coleman proclaimed a break to be near, people anxiously insisted that a confession was useless without a body, and few people believed the FBI would ever locate the body of Mack Charles Parker. Perhaps Parker was still alive, they speculated, living in Cuba or Mexico, and the entire lynching had been fabricated by blacks to get publicity. Such wishful thinking by whites masked their fear that the affair would not go away until so much of the truth was unearthed that their town would be altered beyond recognition.[18]

When the first break in the case came, it was from a most unexpected source. In Chicago, over the weekend of the lynching, John Sengstacke, the publisher of the Chicago *Defender*, had dispatched Lou Palmer and photographer Howard Pulley to cover the lynching. Both men were black and both were old hands at covering interracial matters, although neither had been in Mississippi or had covered a lynching before. Palmer had recently been beaten up by whites in East Memphis, Arkansas, and was not at all happy about going into Mississippi. They slipped into Lumberton in the quiet of the night and attempted to blend in with the local black population, knowing if they made known their credentials, they would put themselves in jeopardy. Although dressed in old clothes, Palmer and Pulley still encountered suspicion and quiet terror in local blacks. It took some effort to get a black to show them around and help them find a place to stay. After several apologies and closed doors, they were finally taken in by a black family in Lumberton, with whom they stayed for the few days they were there.[19]

Palmer and Pulley next went to Poplarville to interview C. J. Mondy. Palmer found the town tense, "and the sight of black reporters in the town did not help one bit." There were dozens of white reporters in Poplarville hanging around the courthouse. "They had all been upstairs in the jail house to talk to Parker's cell mate," said Palmer, "and when we presented our credentials, the Sheriff told us to wait." They were put off for more than two hours, with Sheriff Moody becoming increasingly obstinate until finally in desperation Palmer buttonholed Cliff Sessions, the UPI reporter, on Monday morning. Explaining that the *Defender* was a UPI subscriber, Palmer asked Sessions to speak to Sheriff Moody. Sessions saw Sheriff Moody on their behalf, and a short time later Palmer and Pulley were led upstairs into the cells to interview Mondy.[20]

Much more comfortable with a black reporter, Mondy described to Palmer in lurid detail the abduction, returning time and again to the gruesome scene of Parker's head banging down the iron steps of the jail house. Mondy was released on bail the next day. It was Palmer's account that found its way into headlines and onto radio and television news reports across the country. Later that day Palmer interviewed Mayor Pat Hyde, who boasted to him, in acute contradiction to what Palmer had experienced firsthand, how well whites treated "their negroes." Whites treated Palmer and Pulley as objects of curiosity and then ignored them. Even blacks were cautious in their associations with them, lest they anger local whites. "It was so tense," thought Palmer, "any outsider was immediately looked on with some kind of suspicion. It was hard to get any of them to talk at all. They were terrified, they were petrified." Eventually, however,

Palmer and Pulley, operating on their own, away from white reporters, made contact with Curt Underwood, who, after considerable prodding by Palmer, gave them an account of the night of the rape that differed wholly from the accepted version. But Underwood refused to allow them to make it public as long as he remained in Lumberton. Police officers had threatened his life, he told them. "They made us say it. They threatened to beat me and I know they beat one of the boys. They told me if I didn't say it about Parker, they would send me to Jackson to jail and make me an accessory to the crime." Haltingly, and with considerable anguish, Underwood recounted a tale of police brutality that shed a new light on the case. He now insisted they had not seen the Walters car after all. "And Parker never said he was going to attack the woman. How could he when he didn't even see her?" When asked why he gave evidence to the contrary that sent Parker to jail and eventually to his death, Underwood responded, "They put those words in my mouth. Besides they were all threatening to whip me and beat me and throw me in jail . . . I was plenty scared."[21]

Underwood recounted his apprehension by Sheriff Hickman, emphasizing that he was never beaten, but that Rainbow Malachy had been beaten twice because he refused to corroborate Underwood's story. Malachy maintained all along he had passed out in the back seat of Parker's car. The threat of a beating similar to Malachy's or possible indictment scared Underwood into agreeing to give false details about Parker's activities on the night of the rape. When Palmer first spoke to him, Underwood told him the same story he had been telling police, but Palmer suspected the youth was hiding something and when he contacted Underwood the next day he told the newspapermen, "I can't live with this lie for the rest of my life. I don't believe that Parker raped that woman. I've got to tell the truth."[22]

The truth in Mississippi was subject to various interpretations, white and black, some of which were verified with threats of violence. Underwood had received anonymous warnings himself in the investigation of Parker's disappearance. After considerable persuasion by Palmer, Underwood agreed to leave Mississippi for Chicago, where he would live with his aunt and uncle, who had left Lumberton twelve years earlier for the Chicago steel mills. Palmer concealed Underwood under some blankets on the floor of the car until they crossed the state line into Louisiana. Soon he was reunited with his uncle and half brother and "very happy to be away from the type of justice meted out to Negroes in Mississippi."[23]

Curt Underwood was not the only person who fled Mississippi justice. Rainbow Malachy also received death threats from unknown sources during the days following Parker's abduction. Swearing he would not let authorities "put words in his mouth," Malachy left Lumberton by bus early Tuesday morning after receiving money for the trip from his sister in Chicago. Fearing interference by the police, Malachy met the bus along the road outside Lumberton rather than at the bus station in town. Malachy had heard reports from several sources that a white man who worked near where Parker had worked remarked after Parker's lynching, "They sure did a good job last night. They should have done it long before now. They ought to get the other four next. It would be wise for all of those boys to leave." These rumors and the suspicion that other blacks in Lumberton had been avoiding him for fear of white retaliation persuaded Malachy to contact his sister in Chicago. When he arrived there on Thursday morning, he told the story of his arrest and recounted how Sheriffs Hickman and Moody tried to force him to change his story to a version unfavorable to Parker. "I don't intend to go back to Mississippi," he said.[24]

After these stories surfaced, white Mississippians became more defiant toward their critics and more self-righteous about race relations in the South. Yet Underwood's new version of the events before the rape, coming less than a week after the lynching, failed to stir a controversy over Parker's guilt or innocence. Instead, because of the intense racism of white Mississippians, they chose to see it as a blow to the FBI: the Jackson *Clarion-Ledger* headlined its story "Negro Press Scoops FBI in Poplarville." As further proof of the inherent dishonesty of black people, the newspaper asserted that the reporters resorted to "stealth" to spirit Underwood out of Mississippi. The irony of using the testimony of black men to indict Parker but refusing to believe that they lied to please their interrogators was lost on Mississippians. "A Negro newspaper in Chicago boasted Wednesday that its staffers defied federal agents and Mississippi police in spiriting away a key witness in the Poplarville lynch-mob case." Toward the end of the story was this: "In Chicago, Underwood said he was threatened by Mississippi officers and implicated Parker under intimidation thus refuting his earlier evidence given in Mississippi." The paper gave more space to Sheriff Moody's denial than Underwood's new story.[25]

The aggressive Gulfport *Daily Herald* added spice to the bubbling pot. It re-interviewed Tommy Lee Grant, who "reiterated [that] what he had given against Parker . . . was the truth. Grant said that officers did not intimidate him or any of the other Negro witnesses in the case." David Alfred, the fourth man in the car, supported Grant's version of the story. Even Lee Underwood's father, who, like Alfred and Grant, remained in Mississippi, doubted that either the sheriff or his deputies threatened to beat his son. As far as he knew, no one had tried to keep his son in Mississippi to prevent him from heading north to change his story. Bill Stewart, still trying to please everyone, played tapes of statements made by Parker's companions. Even though the recordings constituted a vital part of the evidence the state planned to present against Parker in court, County Prosecutor Stewart had no qualms about playing them. As for the beatings, Stewart himself felt, "They were definitely not intimidated in any way." Sheriff Hickman admitted hitting Malachy, "but not during questioning."[26]

With local law-enforcement officers furiously denying brutality charges, the Underwood story did have some effect on the course of events.[27] In New York City radio station WMCA announced after receiving word of Underwood's reversal that it would give a $5,000 reward for information leading to the arrest and conviction of Parker's abductors. The station president requested contributions to enlarge the reward and announced that the station, which had a rock-'n'-roll format, would present a special series on the lynching. At the same time the NAACP sent a wire to President Eisenhower, emphasizing the need for positive action to protect the lives and rights of citizens where states refused to do so: "A naked campaign urging defiance of courts and law, including Supreme Court rulings and the Civil Rights Act of 1957, has been spurred by governors, senators and congressmen and state and local public officials. The Poplarville crime is the natural consequence of this behavior."[28]

In response to the NAACP, Erle Johnston published an editorial in his newspaper, asserting the NAACP "must share part of the blame" for the mob's action. Referring to the *Goldsby* case, Johnston pointed out, "The NAACP has been instrumental in obtaining the decision and through its legal actions has made a mockery of our court system. No doubt this was in the mind of the mob members as they spirited the Negro away to face some kind of justice for his crime."[29]

Johnston and other white Southerners had to search hard to find a way to link the NAACP with the lynching. Many Pearl River County residents blamed the U. S. Supreme Court and the NAACP for the lynching and the civil rights bill, incorrectly attributing to the Supreme Court the decision made by the state supreme court in the *Goldsby* case, which led the people in Poplarville to believe that Parker would go unpunished for his deeds. This court decision, not a tendency to lawlessness, they argued, caused the lynching. Since no black had voted in Pearl River County since 1946, Judge Dale concluded they did not care about serving on the jury. He said smugly that the state should change its laws "so that a Negro can be tried for a crime against a white person." Poplarville also mistakenly resented the NAACP for hiring an attorney to defend Parker. No amount of protest to the contrary could persuade local opinion that R. Jess Brown had not been employed by the hated NAACP.[30]

The New York-based organization knew next to nothing about M. C. Parker while he lived. The NAACP gave no money to R. Jess Brown to defend him. It also shied away from an active investigation of the lynching. Whereas in times past it had doggedly investigated lynchings and rumored lynchings, under Roy Wilkins it kept a lackadaisical eye on the proceedings in Poplarville. Wilkins wrote letters and sent a few telegrams to key individuals, and the subsequent write-in campaign was weak and ineffective. As for direct involvement, Wilkins maintained, "Legal action looking toward the punishment of those guilty of the crime of lynching is in the hands of the county and state authorities." This was a weak position to take in light of the bold, assertive anti-lynching activities by the former executive director Walter White.[31]

In Poplarville on Friday, exactly one week after the lynching, with the FBI actively pursuing its investigation, Ralph Bachman broke his six-day silence and asserted confidently that his agents would crack the case. Anyone arrested, he said, would be lodged in the nearest federally approved jail for arraignment before a U. S. commissioner, which tacitly indicated Bachman believed the lynch mob had violated federal law. Simple murder was not a federal offense; kidnapping across state lines was. Since simultaneous prosecution by state and federal authorities constituted double jeopardy, Bachman seemed to be saying that federal violations would take precedence in this case.[32]

In hopes of unearthing witnesses even one week later, the FBI went from house to house, questioning Poplarville residents and attempting to discover at least one person who might have noticed an unusual amount of traffic that night or perhaps a commotion at the courthouse. These efforts came to nothing. The residents, if they knew anything, wouldn't discuss it with the FBI. Agents found it increasingly difficult to get the townspeople to talk to them about the case. They checked and rechecked every retailer in Pearl River County who sold white working gloves. Agents visited one store several blocks from the courthouse four times within the first six days, asking about any unusual purchases of work gloves. The owner told them the same thing each time; he had sold no gloves to strangers or friends before or after the lynching. The search for the source of the gloves eventually extended over three states. Exploring every possibility, Bachman divided the officers into groups of four and instructed them to walk every road in and out of Poplarville for a distance of ten miles, picking up every scrap of paper, every piece of discarded junk, in hopes of discovering one new shred of evidence. On May 3, after receiving an anonymous phone tip, Hattiesburg police discovered a crude effigy of Parker hanging at the intersection of Highways 11 and 49 outside of Hattiesburg. The stuffed dummy was attached to a 4-by-5 feet piece of cardboard with "M. C. Parker" inscribed on it. There were bullet holes through the "C." The police dismissed this, a bit preemptorily, as a prank of students from Southern College, located in Hattiesburg, rather than a sign of shifting local sentiment.[33]

As the investigation slowly but methodically progressed, the lynching began to have its first effects on national and regional racial policy. The head of the Civil Rights Division, W. Wilson White, flew to New Orleans at the last minute to present the government's position in a Macon voting rights case. White reaffirmed administration opposition to any attempt by the federal government "to superimpose any plan for integration of the schools upon the states," but in light of recent events in Poplarville, he urged strenuous federal intervention in the area of voting rights and obstruction of justice by local officials. As the *Goldsby* and *Parker* cases demonstrated, the right to vote held implications far beyond the simple casting of a ballot. It gave one access to the legal system. He felt the lynching had become a test of the willingness of the South to comply with the complete investigation of denial of civil rights to blacks. In this area he foresaw no immediate problem because "Governor Coleman is as outraged as any of us." In fact, Coleman made sure the highway patrol gave the FBI its complete cooperation throughout the investigation. Another governor could just as easily have withheld highway patrol assistance entirely. White also stated he wanted the state of Mississippi to prosecute the mob. This was the first public indication of a split within the Justice Department over the prosecution of the guilty parties. Other officials as high as Attorney General Rogers had expressed their desire that the federal government proceed with plans for trying the men once the FBI identified and apprehended them. The White House had yet to speak officially on this matter, choosing instead to wait and see what the investigation produced before making any final recommendations.

Federal authorities were uncertain what to do in the case. The heinous nature of the crime had created an embarrassing national scandal, which in turn necessitated active federal involvement. But such a high degree of federal involvement in a lynching investigation was unprecedented. As a result it remained unclear exactly which course of action the government would follow. Such a cautious approach produced uncertainty and a lack of direction. The investigation continued in Poplarville, but beyond that, no one, from the citizenry of Pearl River County to the attorney general of the United States and perhaps higher, had a solid idea of what would happen if the FBI succeeded in solving the case. For almost everyone it became a matter of wait and see.*[34]

---

* Across the nation the lynching rekindled the fear that the white South would summon the dread specter of lynch law. Lynching had been useless as a barometer of Southern racial attitudes since the 1930s, when the practice nearly disappeared. According to Harold C. Fleming, executive director of the Southern Regional Council, in an article published before Parker's abduction, "The plain fact is that the dwindling number of traditional lynchings is no longer a reliable index to injustice, racial or otherwise. The lawless spirit of the lynch mob is still with us, but the pattern of violence has changed." Most analysts considered the Parker lynching an anachronism. "Education, respect for the law, and most of all awareness of the rights of the human person under the law— these things have prevailed," explained the Asheville *Citizen*. Once Southern leaders had participated in lynchings. In the 1940s, as more mob members were tried and convicted and given prison sentences, local leaders discontinued the practice of invoking lynch law to punish blacks and to win support from their community. Since 1937, according to Tuskegee statistics, more lynchings were prevented each year than occurred. And there had been no classic lynchings with the mob storming the jail since 1949. Southern leaders recognized the burden such an event placed on America and acted accordingly. Although they may have felt no sympathy for the black man and potential victim, leaders such as Coleman realized the South's position in the nation demanded an end to lynching. For the average white Southerner, on the other hand, the reaction to Parker's death

In Washington a few days later, Senate Majority Leader Lyndon Johnson made the passage of a new civil rights bill one of the major objectives of the current session of Congress. Although Johnson personally favored a moderate bill, the potential influence of the powerful and persuasive Texan dashed the hopes of Southern Democrats that they could sidetrack the issue for another year by threatening a party split before the upcoming presidential campaign. The lynching of Mack Charles Parker precluded such threats and put civil rights opponents on the defensive. Senate Minority Leader Everett Dirksen admitted that Northern indignation over the Poplarville incident improved the chances for passage of a bill strengthening the 1957 Civil Rights Act. The bill's Senate sponsor, Paul Douglas of Illinois, thought, "The decent elements in the South are just as indignant about the Poplarville affair as we are in the North. But," he added, "the tragedy *does* indicate the need for added protection of the colored population beyond that which local authorities are willing or able to give." Johnson wanted to usher through the Senate Judiciary Committee a bill mild enough to avoid a Southern filibuster that might damage party unity before the presidential election. The House had completed its hearings prior to the lynching. The bill awaited Senate consideration.[35]

The Jackson *Clarion-Ledger* responded to news of Lyndon Johnson's intention to usher a civil rights bill through Congress with a stinging editorial requesting a federal anti-rape law. "The entire world is goggle-eyed about lynching," the paper complained. "There is a loud scream going up in Washington to pass a Federal Anti-Lynching Bill. It is argued with deafening illogic that this law is needed because a Negro rapist was kidnapped in Poplarville. . . . The FBI has already swarmed to the case." Claiming lynchings had nearly disappeared until the federal government began interfering in Southern affairs, the editorial added, "While pinkish liberals of both parties weep and moan over Mississippi, these same pious 'gentlemen' show no alarm whatso-

---

put things in a new light. It was one thing for Yankees to castigate the entire South for it and warn it would lead to other lynchings. It was something else again for them to praise Governor Coleman for calling in the FBI and placing the Mississippi highway patrol at the agency's disposal. Southerners demonstrated an increasing awareness in the wake of the move in Congress to provide stronger civil rights legislation that violence hurt their cause; but they remained determined to fend off any advancement by blacks. For this reason they disapproved of Coleman's actions. Harold C. Fleming, "The Law Gains Ground," *New South* 6 (January 1951), 8; Asheville *Citizen*, April 26, 1959; New York *Times*, May 3, 4, 1959.

ever for the sacredness of their own wives, daughters, mothers, and clerical help."[36]

At least one black in Mississippi was still experiencing a bitter struggle with Mississippi's golden opportunities for blacks, however. Liza Parker was to have been the main speaker at a rally hosted by the NAACP in Jackson, but after receiving several threats against her life if she addressed the rally, she refused to attend. After receiving more threats a few days later, Liza Parker hastily packed a battered suitcase and, with the two youngest children, boarded a bus for Merced, California, and the home of relatives. In Lumberton, meanwhile, Parker's arresting officer, Ham Slade, predicted the abduction would remain unsolved for several years.[37]

Mack Charles Parker
(UPI/Bettmann Newsphotos)

Rape victim June Walters and
daughter Debbie Carol
(UPI/Bettmann Newsphotos)

Pearl River County Jail and Courthouse with an "X" marking Parker's cell
(UPI/Bettmann Newsphotos)

Facing page, top
Mack Charles Parker's funeral in Lumberton
(UPI/Bettmann Newsphotos)

Facing page, bottom
Eliza Parker with Sissy and Peanut
after her son's death
(UPI/Bettmann Newsphotos)

Former Deputy Sheriff J.P. Walker
(Copyright © 1959 Cravens/Black Star)

Itinerant Baptist minister James Floren "Preacher" Lee
(UPI/Bettmann Newsphotos)

McNeill barber C.C. "Crip" Reyer
(Copyright © 1959 Cravens/Black Star)

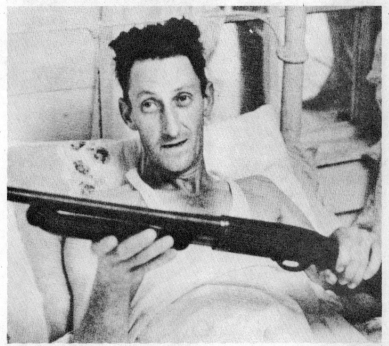

Pearl River County farmer L.C. Davis
(Copyright © 1959 Cravens/Black Star)

Circuit Court Judge Sebe Dale
(AP/Wide World Photos)

FBI agents at their Poplarville headquarters
(Copyright © 1959 Cravens/Black Star)

7

"Don't Let Them Kill Me"

Undaunted by their lack of success, the FBI and the highway patrol continued to search the waterways and bayous in the surrounding countryside on foot, by car, and by airplane. On Monday, for the first time, they were able to use boats on the river. So far the searchers had only turned up a set of bloodied clothes, which did not belong to Parker. They continued checking the waterways because the information gleaned from the people they had questioned indicated overwhelmingly that the mob had dumped Parker into the Pearl River. After the belief that the body would never be found, this was the second most commonly shared opinion in Pearl River County. But nature lent an unexpected helping hand with the end of the spring rains, enabling the agents to inspect in greater detail the river and all its twists and turns. Working in shifts, they scoured the banks once again, hoping the receding waters would leave a clue about Parker's fate. Often they ran into parties of reporters working on their own. Several hours after the search had begun on Monday, May 4, 1959, ten days after a mob carried him from the Pearl River County Jail, Parker's body bobbed to the surface two and a half miles south of the Bogalusa Bridge. It waited, caught in a driftwood jam, for someone to come along and retrieve it.

An FBI agent and a state trooper patrolling the river in a small

skiff about a mile and a half upstream from Richardson's Landing spotted reporters Cliff Sessions and Keith Glatzer along the
bank. The two officials headed toward the reporters to see if
they'd had any luck. As they approached they saw an unfamiliar
object fifty feet away from the reporters in the middle of the
river. The spring rains had brought flooding many miles up
river near Jackson, but here the river crested less than five feet
above normal and began to recede on Sunday without overflow-
ing its banks. The waters were brown with churned silt, and the
currents were considerably swifter than normal. The trooper
sighted what appeared to be a head—facing upstream—a right
arm and right shoulder protruding from the water among the
driftwood. Closer inspection revealed a badly decayed body.[1]

The powerful waters had freed Parker's body from its chains
and swept it along until the left foot caught in the crook of a
fallen tree and rolled over. Another log pinned the entire leg.
The body lay foundering in the water on the Mississippi side of
the river about fifty feet from shore at a point where the river
widened to about one hundred yards. The receding waters exposed the body snared in the jam awaiting discovery. After en-
suring it would not float away, the officers returned to their car
and radioed into Poplarville that they had found a male body
floating in the river.[2]

Agents notified Bill Stewart, the county prosecutor, and at his
request advised Justice of the Peace Walter Davis from Crossroads, Mississippi, a small hamlet a few miles from the river,
about the discovery. Davis contacted six persons to serve on the
coroner's jury, among them Houston Amacker. These six men,
Davis, and Stewart drove to Richardson's Landing to await the
body. After photographing the body, agents set about removing
it from the river. With a heavy log still holding the left leg,
Parker's body proved extremely difficult to free. The decom-
posing corpse was so stiff they could not move its limbs to
untangle it from the wood. Finally, they tied a rope to the
exposed portion of the body, pulled it free from its wooden
net, and towed it across the river, where they pulled it over the
gunwale. The boats proceeded downstream to Richardson's
Landing, where the impromptu jury helped haul the corpse
ashore. They laid it on its back. With its legs cocked slightly,
stiff from rigor mortis, and the arms stretched fully above the
head, Parker's corpse appeared to the half-circle of men standing uneasily around it to be contorted into mock supplication

lying there on the shore, rotted, beaten, and battered. The jury remained at the landing for a considerable time inspecting the body as agents prepared to take it to the hospital. Later that afternoon, law-enforcement officers escorted the body in a caravan of cars, occupied by FBI agents and members of the sheriff's department of Washington Parish, Louisiana, to Charity Hospital in Bogalusa for an autopsy and positive identification. The body was clad only in men's underwear briefs and a torn T-shirt. Since Parker had been wearing trousers when the mob dragged him from jail, word of this missing garment was sufficient to confirm rumors that the mob had castrated him before dumping him into the river.[3]

The coroner of Washington Parish refused to perform an autopsy on the body because it had been discovered in Mississippi, forcing Walter Davis to return to Poplarville and summon Dr. W. F. Stringer from the Pearl River County Hospital. "We apparently hit it just right after the water had fallen," Bachman told reporters. "I don't think the body could have been up for more than a day or so." After word that an adult male body was discovered in the river, 150 people gathered at the door of the small one-story, one-room building in the rear of Bogalusa Hospital to await further news. They milled around anxiously as the minutes dragged into hours.[4]

Authorities made no formal announcement that night, but later, after the autopsy was completed, word spread rapidly among those waiting outside that the body was indeed that of Mack Charles Parker and that he had been dead before he hit the water. Questioned by reporters on his way out, the coroner refused to comment on how Parker died except to say that he had no idea how long the body had been in the river. FBI fingerprint experts identified the body half an hour before Dr. Stringer performed the autopsy, and forwarded their information to headquarters. The official coroner's report declared the cause of death to be "wounds made by two one-fourth-inch high-speed projectiles at the hands of person or persons unknown." Parker's brain had completely deteriorated. Maggots covered the back of his neck and shoulders. The river had so bleached and bloated the body and it was so badly decomposed that facial characteristics were not identifiable. The coroner was unable "to definitely determine whether [the] victim was beaten," but "it appeared that, in view of the lack of water in the lungs, death probably took place prior to the body going into the water." In his report Stringer suggested that the two wounds were caused by jacketed bullets, fired at close range (because they left powder burns on the chest) from a rifle or target pistol, and that Parker was in the prone position "with the person doing the shooting standing at the feet of the victim," because the bullets left the body on a slight upward trajectory. The autopsy showed further "that the decedent's genitalia was [*sic*] intact."[5]

News of the discovered corpse quickly reached Chicago, prompting editor John Sengstacke to ask Lou Palmer to return to Poplarville. Fearing personal injury if he returned, Palmer refused, suggesting Sengstacke send a fresh face instead—photographer Tony Rhoden. Sengstacke summoned Rhoden to his office and told him to fly to Memphis immediately to talk to Lou Palmer before going on to Mississippi. When Rhoden arrived at the Memphis airport, Palmer and Pulley were waiting for him. From them he learned about the severity of conditions in southern Mississippi. Authorities were furious over the statements made by Underwood and Malachy and were still looking for Palmer and Pulley. In fact, Sheriffs Moody and Hickman had approached Curt Underwood's parents and offered them $500 if they would sign a kidnapping charge against the two reporters, since Curt was under twenty-one. Moody was "just as sweet as pie" when he tried to cajole the Underwoods, but they turned him down flat. Palmer and Pulley gave Rhoden as many details about the area as they could and warned him to be especially careful. Palmer asked Rhoden if he had any pictures of his wife in his wallet because he feared the trouble even a photograph of Rhoden's light-skinned wife might cause. Rhoden pulled out his wallet and showed Palmer several photographs of her. Palmer took all the photographs plus all his press identification, leaving Rhoden with only his private investigator's badge.[6]

Such precautions were necessary, Palmer explained, because authorities had banned *Defender* reporters from the area and Rhoden was being sent in undercover. After relieving him of his identification, Palmer said to him, "Tony, we have a surprise for you. We've chartered a two-seater for you to fly you there." The pilot, he told Rhoden, came from Indiana because neither he nor Pulley felt it was safe to trust a Tennessee pilot. In addition, the pilot claimed to be familiar with Poplarville and Lumberton and would play it carefully. Tony shook hands with Palmer and Pulley and headed toward the plane. When he boarded and saw that the pilot was white, he was so shaken he couldn't hide it from the pilot, who looked at him and smiled. "Don't worry," he said. "They paid me enough to get you there and bring you back." Rhoden told him they had to hurry to get pictures of Parker's body before he was buried.[7]

The private plane took off for southern Mississippi with an apprehensive black photographer and a glib white pilot. It was hot in the cramped interior, so hot and so cramped that Rhoden, who was dressed for spring in Chicago, began sweating until soon he was soaking wet and extremely uncomfortable. Adding to Rhoden's discomfort, the pilot couldn't find the airport. Eventually, they found something resembling an old airfield, covered over by thick grass and grazing sheep, with a car parked at the gate as though waiting for them. "Have you ever seen this strip?" Rhoden asked. The pilot shook his head no. He looked out the window. "Down there is the strip but it's full of sheep," he said. The pilot flew the plane lower and lower, trying to scare away the sheep. As the plane circled and dove at them, Rhoden saw two police cruisers approaching. On the last pass the sheep scurried to one side of the field and the plane swooped in for a landing. "OK," the pilot said to Tony, as they taxied to a stop in the middle of the field. "You get into town and I'll wait for you."[8]

The car parked by the gate contained five or six curious white girls. It was soon joined by the two cruisers. When the pilot saw them he exclaimed, "My God! You got company." The plane was parked about a hundred yards from the cars. The pilot reached over and grabbed Rhoden's camera bag and set it outside the plane. When Tony got out and began walking toward the gate, the pilot revved his engines and took off, abandoning Tony. Tony continued to the gate. As he approached, Sheriff Moody got out of his car and said, "Boy, what's wrong?" To Rhoden's surprise, he seemed genuinely concerned. They had stopped, Moody explained, because they thought the plane was in trouble. With his gun on his hip and two carloads of deputies, he looked formidable indeed, but Rhoden braced himself and told the sheriff matter-of-factly that the plane was having trouble holding its altitude and had to drop him off to avoid crashing. Then he told the sheriff, "Now I got to get back out of here and catch a cab or something, get to the railroad station or the bus station."[9]

Moody believed Rhoden's story and offered to help. Rhoden knew arrangements had been made for a black taxi driver to pick him up, so he continued to improvise, hoping the cab would show up soon. At Moody's suggestion he got into the cruiser. As he did so one of the deputies said, "Say, when we was coming down we saw a cab down the way and maybe he can help you." The officers in the other cruiser drove down to get him while Sheriff Moody asked to see Rhoden's identification. Rhoden showed him his badge, silently thanking Lou Palmer for his foresight. The sheriff looked it over. "Oh, you're an officer too, huh?" "Well," Rhoden responded, "I'm a private investigator from Chicago and we have to investigate some trouble down at Atlanta University." That seemed to satisfy Sheriff Moody, and when the taxi arrived, he helped transfer Rhoden's bags and waved goodbye to him.[10]

After Moody and his deputies drove away and they were alone, the cabbie turned to Rhoden and said, "Man, I was scared to death! I started to leave, but I was scared. I didn't know what to do, because if I'd left they would have figured I was coming to pick up somebody. But what I did I raised my hood like my car was heating up, and when they came back to get me, they told me there was a nigger up there trying to get out. He's stuck here and the plane was having trouble." The driver thought for a moment and added gravely, "Now listen, they were trying to find someone coming in. What did you tell them?" Rhoden repeated his story. "Well that's good," the driver responded. "Now what we'll have to do, we gotta go down to the black area where the boy lived."[11]

They drove to Lumberton and on into the black neighborhood, with its tin-roofed tar-paper shacks and roads of thick red-clay dust and ruts from horse-drawn wagons. "If you step in it when it rains," the cabbie explained to Rhoden as they crept along, "you can't even walk because the red clay will pull your shoes off. So the black people go barefoot. Then they don't have to worry about it." Tony asked him where M. C. Parker's home was. "I don't know where it is. You'll have to ask somebody," the cabbie said. As they made their way along the bumpy road into the woods through the black section, they saw people sitting out on their porches, young people, old people, watching them with equal curiosity. The cabbie pulled up. "Well, you can try it, but I don't think these people are going to tell you anything." "Why?" Rhoden asked him. "Look at you, look at the way you're dressed. They've never seen nobody dressed like you coming down here asking no questions." Tony looked at himself. He always dressed well—white sports coat, black slacks, white Panama hat. He never dressed casually. "OK, fine," he mumbled, and got out. It was late afternoon and he wanted to find Parker's home quickly. He walked over to the first two people he saw. "Do you know where Mack Parker lived?" he asked. They looked at each other and said nothing. Rhoden went to the next house: The people closed the door on him. It was then that Palmer's warnings finally sank in. The black people really were scared to death. Rhoden gave up and went back to the cab.[12]

"Well, it looks like we're not going to find out anything," he complained. The cabbie thought for a moment and said, "I'll tell you what to do. I have some overalls in the trunk. Take these, and we'll go down the street and you can put them on and come back. Take your hat off. And then just try to act like a nigger. You act like a white!" Tony changed clothes and even removed his shoes, remembering how he had scoffed at Lou Palmer's stories of how he and Pulley had to dress down. Leaving his camera bag and his urban manners in the cab, he shuffled up to a group of old men sitting in front of a small shop, playing checkers. The old men didn't look up. To Tony's surprise, they were talking about Parker. One old man was saying, "You know, they found him and he's up there at Hall's funeral home." Another man related that Lumberton City Marshal Ham Slade had come to the Parker home the morning after the rape and pulled M. C. out and taken him into the woods and beaten him. Tony took it all in, not saying a word. It turned out he was about two city blocks from the Parker house. He stepped off the porch into the dusty road and headed up the street to a store where he bought some candy. Several men were looking out the window at the Parker house. Tony looked; sheriff's deputies were there keeping watch. I wonder what they're doing? he thought. Mimicking the local dialect, he asked, "Think they doin' somebody else?" The men told him the deputies had been there all day. As he left the store, he pulled the camera from the bib of his overalls and quickly photographed the Parker house. He turned and shot a few pictures of the store and the men on the porch before returning to the cab. "They have the body at the funeral home," he told the hack. "I'm going to try and get some pictures."[13]

By that time, nearly six o'clock, Rhoden had to report to Chicago and his wife that he was safe. The cabbie took him to the black barbershop in Poplarville, where Lou Palmer had earlier relayed his information to Chicago. Tony reported to Chicago that the body was at the funeral home and he was headed there as soon as he hung up. He would try to get some pictures of the corpse, even though he had been warned the police had the funeral home surrounded and weren't letting any blacks in except family. As the sun began to set, Tony and the cabbie headed back to Lumberton and drove up to the funeral home and the four squad cars parked by it. Still dressed in overalls, Tony got out, walked up to the front door, and asked one of the highway patrolmen on guard if he could slip inside for a quick picture and possibly speak to the funeral director. The trooper responded curtly, "Go away. You can't come in here." A lot of white newspaper photographers had been trying unsuccessfully as well, the trooper added. Tony walked around back to find someone who would let him in another door or who could help him convince the police to change their minds. He tried every trick he could think of, but to no avail.[14]

As he was about to give up, he struck up a conversation with a state trooper who had just come on duty. They began talking and became friendly in the way strangers in a time of stress sometimes do. The trooper asked him where he was from. "I'm from Chicago," Tony told him. The trooper said he lived in Indiana and added, "But I'm down here. It's the only way I could get a job." They talked a little more and the trooper told him about the black friends he made in the service and how one had saved his life. Then he said quietly, "Now, I'll tell you what. What I'm going to do for you is what I wouldn't do for nobody else but because somebody saved me and he was black when I was in the service, I'll help you out." Tony was skeptical but pretended to be interested, having learned long ago never to trust whites unless he absolutely had to. The officer said to him, "At twelve o'clock, you watch what happens and when the officers leave the funeral home, you be ready. I'm going to leave this side door open for you because you can see the body covered up. You're going to have to do it in a split second." Tony told him he was used to that from his work on the streets of Chicago, photographing everyone from bank robbers to presidents. In fact, Rhoden added proudly, he'd taken pictures of every president since Roosevelt. "You have to go in there," the trooper warned, "pull the sheet back, and shoot the picture with that one flash, and if you miss that's it."[15]

At midnight, as the next shift of officers was coming on duty, Tony was waiting patiently in the cab down the street. Suddenly all the officers rushed into their cruisers and sped away. They had received a call that a black man was raping a white girl down in the center of Lumberton. They all left at once. Tony ran inside, pulled back the sheet, shot a picture of M. C. Parker, put the sheet back, tore out the door and into the cab, and took off. He learned later that the trooper had arranged the bogus call. When the police returned to the funeral home, the assistant funeral director, who had been on duty at the time, told them about the sneaky black photographer who had come in when they were gone and photographed the corpse. The police immediately began searching for Rhoden, who by this time was on his way to the barbershop in Poplarville.[16]

The police scoured the black sections of both Poplarville and Lumberton for him, running like wounded animals up and down the streets in their frenzied search, looking everywhere, questioning anyone they saw. Eventually, they came to the barbershop. The man who owned the shop put Tony, who stood only five feet, eight inches tall, into a wicker basket and covered him with used towels. "Now, you're going to have to stay quiet until these guys stop running through the town," he said. "Then I gotta get you out of here." Tony hid in the basket, listening to the cruisers driving up and down, back and forth, until 2:00 a.m., when he finally escaped in the trunk of the cab. He spent the rest of the night in the cabbie's home. The next morning, after learning that police had obtained a description of Rhoden, the cabbie wanted to take him across the state line to safety, but Tony said no. He had come for a story and he was going to stay until he had it all, redneck police be damned. Besides, Tony pointed out to the cabbie, the *Defender* was paying both him and the barber well for their services. The funeral would take place soon and then they could leave. "You're not going up there, are you?" the cabbie exclaimed. "Just let me have your overalls," Tony responded. "I won't get up close because someone might have told them what I look like."[17]

The coroner's inquest convened at two o'clock that afternoon at the Pearl River County Courthouse. People in the sweltering courtroom strained forward to hear Bill Stewart quietly, almost diffidently, read the technical details from the report. Although the top layer of skin was missing from the body, the FBI's fingerprint expert had been able to match the fingerprints from the body with Parker's army enlistment records as well as the more recent prints. Upper parts of the torso showed evidence of bruising; four holes in the body, two in the chest and two in the upper back, indicated Parker had been shot to death by two bullets, one of which pierced the pulmonary artery. The other entered the chest, fractured the rib, and exited through the back. Parker had not been castrated, Stewart added, well aware of rampant rumors to the contrary. Earlier the Bogalusa chief of police had publicly announced there had been no emasculation of the body, which the coroner's jury confirmed. Nevertheless, the rumors persisted. Authorities agreed that the murder weapon had been a .38 caliber pistol, because slugs from a .38 fired at close range generally made quarter-inch holes. The jury deliberated for just over twelve minutes and then read its simple verdict. "Death was apparently caused by two 1/4 inch high speed projectiles that entered the victim's body." Stewart added "Death occurred at the hand of a person or persons unknown." Aside from a mark on the head, which Vernon Broome thought was caused by the pounding the body received while in the rough water, no other substantial marks appeared on the corpse.[18]

Two hours after the inquest Parker's body was laid to rest in the black cemetery at the northern city limits of Lumberton. The weeds were so high in the old, untended cemetery that they covered most of the gravestones. Of the fifty people at the funeral, half were white newsmen. Tony Rhoden stood a safe distance away, quietly taking pictures. From Parker's immediate family only Dolores attended; she had tried and failed to contact her mother in El Paso, where her bus was scheduled to stop. So Parker was buried before his mother learned her son's body had been recovered. An American flag draped his gray, metal-trimmed coffin. The Reverend J. W. Watkins, the eighty-six-year-old retired minister of the Lumberton Tabernacle Baptist Church, where Parker attended services and where he had planned to marry Ruth White in June, had wanted some sign of respect for the ex-soldier, so he secured a flag through the local post office. The slight minister dug Parker's grave himself in the side of the red-clay hill of the cemetery, about a mile from the Parker family home. He urged the people in attendance to trust in God. "We realize that all of us is on a funeral train and some day or some night we are going to move on. Every one who is in trouble ought to feel his trouble too." Then the Reverend W. D. Burns of the Mount Zion Baptist Church in Bogalusa and radio minister Nathan Wheeler led the group in a short prayer. "I pray God will have mercy on everyone," Wheeler intoned.

"Won't you help us to be a stronger people? Give us the power to love everybody."[19]

As the pallbearers attempted to lower the coffin into the ground, they discovered that Watkins and his helper had dug the grave four inches too short. So after he finished preaching, Watkins, who "was paid for the grave diggin' but preached for nothin'," jumped back into the grave and lengthened it with a shovel. Nathan Wheeler gave the final invocation. As he did so, Parker's sister began crying and had to be led from the grave. As the coffin was being lowered for the second and last time into the ground, the Reverend Mr. Burns stepped up to the sobbing relatives and told them, "God is too just to do any wrong. I want you to know that." He placed his hands on Dolores's head and murmured a silent prayer and the grieving blacks filed away from Parker's grave, followed by reporters and cameramen. After everyone had gone, Tony Rhoden ran up and quickly photographed the grave site before climbing into the trunk of the cab and heading to Jackson and the home of his sister-in-law. The small marker placed in the dirt at Parker's head bore the unfortunately incorrect inscription: Mike Charles Parker, Died April, 1959, aged 23 years.[20]

It was not until early the following morning that Liza Parker learned of the discovery and burial of her son's body. Her sister, Lola Peters, met her at the Merced Greyhound bus depot and gave her the news as she stepped off with the two children. Mrs. Parker had been sickened with grief since the abduction of her son and, upon hearing the final news, collapsed into her sister's arms. "Even before they dragged him from the jail," she told her sister, "I was afraid of what might happen. Poplarville had always been a dangerous place." In giving her reasons for fleeing Mississippi, she complained, "After it happened I couldn't even get anyone to take me to the grocery store or be seen with me. Everyone was afraid that something more would happen, so they gave me money and told me to leave." After locating Parker's mother in California, reporters placed call after call to the home of Lola Peters, who told them that Liza was too scared to come to the telephone. "You can't blame her," she explained. "She left because threats were made against her life." A week later, recovering her strength and indignation, Liza Parker accused local authorities of complicity in the lynching. "I feel that Mr. Moody the sheriff should have known what might happen. The town was just too small for him not to have some idea that trouble was afoot." As for the identification and punishment of the mob, she had no hope whatsoever. She feared no one in the Poplarville area—white or black—would talk. "People down there are just scared to death." She stoutly maintained her son's innocence. When she had asked him if he had raped June Walters, he had responded, "No, mother, I did not. I don't know why they put this on me." Mrs. Parker added sadly, "I hope justice is served."[21]

With her mother planning to find a job and remain in Merced, Dolores decided to move in with her aunt in Bogalusa. Although Dolores also denied that the NAACP had offered her or her mother financial support, she was very much aware of the death threats her mother had received. "She went to live in California," Dolores explained somewhat defensively, "because her sister lives there. I am staying here because my closest relatives live here." With Dolores's move to Bogalusa, every remaining member of M. C. Parker's family had left Lumberton as a result of his death.[22]

With M. C. safely buried, blacks and whites alike hoped life would return to normal. This was not to be. Even though television news films proved the contrary, word spread among whites that the government had financed a lavish funeral for Parker, and white people felt he had somehow managed to escape his just punishment by having an expensive funeral. In addition, the American flag draped across the coffin seemed to legitimate his claims of innocence. Citing E. T. Hall's guess that the government would finance the funeral, whites complained Parker did not deserve government funds for it. Since he left the army with a dishonorable discharge, whites erroneously claimed, the postmaster erred in issuing an American flag for his funeral.* People were also beginning to complain about the resurgence of hate mail, which they blamed on national attention to the discovery of Parker's body. "Frankly, you people are a disgrace," wrote one man after watching news reports of the body's discovery. The mayor and Sebe Dale again received letters castigating them and the town for permitting such a thing to happen. For everyone in Poplarville, the lynching had become a nightmare, and the townspeople only wanted to let it fade away.[23]

---

* Although twice convicted of theft and of disobeying superiors, Parker received a general, not a dishonorable, discharge from the army, and was thus entitled to the military honor at his funeral. FBI memorandum, undated. A general discharge differs from a dishonorable one in that in the former the person is deemed by the military to be unsuitable for military service but not necessarily to have committed a crime.

The discovery of Parker's body had been a shock to the people of Poplarville. Citing the confidence shown by town leaders, residents were certain the body would not turn up and the investigation would soon die. One chagrined man suggested that had the lynch mob taken Parker to the Honey Island swamp behind Picayune, "no one would ever know about it but the water moccasins." Those few who felt the body would eventually surface in the Pearl River openly predicted that it would be beyond recognition once discovered. They were wrong. Positive identification led to immediate John Doe murder warrants in addition to the pre-existing charges of kidnap. With Parker proven dead, it remained for the FBI to bring his murderers to justice.[24]

At the beginning of the week citizens began surreptitiously and cautiously mentioning the names of several participants. One man was mentioned most often—J. P. Walker. The FBI already suspected him, Preacher Lee, and Francis Barker. But this was unknown to residents, who whispered that L. C. Davis and one or more of Preacher Lee's sons might also have been involved. No one said a word in public. Francis Barker died of a heart attack in the Bogalusa Charity Hospital on Thursday, April 30, several days before the body was discovered, and his death made his name the first to be brought into the open. He might have ridden in the car that followed Reyer's car, people guessed. The FBI knew and refused to say. Agents had arranged for new offices over the weekend, moving to larger rooms above the Mississippi Power and Light Company on Main Street, two blocks from the courthouse, in order to accommodate the large number of agents and the growing body of evidence. Of the investigation, a local storekeeper's comments typified the exasperation in the town, "The agents at Poplarville were busy at telephones, scribbling on pads. They were, as usual, extremely polite, but you could have learned as much from the telephone pole on the corner."[25]

When the body turned up, some residents were displeased, fearing its discovery would increase the length of the FBI's stay. Others hoped it would bring a quick end to the investigation. No one fully anticipated the increase in anti-Poplarville sentiment throughout the country.[26] More than one resident came to share the feelings of one irate citizen who complained. "When that lady was raped, you didn't see no FBI men around here." Newsmen were being told constantly that they failed to give enough attention to the gravity of Parker's crime, and ru-

mors of the expensive funeral caused even more heated criticism of the press. The unblinking glare of national publicity,
the relentless questioning of people in the county, the hate
mail, and the uncertainty whether those being questioned were
suspects or witnesses began to have an effect on the populace.
The Reverend Frank H. Thomas wrote a letter to the editor,
defending himself for deciding against preaching a sermon
about the lynching on the Sunday following. "You seem very
concerned with M. C. Parker's abduction," he wrote. "The national rape rate was 76 times greater than that in Mississippi.
Does that concern you?"[27]

In support of those pointing with increasing anger to the nature of Parker's alleged crime, Bill Stewart re-emphasized that
his case against Parker had been absolutely ironclad. Governor
Coleman had already made it clear he believed Parker raped
June Walters. In spite of their political rivalry, Sebe Dale went to
great lengths to cite Governor Coleman's post-lynching indictment of Parker while lending support to Stewart's claims. These
men intended such arguments to justify the lynching to the rest
of the country, not to sway southern Mississippi. They failed to
realize that Parker's guilt or innocence or the nature of his crime
was by now a secondary factor. If the national press provided
any indication, most Americans already believed Parker guilty if
for no other reason than the color of his skin. But Parker's guilt
made little difference to the public in its view of the lynching.
The nation was outraged by the lynching, not the rape. Southern
Mississippians found it very difficult to come to grips with this.
Their desperate pleas about interracial rape fell on deaf ears and
left them even more isolated in their insistence that rape justified
lynching. Poplarville convinced itself it had been wronged, that
the town itself had become the ultimate victim of the lynch mob.
Another local circuit judge went so far as to comfort his courtroom that Parker had not been lynched at all. The crime his
abductors committed was merely "conspiracy to commit a crime,
the crime of murder." The judge said a mob had to be operating
in public after having been drawn together with "no fear of
detection, nor intent of secrecy, similar to the throngs in the
Northern urban race riots," to constitute a lynching. He blasted
Northern politicians and liberals for labeling a murder a lynching and added, "The party of politicians that heaps the most
venom on the people of the South will get the most Negro or
Socialist votes."[28]

While Parker was being buried, President Eisenhower was holding a press conference in the East Room of the White House. Wary of racial issues since the 1957 Little Rock crisis and still somewhat apprehensive about the *Brown* decision, Eisenhower wanted to avoid comment on the lynching. But Robert Spivack, then of the New York *Post*, pinned him down as much as the elusive man would allow. "Mr. President, I believe it was a week or so ago that you expressed your indignation through Press Secretary James C. Hagerty over the kidnapping by a Mississippi mob of a Negro prisoner, and according to some reports the FBI has now found the body. I wonder if, as you review this episode, that you feel that it emphasizes a need for stronger civil rights legislation, or if you have any other specific conclusions you draw from this affair?" Eisenhower responded in his halting, elliptical way with some irritation: "Well, I hadn't thought even about the idea that it needs a new law on this particular case. The state authorities went on, got on the job immediately, they called in the FBI, they have been working in cooperation and law has been violated, and I don't know how you can make law stronger except to have it, when you make certain that its violation will bring about punishment. Now I know the FBI is on the job, and I have every confidence that they and the State Department—or the state authorities— will find some way of punishing the guilty, if they can find them." In reporting this press conference, the Jackson *Clarion-Ledger*'s headline revealed the paper's deepest concern for the South—not the triumph of justice, but rather "Ike Sees No Need for 'Lynch' Law."[29]

Radio Moscow wasted little time in taking advantage of its international rival's awkward position. In a broadcast to Africa it charged, "It is perfectly clear that none of the criminals concerned will be punished, for in the United States those who murder Negroes are not punished. The Ku Klux Klan lynchers who are intensifying racialist terror in the U.S. enjoy the advantage afforded them by complicity of the authorities." Because "Mississippi authorities took no measures to punish the murderers of Mack Parker," the broadcast claimed, "the whole thing was premeditated and prearranged." Moscow warned Africans, "It is characteristic of American imperialists to bring into countries not only their goods but also their racialist laws." American imperialists inflict "their racialist laws" on the people of Asia and Africa at the same time they "grab the resources of other countries and exploit the people. And to crown it all, an African Ku Klux Klan also made its appearance."[30]

Radio Moscow's accusations provoked an unusual response among Mississippi's citizens. When Gary Moore, the commander of the Mississippi American Legion, saw television reports of Radio Moscow broadcasts and of Parker's funeral and then heard the rumors that Parker had been court-martialed for theft, he demanded return of the flag used at Parker's funeral, as though this would somehow negate Radio Moscow's charges and make Parker less of a victim. He asked the Lumberton postmaster to obtain the flag from the Parker family. The chaplain of Picayune's American Legion also joined the effort to retrieve the flag. In most states the Veterans' Administration provided the flag, which the local post office then issued to the family of the deceased military man. The army had no control whatsoever over the procedure. Customarily, the family presented the necessary papers to the postmaster after the funeral. In Parker's case the assistant postmaster, Malcolm Dickson, of the Hattiesburg Post Office issued the flag to E. T. Hall, the funeral director. Learning of Moore's actions, NAACP Field Secretary Medgar Evers indignantly charged, "It should be quite apparent to every Negro just what the American Legion stands for and condones. Lynchings. Since Moore and his bunch want to do something patriotic, he should issue an order for the capture of the band of cowards that lynched Parker rather than further discredit his state and his group by his proposed action."[31]

Moore did not take such insults from a black man lightly. "The statement by Evers was the most unfounded, ruthless, damnable falsehood that was ever issued by any person or organization," he replied. "Among things other than lynching the American Legion does not stand for the NAACP and their tactics . . . for rape . . . or for the flag of our great country to be draped on the casket of any man who has been discharged from the armed forces of our country dishonorably." Despite Moore's erroneous information about Parker's discharge, he went on to insist that the American Legion will not allow "any person or organization to trample its good name."[32]

Moore was so enraged at Evers's accusations that he ordered the Lumberton chapter to recover the flag. The burden for its recovery fell upon the man who had first issued it to E. T. Hall, but Malcolm Dickson claimed not to know what to do. The American Legion had no authority. "If the VA wants it recovered, I'll tell the undertaker," said Dickson. Repeating the incorrect rumor, he lamented, "Nobody knew when the flag was issued that the boy was dishonorably discharged." In further support of the action, Lumberton City Marshal Ham Slade, who previously stated publicly that Parker had no record of arrests or of getting into trouble, asserted that Parker had been a "trouble-maker" since coming home from the army. Poplarville police officers, who swore a week and a half earlier they had never heard of Parker before his arrest, now claimed Parker had been known throughout the black section as a "clown" who had been arrested several times for drunkenness. Bill Stewart claimed that as an ex-service man Parker was not entitled to the honor of the flag because he had two minor convictions and had "also been in other trouble while in the army."[33]

The debate raged for a week and a half following the burial. As charges of brutality and harassment by FBI agents began to surface, the Veterans' Administration ordered Malcolm Dickson to retrieve the flag from the Parker family. Following his instructions on May 13, Dickson, E. T. Hall, and both the commander and adjutant commander of the Lumberton chapter of the American Legion traveled to Bogalusa to get the flag from Dolores, putting a final, unsavory ending to the funeral. Self-righteous whites claimed Parker had a lavish funeral at the taxpayers' expense. To prove he had not deserved it and to discredit criticism from outside the South, they made sure the flag that covered his coffin was returned to its shelf in the Hattiesburg Post Office for the next, perhaps more fortunate, ex-GI.[34]

8

The FBI in Peace
and War in Mississippi

The flurry over the flag quickly became secondary to a much more serious problem by Southern standards: charges of citizen harassment by FBI agents, which were growing increasingly widespread and increasingly vehement. When several suspects entered the hospital after being grilled by the FBI, Mississippi politicians began demanding an investigation of the FBI, arguing without any sense of irony that the agents had violated the civil rights of the people they questioned. As a result, the initial purposes of the investigation became lost, momentarily, in a cloud of invective.

Outwardly ignoring these charges, the determined lawmen began following up the discovery of the body. While Parker was buried and the storm over the flag rose and subsided, the FBI and the highway patrol continued their investigation. Since lynching was not a federal crime, the Justice Department had to identify the mob and prove it had crossed the Mississippi-Louisiana border. Otherwise, Parker's death was a simple case of murder, not punishable under federal law. Federal officials had to have credible evidence of interstate flight to have jurisdiction and an eventual conviction under the Lindbergh law.*

---

* Southern filibusters defeated attempts to pass federal anti-lynching laws in 1922 and again in 1937. In any case, those laws were probably unconstitutional. Since it had begun

Beginning where they discovered the body, agents combed both sides of the river for traces of the mob, looking for gloves, hoods, and perhaps the murder weapon, although no one thought the lynchers would have been careless enough to leave that behind. The foot-by-foot search disclosed a burned-out car that turned out to have been incinerated at least two weeks prior to the lynching. Ralph Bachman calmed newsmen aroused by the find with the terse comment that there had been no new developments since the discovery of the body. In the meantime, an air of tension settled over Bogalusa. June Walters's family lived in Bogalusa, and since the FBI had set up a second head-quarters nearby, some observers believed that the FBI suspected the mob to have originated at least in part from there. Residents of Bogalusa complained the FBI was drawing them into the un-pleasant affair. Remarked one Bogalusa woman, "I wish that they could have kept this thing in Mississippi instead of droppin' it in our laps."[1]

With the discovery of the body, the FBI moved one important step closer to success. Several of the more arrogant mob members, confident of their invulnerability, helped the FBI along a little further. When agents came to Crip Reyer's barbershop the day after the body was discovered, he met their questions with jokes and wisecracks. Reyer knew he was asking for trouble, but like the others he reflected confidence that he would never be arrested. He believed he had the community on his side and that in his mind was the crucial factor. Agents returned to McNeill to question Reyer on May 6 without positive results. He refused to make any statements. Similarly, they subjected Arthur Smith, Preacher Lee, his son Jeff, Herman Schulz, and J. P. Walker to long grilling sessions without any immediate results. Others whom they questioned and whom agents believed played no role in the lynching mentioned these men. It appeared as though almost everyone in town had heard of some or all of them. Between April 30 and May 8 the FBI questioned at least once every man (except Francis Barker, who had died) who had en-tered the courthouse to abduct Parker. None of these men con-fessed. Walker, for example, told the agents he first heard of the lynching on Saturday morning between 8:00 and 9:00 when

involving itself in interracial violence, the Justice Department had been forced to use anti-conspiracy laws first passed in 1870 and 1871. These laws made it illegal to conspire to deprive an individual of his civil rights.

he went to Hickman's Drugstore in Picayune for coffee. Eddie Walters told agents his brother had been approached by two men from Poplarville the day of the lynching, but swore neither he nor Jimmy had participated in their schemes. Jewel Alford had so far denied any knowledge of the lynching. When agents questioned Marshal Orr on May 8 about why he and Petey Carver had stayed away from the jail for so long the night of the lynching, Orr volunteered that he knew nothing about the lynching beforehand but had he known he would not have gone anywhere near the vicinity of the courthouse or the jail attached to it. He explained it was not his duty to protect the prisoners at the jail. That duty belonged to Sheriff Moody, and Orr did not want to get involved with anything having to do with an abduction. Under persistent questioning from FBI agents, Petey Carver finally admitted to falsifying his earlier story of his car stalling out around midnight, just at the time of the lynching, as the reason he was late getting to the jail. Carver's car never stalled out. The Justice Department found his "meanderings" around the Poplarville area at the time of the lynching "questionable" and remarked about Carver's failure even to "alight from his car upon arrival at the hospital after the abduction."[2]

In the first two weeks after the lynching, the FBI questioned hundreds of potential witnesses and suspects and gathered dozens of items as possible clues. In addition to this, agents discovered Parker's body when no one, especially the mob members, thought they would. Nevertheless, after two weeks of investigation in which several county residents underwent intense scrutiny, no one had confessed. This stemmed in part from the stiffer opposition investigators began to encounter. But the FBI was not about to allow itself to be defeated by local intransigence. The investigation was progressing well and the FBI planned to stay in Poplarville until it obtained results. It was precisely this that concerned town leaders, who worried the FBI might keep agents there throughout the summer, disrupting the life of the sleepy town that considered one stranger cause for discussion and now faced sixty FBI agents, forty highway patrolmen, and thirty newsmen. Rumors of new developments persisted, as they had since the first day of federal involvement. Meanwhile, Attorney General Rogers received a petition from the AFL-CIO to use all the powers of the government to investigate vigorously "the most atrocious crime in the history of this or any other nation." This petition, one of many from interested organizations and concerned citizens, prompted governmental assurances that the investigation would proceed quickly. In the past with other lynchings, especially those before the 1934 lynching of Claude Neal, the government ignored petitions of this kind or gave them a halfhearted response. In 1959 in light of increasing civil rights disturbances in the South and increased concern over America's image in the Third World, the White House, the Justice Department, and other agencies found themselves constantly reassuring the nation that justice would be done in Poplarville. Such reassurances failed to mention that even limited success depended upon local cooperation.[3]

In Poplarville the fear of retaliation by local blacks, which had existed since the lynching, was rekindled by the discovery of Parker's body. Noticing an increase in tension in his congregation, the Reverend Frank H. Thomas preached against the pistol practice that had begun in the surrounding countryside, but to little avail. The Poplarville hardware stores sold all their handguns. Said the owner of one store, "Women have been coming in here in droves buying pistols for protection."[4] The Chicago *Defender* had scored a coup of sorts with Curt Underwood's account of his ordeal with Mississippi lawmen that further exacerbated tensions in Poplarville. The newspaper also printed a wholly false story Tony Rhoden had heard in Lumberton that June Walters had never been raped, but had tried to conceal a "love tryst" with another man, a white man. The unsigned story, which ran on the front page of the paper the week after the Underwood story, claimed the unnamed source, who feared for his life lest he be identified, knew the "phantom lover" and asserted that he and Mrs. Walters had been having an affair for several months. The affair led to June Walters's estrangement from her husband. On the night of the rape, so the informant claimed, she had gone to Bogalusa, where her husband was playing, to get some money from him. Jimmy agreed to drive her home and on the way the car broke down. Walters left to get a tow truck. Parker did not happen by a second time. Instead, June's lover stopped and drove her back a deserted road, where they had a "secret tryst in the woods." When the lovers returned to the highway, they found that "the husband had returned and left the scene" again when he found his wife and child gone. The man said it was then that June "cooked up" the rape story in order to explain her absence.*[5]

---

* The Walters filed a one-million-dollar lawsuit against the *Defender* because of the story. The *Defender* settled out of court, agreeing to pay the Walters $5,000 in damages.

The first indication that all was not well between southern Mississippians and the FBI agents appeared several days after the discovery of the body, during the controversy over the flag. On May 10 the *Clarion-Ledger* devoted an unusual amount of space on its Sunday editorial discussing in vague terms the role of the FBI in the lynching investigation. The paper mused, "While little is said on the subject, there is considerable sidewalk comment in Mississippi over the fact that the FBI is active in the kidnap-murder case down in Poplarville." After lauding the agency for its well-earned worldwide reputation, the paper pointed out that the FBI discovered Parker's body only because it had lodged in driftwood as the Pearl River lowered. The editorial complained that the Bureau had been less successful in apprehending communists than kidnappers—only two kidnapping cases remained unsolved since 1932. But, "just because the . . . Supreme Court saw fit in its broad judicial wisdom to free the FBI-trapped Communist conspirators against America is no justifiable reason why Mississippians should not want to see justice done in any given case. Therefore, it is hoped that the nation's press will concern itself with equal vigor to defending the lives, homes, factories, farms, churches, schools, and shores of America against political world conquerors as it does defending a dead rapist and in demanding that justice be done to suit its conscience in one reprehensible act of kidnap-murder down here in Mississippi."[6]

Its sister paper followed this up three days later with a story about June Walters's four-year-old daughter, Debbie Carol, who "cries with fear every time she sees a negro. Any negro. Anywhere." Entitled "Rape Victim's Child Can't Erase Night of Horror," the long and detailed account of the rape from the child's point of view played to white racial phobias. It told of Debbie continually asking her mother if a "negro" had raped her. " 'I have to tell her "yes," ' said the victim of M. C. Parker's savage assault. . . . 'Every time she sees a negro now, she'll ask me, "Mommy, is that the one who raped you?" I tell her, "No, that's not the one." ' " The paper considered June Walters "the sort of typical young housewife whose main interest is building a home, keeping it spotless and taking care of her little girl. In her spare time she works jigsaw puzzles and occasionally reads the Bible kept conspicuously in her living room because 'Every home needs a bible in it.' " The lynching left the woman, who already suffered from a mild heart condition, in a state of se-

vere anxiety. "She seldom works jigsaw puzzles anymore because she's too nervous to sit still. She has good reason to be
nervous."[7] In reality June was suffering more from the increased strain the lynching had put on her already shaky marriage. Jimmy had been drinking more than ever and missing
work. Worst of all, there was talk that Eddie had been involved
in the lynching.[8]

Attacks against the FBI and the news media in the North
brought into the open the conflict between the FBI and the press
and citizens of the state, a conflict that had been brewing since
the very first day the FBI entered the case. Reports surfaced of
harassment and rough treatment of suspects and witnesses, and
local papers obliged by promulgating them. The FBI came into
isolated and clannish Poplarville in large numbers—sixty agents,
forty from the New Orleans office, twenty more from other
Southern districts—dressed in wash-and-wear suits, wearing
neckties and straw hats, as though purposefully calling attention
to themselves. They showed little concern for the sensibilities of
the local population and appeared by their attitude to have indicted the entire county, which served only to reinforce preexist-
ing prejudices and to increase support for the lynchers as a way
of expressing contempt for meddling outsiders.[9]

Although disquiet spread throughout the state during early
May, neither of the major gubernatorial candidates, Ross Barnett or Carroll Gartin, had yet mentioned the issue. Both ardent segregationists, they waited to see the outcome of the investigation. A third man, Charles Sullivan, a two-time candidate
who had little chance of winning, spoke freely of the lynching
and the FBI. "I don't personally know that it was necessary to
call FBI agents and open the county up to them," he complained. "Anyhow, such requests should come from local officers rather than the governor." With this kind of comment
becoming increasingly common, Coleman's actions were beginning to have a negative impact on Gartin's campaign, as Gartin
became linked with the FBI and outside involvement in local
affairs. Privately, Gartin's workers were now expressing concern
over his election chances.[10]

Suspicious Mississippians considered President Eisenhower's
rare words of praise for their state to have been the result of
Coleman's cooperation with the mistrusted national government.
They viewed the president's attempt to block demands for
tougher civil rights legislation containing anti-lynching provi-

sions as an attempt by a Republican to win support in a state temporarily at a disadvantage. Voters considered the telegrams exchanged by Coleman and the president over the lynching to be written proof of Coleman's (and by inference Gartin's) questionable loyalty to their state and its noble cause of segregation. U. S. Senator Philip Hart of Michigan remarked upon introducing an anti-lynching bill that he did not intend to criticize Mississippi authorities, and Senator Jacob Javits of New York said he was pleased by the close association of the FBI and the state authorities in the probe. This angered loyal Mississippians and further alienated them from Coleman's handpicked candidate, Carroll Gartin.[11]

Just two days after the body had been buried, amid rumors that two inmates of the Poplarville jail had identified Preacher Lee, two people attempted suicide. Thirty-two-year-old Helen Van Ness, who had been in jail the night of the lynching, slit her throat with a razor blade. Dwight Ladner had told her to hide her face in her pillow the night the mob entered the jail so she would not see anything. Nevertheless, she was able to identify several of the mob members to the FBI. On Thursday, May 7, two FBI agents questioned her for over an hour, during which time she identified Jewel Alford and Herman Schulz. She told the agents she had been warned several times not to tell anyone what she had seen, and then realizing what she had done, several hours later the despondent woman tried to kill herself. She missed her jugular vein, and officers took her to the hospital in time to prevent serious loss of blood. She was released a few days later and returned to jail. Later she paid her fine for selling mortgaged property and returned to Houston. People dismissed her statements to the FBI as the trick of a woman "just trying to get out of jail."

The other suicide attempt was by a man with knowledge of the activities of the police force the night of the lynching, Houston Amacker, one of four Amacker brothers. During the lynching his brother Jeppie, a town constable who lived with his son-in-law, R. J. Wheat, was sitting in his car and drinking beer with his brother Hubert "Goob," in the black section. When the third Amacker brother, Aubrey, met them there with a friend, they all drove past the courthouse. It was around 12:30. Even though they saw lights on in Sheriff Moody's office and activity on the south steps, they didn't stop. Houston knew this and more, and the FBI had little trouble extracting it from him. At fifty-four,

Houston Amacker was the village idiot of Poplarville. He stood under five feet tall and suffered spells of fainting and vomiting and "falling out", and, according to Dr. Stringer, had generally poor health. The FBI questioned him on Thursday, May 7, and took him to its offices on Friday morning. Later that day friends heard him repeating to himself, "I don't know nothing about it." Early Friday evening he drank a bottle of toilet bowl cleaner containing hydrochloric acid.[12]

Townspeople dismissed Houston's suicide attempt much as they had Van Ness's. "Amacker was tired of people laughing at him," they said. He "was worried about a lot of things," said his brother Goob. "He had been sick for a long time. He and his wife separated a couple of years ago. People kidded him about his spells and his small size and he couldn't stand the kidding. He was in an automobile accident a year or so ago and hasn't been the same since. His back and neck were hurt." The suicide attempts of two whites—one a witness to the abduction, the other a courthouse fixture with a brother on the police force—appeared to have been prompted by fears of mob retaliation against persons cooperating with the investigation. Local residents condemned the FBI, perhaps a bit too self-servingly, for driving those they questioned to suicide. The investigators, however, knew they were on the right track. They continued interrogating and re-interrogating people in and around the county, sometimes escorting them to their temporary offices on the outskirts of Bogalusa or south to Bay St. Louis for longer and more arduous grilling sessions.[13]

On Saturday, May 9, Crip Reyer admitted to the FBI that Arthur Smith had accompanied him to the meeting on the Wiggins Road and that they had met later that night at Crossroads with J. P. Walker and others. The FBI had approached Smith with similar questions the day before, but he had denied everything. On the 11th, armed with the new information supplied by Reyer, agents went to Smith's home in McNeill at eleven o'clock at night and took him to Bay St. Louis, where he continued to deny his role in the lynching. This time, however, he supplied the names of Walker, Preacher Lee, L. C. Davis, and others as being in the two cars.[14]

The agents maintained a day-and-night watch on Smith from a car across the road from his house and brought him back the next night to have him sign the statement he had given the day before, but Smith, who was barely able to write, refused. Hearing it read to him, he found no discrepancies in it, but told agents that because of his limited education he lacked an understanding of what he was doing. During the following days of questioning, the agents kept at the young man, at one point interrupting him and his wife during sexual intercourse late at night, until he weakened and furnished them detailed information on everything but the actual killing and the dumping of the body into the river. From his vantage point, Smith had watched Walker drive the car containing Parker into Louisiana, but had not seen the car again until after Walker recrossed the bridge onto the Mississippi side of the Pearl River. Day after endless day and night after endless night of constant hounding by determined agents took its toll on the hapless stump hauler. His nerves were frayed by the grillings and by his own fears of what might happen to those who betrayed the mob. Walker's reputation was a strong warning. Agents brought Smith back on Wednesday night, May 13, and he elaborated on his activities before and during the meeting at the Davis farm. Agents questioned him again on Thursday, Friday, and Saturday, each time waiting until the lights went out in his home before knocking. On Saturday the emotionally overwrought Smith took agents to the Davis farm and showed them the area in front of the house where the meeting had taken place. Afterward, they drove him to Walker's home and the homes of other mob members, where Smith confirmed their role as participants.[15]

The FBI took Smith's confession of Wednesday night to Jewel Alford on Thursday, and the wall of resistance crumbled further. Alford had been increasingly troubled by his own role in the lynching, and when agents read to him from Smith's statements, he could no longer remain silent. After telling Sheriff Moody about his role in the affair, Alford admitted to the FBI agents that he gave the keys to the mob. In addition he named those men who came to his house and named the owner of the car in which they had been riding, the car that eventually transported M. C. Parker to his death, Crip Reyer's Oldsmobile.[16]

It seemed that neither the FBI nor the weather in Poplarville would let up. The intense heat forced the FBI to seek new, air-conditioned quarters at the same time agents were putting the heat on the third man from whom they expected to get a confession. Armed with new evidence from Smith and Alford, they brought in Crip Reyer late Thursday, May 14, along with six other men who were suspected of being deeply involved in the lynching. All the men hid in the back seats of cars driven by federal agents and shielded their faces from reporters as they rushed inside. The FBI hoped that by rounding up Crip Reyer, L. C. Davis, Preacher Lee, Herman Schulz, J. P. Walker, and Arthur Smith and presenting them with the new evidence, they could wrest confessions from some of them. They advised each man, as they fingerprinted him and took his photograph, to hire an attorney. They held all of them throughout the night, trying to extract confessions.[17]

No one confessed to participating in the actual abduction and murder of Parker in spite of agent-administered browbeatings. In the early hours before dawn, agents escorted the men to the waiting cars. All of the men wore work clothes; all of them hid their faces from reporters, who had held an all-night vigil on the sidewalk. Ralph Bachman commented with unusual candor, "We're not going to identify anybody as a suspect until we have something definitely to go on. For one thing, we don't want to blacken a person's reputation and secondly, when we identify someone as a suspect, you can be sure we've got something definite to go on." Bachman's relatively lengthy comments prompted J. Edgar Hoover to have him instructed to say "No comment" and nothing more to reporters. Feeling the FBI's work was about over, Bachman sent half of his agents home after the Thursday night session. Townspeople were "sure something [was] going on."[18]

During the long Wednesday night session, they had subjected Crip Reyer to a three-hour interrogation that resulted in a mixed confession. Isolated in one small room with three agents while in other rooms other agents questioned other mob members, Crip admitted his car had been used in the lynching, admitted attending the meeting, but denied having anything to do with the abduction or killing of Parker. Succumbing to pressure from the agents, Petey Carver had informed them that a man named Crip owned a red and white 1957 Oldsmobile 88 similar to the type used as the getaway car, and asked them not to reveal his cooperation because of the "embarrassment" it would cause him in the community. On May 7 agents had approached Reyer at his barbershop. He admitted that he owned a red and white Oldsmobile 88 and consented to an examination of it by agents. Without being asked, he also volunteered that a lasso used on some cattle and some game fowl he had shot four days earlier had left bloodstains in the trunk. When the agents asked him why he volunteered such information without being asked, Reyer said he had heard they were looking for cars with blood in them. When agents told him their laboratory could easily distinguish between human and animal blood, Reyer added that he had cut his finger and some human blood might be in the trunk as well. Agents made a quick inspection of the car and placed it under surveillance until the next day to prevent anyone's tampering with it.[19]

The next morning, after staking out the car overnight, the FBI dusted for fingerprints and removed a pair of white gloves, a hood, paint scrapings, blood samples from the rear seat, rope from the trunk, hair from the trunk, and various other bits and scraps of evidence. The blood residue in the rear of the car, however, proved to be "insufficient for grouping purposes" and the blood and hair in the trunk and on the rope were of bovine origin. Crip remained unaware of the FBI test results.

Reyer's wife received a visit from the FBI the same day as her husband, but at a time when he was away from the house. Mrs. Reyer confirmed Crip's story that he had returned home from the barbershop at 8:00 p.m. on the night of the lynching and had watched television the entire evening before going to bed. But Reyer's stepdaughter, whom agents also visited, told them she and her husband had been at the Reyer home when Crip returned from the barbershop and that he had left again almost immediately for Poplarville, "to see about some cattle," and returned around 10:30 that night.[20]

Crip admitted that the lynch mob used his car to carry Parker from the jail to the Bogalusa Bridge, but he refused to sign any statements to that effect. Different agents returned to his farm and barbershop on May 11 and 12, but they could not persuade him to sign any statements or elaborate further. Nevertheless, the agents believed it was only a matter of time, and they persisted until he finally broke. On the night of May 14, after hearing Alford's confession made earlier that day, Crip agreed at first to sign a lengthy confession of his own in which he admitted to attending the meeting before the lynching and allowing his car to be used. He also identified Preacher Lee, L. C. Davis, J. P. Walker, Francis Barker, his nephew Arthur Smith, and, tentatively, Jeff Lee as part of the lynching conspiracy. As for his own activities, he insisted he had been with Francis Barker when the raid on the jail occurred. Over the course of the next several days, agents visited Reyer repeatedly until he made a positive identification of the main members of the mob. Then the realization of what he had done proved too much for him. On Sunday, May 17, he suffered a nervous breakdown and entered the Picayune hospital screaming incoherently. By that date, the FBI possessed two nearly complete confessions, neither of which were ever signed.[21]

Crip Reyer was a jovial man with a reputation of being a good-hearted buffoon. On one occasion he was sitting in the Star Cafe talking freely about his role in the lynching when his companion told him an FBI agent sitting behind him had overheard everything Reyer had said. Reyer turned to the agent. "Do you know who I am?" he asked. The agent answered, "Yes." Reyer replied, "Well, I'm the biggest goddam liar in the state." Then he got up and walked out. "All the agents have been pretty nice to me," he said during the investigation, "except one who almost came right out and called me a liar." Sitting comfortably in his home fifteen miles southwest of Poplarville the day before agents read him Alford's confession, Reyer admitted that he had been in Poplarville on business the night of the lynching. "But, I don't know that my car was used in the lynching," and "I certainly didn't put a hood over my head and take any Negro out of jail." Reyer had tried to laugh about the tightening noose of evidence, but his hands shook as he spoke and a light tremor passed over his lips. "I've been joking with some of them," he told friends. "I started to drive away the other day when I noticed them behind me and I told them they'd better gas up because I had a lot of places to go that day."[22]

Jeff Lee was a man with a "detective complex who often hung around the courthouse nosing in on police matters," according to Sheriff Moody. One of the people questioned by the FBI characterized him as a "mean and dangerous individual."[23] Agents first contacted Lee on May 4, after Alvin Gipson told them that a man who looked like a Lee was in the back seat of the Oldsmobile the night of the lynching. "I gave them a signed statement [on May 7] about where I was the night of the crime," Lee complained, "but they came back later and wanted me to tell them again. I told them to read that statement." As for his pre-lynching trip to visit Jimmy Walters, "they said witnesses told them I was in Hattiesburg the day before the lynching looking for somebody to join the gang, but I was seeing about a job." Agents trailed Lee into the Star Cafe, as they had Reyer, but Lee turned to the agent who sat down in the next booth and said loudly, "I didn't come in here running and I ain't leaving running, so you can just sit there all day." To his friends he boasted the agents "can follow me to hell and back, I don't care." But Lee was rattled by the FBI's persistence, and his mood grew steadily worse. He complained the investigation of him "has got everybody around here talking about me." Investigators placed his home under surveillance and monitored his every action. Lee refused to take a lie detector test, as he said, because, "I don't believe in them."[24]

Bureau agents made the rounds of Lee's friends and neighbors, trying to find a flaw in his story. His friends stuck by him and told agents nothing damning, nothing they could use at all. Agents told his wife that her "husband was involved in this thing, that he helped make plans for the lynching." Lee, whose tough nature was belied by his soft voice and his chain-smoking, maintained he had been home in bed the night of the lynching. The first time the FBI came to his house, he said, "I was already in bed, but I got up and went to town with them." They took Lee to their new headquarters, where they told him they knew that his trip to Hattiesburg was to enlist Jimmy Walters in his plans. The questioning was "sometimes rough and sometimes nice," Lee reflected, "but I guess that's how they operate." When one agent asked him if he was ready to tell the truth, "I told him I had already told the truth and I wasn't going to tell anymore." Three days later two other agents questioned Jeff and his wife together. The frightened man thought his house had been secretly searched. "I know it has, but I just can't prove it. But they can search my home any time if they come up like gentlemen and ask."[25]

Unlike his son, Preacher Lee talked freely to anyone about the lynching. He proclaimed himself the "prime suspect" and proudly boasted both he and his son Jeff had refused to submit to lie detector tests. When agents had asked him, Lee said he replied, "I will die and go to Hell first." Posing for photographs with a poised shotgun, Preacher Lee recounted that someone had hit his dog on the head one night and so the next night when he heard noises in the bushes behind his house, he fired his gun into them. The next morning he found cigarette butts and a trail of dried blood leading away from the bushes, which led him to conclude he had wounded an FBI agent. The Missionary Baptist minister admitted, agents "bothered me with long questioning sessions" and had been able "to make me say words I'm ashamed of." Still, he freely admitted his views on racial matters. He thought "communists and the NAACP" were stirring racial tensions and insisted that "God's word set forth that the Negro is a servant." Lee also admitted he had entered the hospital the morning after the lynching because a board had fallen on him while he was doing carpentry.[26]

The physician who examined Preacher Lee termed him a "58 year old white male neurotic," who complained of chest pains, which the doctor found of psychosomatic origin, and weakness on the left side. Lee had scratches on his left hand, which he said were caused by nails in the same piece of lumber that fell on his head. He also had a bruise with a slight break in the skin over the left mastoid bone. Parker had wrested Preacher Lee's club from him and hit him with it on the left side of his head. The scratches on the left wrist were caused by Parker's fingernails as Lee and Walker tried to force Parker from his cell. The attending physician's impression was recorded as "? cerebral concussion vs. small hemorrhage."[27]

Agents first approached J. P. Walker on April 29, wanting to know where he had been on Friday night. They learned from jail inmates that Walker had been to the jail on the day Parker was arraigned and had returned several times afterward, including the day before the lynching. Nevertheless, they did not question Walker again until Thursday, May 14, after Jewel Alford made his statement incriminating Walker. On Thursday they escorted him to Bay St. Louis. After questioning him, they followed him home, waited overnight, and took him to Poplarville on Friday to question him again. Walker told the FBI he had been in Poplarville the night Parker was lynched "politicking" for the August 4 primary. He too refused to submit to a lie detector test. When agents pressed him to learn why he had been spotted in Reyer's Oldsmobile, he swore vehemently and finally became so irate that he refused to answer any more questions, threatening to strike one of the agents. "They called me a liar," Walker challenged, "and I told them to bring me home. I ain't going with them no more unless they arrest me. They threatened me and talked to me like I was a nigger or a dog or something." Walker expressed outrage that the government was "spending $100,000 [on the investigation] because of that nigger who wasn't worth two cents." He later apologized to the agents for losing his temper.[28]

"When I was deputy sheriff," the body shop owner mused, "I worked with the FBI agents and found them to be a nice group. That is why I agreed to talk with them." Walker had agreed to accompany them to Bay St. Louis and later to Poplarville, but, he now said flatly, never again. Walker also tried to improve upon his alibi by explaining that he had been in Poplarville politicking and drinking coffee several nights during the week before the lynching, adding sarcastically that he thought it would help his election chances if voters knew about his encounters with the FBI agents. He finally told them he had been to the meeting at the Davis farm but admitted to nothing more.[29]

Agents continued bringing men in and out of the office in Poplarville in a flurry of activity as intense as that on the day they discovered Parker's body. On Thursday afternoon, May 14, the FBI whisked three men away from headquarters in the back of a car. As the men left Poplarville, they held large squares of cardboard in front of their faces, supplied by the agents for just this purpose. The car headed north toward Hattiesburg and was reported to have passed through that town, giving rise to the rumor that FBI agents had already arrested three men and were taking them to jail in Jackson. In reality, agents were merely returning several suspects to their homes. By Friday morning, May 15, the FBI had completed the questioning of most of its main suspects.

Every act by the FBI heightened speculation. Despite the almost constant denials from agents as the weekend wore on, some newspapers claimed arrests had occurred, and others predicted arrests of as many as seven men before Monday. The town itself remained unusually quiet on Saturday, May 16, after word spread that the FBI had obtained several confessions after the night-long grilling sessions. Generally, sleepy Poplarville bustled with activity on Saturday afternoons as rural folk came to town for relaxation and to catch up on the latest gossip. But the gossip of late had not been cheerful, and there were disquieting rumors that the FBI would make arrests during the weekend.

Even though the Sunday papers trumpeted impending arrests, no arrests were made. The FBI had been unable to obtain the confessions that would warrant them. Agents had solved the case by Saturday, less than three weeks after being called in, and had a complete story of the lynching, but they were unable to extract a full confession from anyone who had ridden with Parker. Bachman and his men did not give up the investigation, however. They discontinued tailing their prime suspects and instead tried to refine their existing evidence for presentation to a grand jury. They lacked signed confessions incriminating the men who actually helped kill Parker, which was what the agents had been working for; otherwise, they had names, times, places, and events in great detail.[30]

No one, including the suspects, knew the investigation had reached an impasse. The agents skillfully concealed the extent of their knowledge from everyone to whom they talked. The closest they ever came to making any arrests was when they advised each man they questioned during the all-night session to hire a lawyer. They neither asked Sheriff Moody to supply arrest warrants nor informed him that they would soon be asking him to do so.[31]

Although the mob members had avoided arrest on state murder charges and on federal charges of kidnap and conspiracy to deprive Parker of his civil rights, the strain was so severe that several succumbed anyway. Amacker was already in the hospital after his suicide attempt. Arthur Smith had entered the Poplarville hospital for what was called a cerebral hemorrhage after he collapsed at his home on Saturday afternoon an hour after FBI agents left. Smith had returned home from Poplarville after a morning with agents and had gone to bed feeling weak and dizzy. His wife noticed a glazed look in his eyes but said nothing to him about it. She continued preparing lunch and, after making coffee, walked to a neighbor's house just up the road. As she returned home, she spotted an FBI car near her house. FBI agents were still watching their home. Inside, she found her husband lying stricken and unconscious. She complained to the doctor that her husband, who was in good health normally, had been feeling bad since Thursday night, May 14, when the agents kept him in Poplarville until 6:00 a.m. Smith's brother Cecil said, "Arthur was a husky, healthy man who's never been hospitalized. It looks to me like they've got to leave Arthur alone now." Cecil added that his mother was "on the verge of a nervous breakdown" because of the FBI's grillings.[32]

A local doctor suggested that the possible "cerebral hemorrhage" was brought on by extremely high blood pressure, caused by intensive questioning. The doctor placed Smith in a private room with orders to the staff not to allow any visitors but immediate family. Smith lost his power of speech and could only mutter and make noises. He appeared to recognize only his wife. The doctor expected him to reach a crisis stage in seventy-two hours and wanted him undisturbed until after that time.

When word leaked out about Reyer and Smith, townspeople began to show open hostility toward the FBI. Considering the intensity of the investigation, residents had been slow in showing their feelings, but once they surfaced, they spread rapidly. One man who had attended the meeting at Gumpond admitted to being questioned by agents on several occasions, but seizing the new attitude of defiance in the county, he attacked the agents rather than defending himself. He quoted agents as saying, "All right, when did you bend your gas tank? When you were taking Parker away from the jail?" One resident jokingly reported that when agents asked him if he had participated in the lynching, he had replied, "No, I wasn't invited."[33]

As Smith lay in the hospital, unable to speak coherently, nodding his head in response to questions, a sign across the door barring everyone but his wife, Vernon Broome delivered a ringing denunciation of the FBI's conduct in Poplarville. His remarks diverted attention from the lynching and the certainty of arrests. "I have several complaints about the FBI's tactics and we are seriously considering what to to do about it," Broome declared. "We had hoped the FBI would respect the rights of individuals and the privacy of their homes. We didn't know they would harass people and call them liars."[34]

Under these stressful circumstances, Poplarville viewed Preacher Lee's claim of having wounded an FBI agent as a minor coup. The FBI denied an agent had been wounded, but reports circulated that a doctor in Bogalusa had treated an agent for gunshot wounds. Citizens of Poplarville, who felt the FBI had treated them shabbily when they had extended every courtesy, felt the wounded agent got what he deserved. The FBI had alienated almost every one in the town, and an agent confessed later that the Bureau had indeed been "overzealous in its investigation." Nevertheless, townspeople continued shielding the guilty men. They never extended their initial cooperation as far as giving the agents specific information about the lynching. In that way, the entire town implicated itself and forced the FBI into questionable tactics in order to solve the case. By the middle of May, almost everyone had a good notion of the affair or possessed some information that would have enabled the FBI to piece together a strong case without having to go to the lengths it did. But residents never felt obligated morally or legally to assist the lawmen.[35]

Crip Reyer's physician added to the distress by commenting

publicly, "Definitely the FBI questioning put him in the hospital. Crip was completely off his rocker when he was brought in. It's a dirty shame." The doctor also placed Reyer's wife under his care because she was on the verge of a nervous breakdown. The FBI's methods caused such concern in the town that Bill Stewart, never one to keep his thoughts to himself, made it known that agents had threatened one man with three years in the federal penitentiary unless he divulged certain information. As for Smith and Reyer, "I am checking these reports," he said. "If they are true, we'll see to it the FBI gets no further cooperation." Mayor Pat Hyde said from behind the counter of his grocery store, "People are getting fed up. It seems that they are harassing people who don't know anything about this crime." The FBI's tactics are "a lot of foolishness. This has ruined business here in this town. People don't want to come to town because they would meet up with these agents."[36]

Poplarville attorney David R. Smith, a candidate for county attorney, began advising residents of their rights "if approached or interrogated or intimidated by the forty or more FBI agents and state officers" who were in Pearl River County. "I have uniformly advised them that they have, under the state and federal constitutions, the right to secure the advice and assistance of their lawyer or lawyers; the right to refuse to answer any and all questions and the right to forbid and prohibit any search of their homes or premises without such officer exhibiting a search warrant. I further advised them of their rights to refuse to be fingerprinted or photographed without first being arrested and, if arrested the right to refuse to answer questions without first consulting their attorney or attorneys as to their rights, and that they cannot be compelled to submit to a lie detector test or to give evidence against themselves." Smith added that if the FBI violated any of these rights, the officers were "exceeding their authority and the citizens of the county should be made aware of that fact." Many residents sought legal advice after having been questioned by the FBI, especially after hearing that Crip Reyer's and Arthur Smith's illnesses were related to the questioning. Several worried suspects came to one prominent Poplarville attorney, put $3,000 on his desk, and asked for help. The cautious lawyer shoved the money back and said, "Now get the hell out." Only later did he agree to represent them before a federal grand jury.[37]

The anger of the citizenry caused concern throughout the

state and led Congressman William "Buddy" Colmer to demand a probe of the FBI's conduct in Poplarville by the Civil Rights Commission. Colmer did not question the right of the FBI to investigate the case, but maintained that if his constituents' complaints of intensive grilling and harassment were true, the FBI was violating their civil rights. Colmer sent a telegram to the chairman of the Civil Rights Commission, stating: "While I in no way condone and was first publicly to deplore the violence in the Poplarville, Mississippi, Parker case, nor do I question the authority of the federal government to investigate it, I do seriously question the alleged conduct of federal agents as reported in today's press reports. By direction of the Civil Rights Act of 1957, your commission is charged with responsibility to study and collect information regarding denial of equal protection of the laws under the constitution and to appraise laws and policies of the federal government with respect to equal protection of the law." After listing the reported complaints, Colmer concluded, "It would be appreciated if you would advise whether your commission is investigating such reported conduct of these federal agents which, if true, indicates that the civil rights of my constituents are being violated." Colmer was aware, as were most people following the case, that one of the potential federal charges against the mob was conspiracy to violate Parker's civil rights. It seemed to give Colmer satisfaction to be able to make similar charges against representatives of the mistrusted and disliked Yankee-dominated federal government. The truth or falsity of these charges became almost a moot point because their mere stipulation sufficiently discredited the FBI and diverted attention from the central focus of its investigation. Ironically, these charges surfaced after the investigation had all but ended.[38]

Governor Coleman was caught in the middle once again. In a news conference announcing his intention to accept Sam Ervin's invitation to testify against the Civil Rights bill, he defended his close cooperation with the FBI. "I understand some small opposition has been expressed to the presence of the FBI in Pearl River County," the governor said, asserting the Bureau's presence in Poplarville assured the nation that the lynching had "not been winked at." He claimed a responsibility to the entire state; the "side issue" of his requesting FBI assistance had nothing to do with their presence there. "I want to point out that under the United States law the FBI could have come in anyway after 24 hours. The question," he said, "is to prove that Mississippi is not guilty of supporting lawlessness." Coleman recognized the political mileage Ross Barnett was getting out of the charges against the FBI in Poplarville and the governor hoped to mitigate it to some extent by traveling to Washington. Unfortunately, his press conference backfired when news surfaced of the hospitalization of Smith and Reyer. Colmer, who supported Ross Barnett, further damaged Coleman's position with his telegram to the Civil Rights Commission. As a result, President Eisenhower's remarks that Coleman had cooperated fully with him now assumed a new meaning. Coleman made matters worse by refusing to ask the FBI to withdraw from the case. He asserted that the investigation would free Mississippians of the stigma of guilt by association. "I am also trying to keep the state from being engulfed in a torrent of federal civil rights legislation." But his protests fell on deaf ears.[39]

On Monday, May 8, Coleman had to confront another anti-FBI petition, this time by state auditor Boyd Golding, an arch political foe and supporter of Ross Barnett. In an open letter in the *Clarion-Ledger,* Golding accused the governor of refusing to demand the withdrawal of the FBI, because "to do so Coleman would seriously damage his stand with the National Democratic Party, especially with such men as Paul Butler and Brooks Hayes, the moderate of Arkansas who Coleman tried to elect over segregationist Dave Alford." Golding said, "I think the chief reason that the FBI is staying in Poplarville at so much expense to the taxpayers is that they are trying to make an example of Mississippi because we have refused to swallow integration." J. P. Coleman was considered a moderate *only* because he refused to advocate extremist or violent resistance to desegregation as he quietly sought to enhance the South's national image. The controversy over the lynching investigation enabled ardent segregationists to gain center stage and from there to conduct a successful attack on the moderate wing of the party. "I am glad," wrote Golding, "that Congressman Colmer has started action to protect the people of Pearl River County. It is strange that the FBI wasn't invited to help catch the Negro Parker when he raped a young pregnant white mother while her little daughter was forced to look on." He took a final swipe at the governor: "I would like to witness the invitation of outsiders to come to the sovereign state of Mississippi to harass, browbeat and torture people to the brink of death. However, since you as governor invited the FBI into the state, I think you owe it to Mr. Arthur Smith Jr., his family, the people of Pearl River County and Mississippi the decency of now asking President Eisenhower and J. Edgar Hoover to immediately take the FBI agents from the borders of our state. The Federal Bureau of Investigation has amassed a great record in the past in fighting crime, but it was never intended the 'behind the iron curtain tactics' be used on Mississippians." The besieged governor responded by saying that these charges were "typical of the tactics which Mr. Golding has been using against me ever since I became governor. I am doing what I can to keep all the people of Mississippi from being convicted of mass guilt and paying the penalty for what somebody else did."[40]

J. Edgar Hoover instructed his assistant Clyde Tolson to prepare announcements in the event the FBI had to pull out of the case and to initiate an intra-agency examination of the harassment charges. Hoover was extremely sensitive to these charges lest they damage his Bureau's image, especially in light of the impending withdrawal and apparent failure of the FBI to get the guilty men. Another Hoover assistant, Cartha DeLoach, confronted Buddy Colmer outside of the House chambers about the telegram. Colmer apologized for sending it, claiming he was pressured to by several Mississippi associates. He also admitted that there was no factual basis for the harassment charges, and he promised to refrain from future attacks on the FBI. Hoover commented dryly, "He has the guts of a jellyfish."[41] Governor Coleman meanwhile dispatched Attorney General Joe Patterson to Poplarville to investigate the charges. Coleman's prestige had declined considerably with Golding's attack, and he sought to restore it with Patterson's visit. After a twenty-minute "surprise" visit with County Prosecutor Stewart, District Attorney Broome, and Mayor Hyde, Patterson accompanied the men to FBI headquarters. The attorney general had expressed public concern as early as May 13 over the tactics of the FBI. "The power to investigate is one thing and the power to harass and nag citizens is another," Patterson said of complaints by several people that the FBI had been "camping on their trails." And that had been before Smith and Reyer fell ill. But emerging from the forty-five-minute meeting with head agent Ralph Bachman, Patterson confessed he "didn't know anything about these reports except what [he] read in the papers." He reported that Bachman spoke frankly with them and conducted himself with courtesy. Vernon

Broome felt otherwise. He claimed Bachman flatly denied any unjust treatment of the suspects and refused to say more. All four men had publicly castigated the FBI for mistreatment of citizens; after the meeting they refused to criticize the FBI further. Later that day, after taking time to discuss the meeting via telephone with Governor Coleman, Patterson concluded that the FBI had not mistreated anyone in its efforts to solve the lynching. Since no one had filed an official report about harassment, reasoned Patterson, and since his visit was purely personal, he decided against making an official complaint.[42]

Patterson's visit to Poplarville proved to be a well-executed political move designed to demonstrate to Mississippians the Coleman administration's concern about the reported harassment. While Coleman did worry about these reports, he was more concerned over how much damage such complaints caused him. Patterson had assured Bachman he had not come to Poplarville to cast doubt on the FBI but merely on a "personal visit." Patterson claimed he personally had no complaints about the agents because he knew they never conducted their investigations in such an unseemly manner. He suggested the FBI issue a statement rebutting the allegations because the people of Mississippi were beginning to get the wrong impression of the FBI. Events had forced a Southern segregationist governor and his lieutenants into the uncomfortable position of defending the FBI against harassment charges in order to defend themselves politically within the state.[43]

On the same day as Patterson's visit, another suspect succumbed to FBI zeal: L. C. Davis. His complaints first arose May 7, when agents backed a car up to the side door of his home, put the ailing man in the back seat, covered him with newspapers to hide him from reporters, and drove him to Poplarville. His hemorrhoids were so painful that agents had to take him to his doctor before they could question him. When he returned from the doctor, he was fingerprinted and photographed and held throughout the night. Davis refused, as the others had, to submit to a lie detector test. He came forward with his account of FBI mistreatment after hearing about Arthur Smith and Crip Reyer. He swore he had been home in bed with a toothache the night of the lynching and complained that his last encounter with the FBI sent him back to bed for several days. He allowed the FBI to search his farm but not his unpainted, weather-beaten cabin. When agents returned on Tuesday the 12th, and accused his wife of making coffee for the mob, he told them, "I don't want you here no more. You're not to return without a warrant."[44]

The bed-ridden farmer was well enough to pose for photographers as he lay in bed, holding across his chest the shotgun he kept nearby to ward off the FBI. Davis felt his action was justified by the confusion the FBI had created on his farm. His dogs barked and ran around nervously inside and out of the sparse cabin, his wife complained. "We got bird dogs, deer dogs, hog dogs, and coon dogs," she said, and all of them were in a frenzy. "I got dogbit on Easter Sunday and I took me a club to beat off the dogs, and they [the FBI] took the clubs," Davis complained. "The FBI has been aggravating people and worrying them to death." Agents had been to see Davis nine times and scoured his small farm, picking up cigarette butts, cigar butts, and matches "that anybody could have throwed out the window going by. It's a shame and a disgrace to the people of Mississippi. We ain't got no governor. If we had, he would get them out of the state." Davis had to admit, however, that his interrogators may have made him "hopping mad, but they haven't mistreated me. I told them hell no they didn't have any meeting here." Davis said of the agents he talked to, "Some of them have been mighty nice but I'm fed up and damn tired of it all and told them that I didn't know nothing." But Davis was frightened by the depth and detail of the questioning about the meeting at his farm and his attempt to jimmy the window to Sheriff Moody's office. Finally, he refused to answer any more questions, saying, "Take my knife; you might just as well cut my throat."[45]

Other suspects also complained of unacceptable treatment by the FBI. A Picayune man who had ridden with Crip Reyer and Arthur Smith to the meeting at the Davis farm related that he had returned home late at night from a business trip to New Orleans to find his wife, her ailing mother, and his sister-in-law awake and upset. Four FBI agents had appeared at the door, and before his wife "could say yes or no or anything they were in the house." Even Preacher Lee was upset about his treatment at the hands of the agents. Lee sat on the porch of his tar-paper cabin, telling how much "it hurts when your own color joins up with the Russians."[46]

After the addition of L. C. Davis and others to the list of complainants, people stopped talking to the FBI at all unless they absolutely had to, and then they treated them "coolly but politely." Sebe Dale had a stronger reaction to the harassment charges. He declared that the methods used by the FBI "would very likely be overruled by the United States Supreme Court if they were used on Negroes." But the cantankerous judge hastily added that if the agents had been indiscreet, it had not been intentional.[47]

The FBI soon countered these charges. On Wednesday morning, May 20, it released a statement in Hoover's name explicitly denying every allegation of harassment and improper conduct. "When examined in the light of the facts, the ludicrous nature of these charges becomes obvious," the statement said. "We have been advised by medical authorities that Smith had *not* suffered a cerebral hemorrhage, and the person primarily responsible for the circulation of the false story regarding Smith has known from the very outset that he was not telling the truth." Smith's doctor had begun hedging on his original diagnosis of a cerebral hemorrhage several days earlier. The statement continued, "In like manner other distortions and misrepresentations concerning our investigation have been circulated—many by persons who obviously do not desire this case to be solved." The FBI lauded Governor Coleman and the highway patrol for their cooperation and concluded, "Our agents work as diligently to remove suspicion from falsely accused persons as to identify and apprehend wrong-doers. No innocent person ever need fear being investigated by the FBI."[48]

Hoover received help in defending his Bureau from an unexpected source. Speaking to the North Side Civitan Club in Jackson several days earlier, the chief investigator for the State Sovereignty Commission, Zak Van Landingham, defended the FBI against harassment charges, declaring that agents do not use Gestapo tactics. Van Landingham was a 27-year veteran FBI agent, and he specifically ridiculed Boyd Golding for his comments, saying, "How absurd can you get?" Criticism of the FBI being brought into the Poplarville case is a political issue in an election year." He defended the governor for calling in the FBI and added, "An innocent person will have no trouble in establishing his innocence, if he cooperates with the agents ... the FBI is dedicated to identifying the mob who took the law into their own hands. Do those who criticize really want the mob identified?" And to reaffirm his credentials as a Southern white man, the former FBI agent declared that he favored "total and complete segregation of the races in Mississippi. No one would rather see agitators, both in and out of the state, taken care of more than I would." Van Landingham also wrote to Hoover declaring his continued loyalty to the FBI.[49]

Following the FBI's vehement self-defense, Dr. Stringer admitted there appeared less and less chance that Smith had suffered a cerebral hemorrhage. On Wednesday, Ralph Bachman held a press conference to defend his agents. "You fellows know," he told reporters, "that the FBI doesn't operate that way. Our agents ask persons if they mind being questioned, and if they do, we leave them alone. We checked out these reports and found they weren't true." A somewhat relieved J. P. Coleman concluded, "There just isn't anything to those charges. The FBI has not violated anyone's constitutional rights." Even so, the political damage to Coleman's protégé, Carroll Gartin, was already done.[50]

Writing in the Washington *Daily News,* columnist Lyle C. Wilson summed up the situation: "The reasoning of lawmen that they would take the lynchers into custody went like this: There were nine of them and the community is small. Among nine conspirators in such an event, one at least, is bound to talk. The talk will get around and in time it will get around enough so that the lynchers will become known by name." But, Lyle continued, "there is a smell of collusion in the developments reported from Poplarville—a smell of collusion among some of the townspeople to discredit the FBI quickly before the agents can bring to justice the lynchers of Parker. If the FBI could be sufficiently discredited, it might be that the lynchers would get off unharmed, even if their names became known."[51]

9

Bad News from Bilboville

In the midst of the storm over the mistreatment of suspects by the FBI and the growing issue of race in the upcoming gubernatorial race, Roy Wilkins ventured into the tumult of Mississippi to address a NAACP meeting in Jackson. The visit further complicated the situation for Mississippi's embattled governor, who was still determined at least publicly to bring the mob members to justice. On Sunday, May 17, Wilkins spoke to a packed house in the twelve-hundred-seat Lynch Street Lodge in observance of the fifth anniversary of *Brown v. Board of Education*. Wilkins told the crowd that blacks had a long way to go before they would realize the promise of the 1954 decision. Racial tranquility in Mississippi, he said, was "the tranquility that exists between the jailer and the jailed. Nothing we on the outside can say about Mississippi can condemn the state as soundly as the guilt feelings revealed in the utterances of its own citizens and newspapers." The NAACP's executive director reminded the audience that both J. P. Coleman and Sebe Dale "cried out against stronger federal civil rights legislation." In the old days, "When the South exercised total control over their racial situation, no Mississippi governor or circuit judge would have felt the need to say anything." As he spoke eight plainclothes deputies from the Hinds County Sheriff's Department arrived at the front door with pistols strapped outside their coats. They were carrying warrants for the arrest of Wilkins and field secretary Medgar Evers for advocating the overthrow of state segregation laws. A tense hush fell over the auditorium, but Wilkins continued speaking. The policemen waited nervously by the door for the order to close in on the podium.[1]

Elmore Greaves, well-known segregationist figure and Citizens Council member, had taken out warrants for the arrest of Roy Wilkins and "the Mau Mau admirer" Medgar Evers for violating the 1954 state law that made it a crime for two or more people to conspire to "overthrow or violate segregation laws of this state through force, violence, threats, intimidation, or otherwise." The penalty for violating this law, passed in response to *Brown v. Board of Education,* was a twenty-five-dollar fine and one to six months in jail. When Governor Coleman learned about the warrants, he instructed Joe Patterson to have them withdrawn. As a result of Coleman's last-minute action, Wilkins completed his speech and left the state. Claiming the arrests would "stir up too much trouble when Mississippi already had enough at Poplarville," Coleman demonstrated rare good sense for a Mississippi governor, yet he succeeded only in further alienating himself from influential white racist organizations and the voting public, which accepted assertions by the Citizens Council that their state was under siege and Coleman was aiding the attackers.[2]

Recognizing the potential damage to the Gartin campaign from the Wilkins controversy, the next day Coleman made a plea to the gubernatorial candidates to keep race-baiting to a minimum. Over the weekend Ross Barnett had made several speeches attacking Coleman and Gartin for, in effect, acquiescing on civil rights. Although neither major candidate had yet mentioned Parker by name, clearly the lynching was of growing importance in the election. "Mississippi cannot afford to take a black eye and invite civil rights legislation," warned Coleman, "because of the mistakes of a few men who took it upon themselves to violate the law." But Coleman was pessimistic. He lashed out at state auditor Boyd Golding and Bidwell Adam, the elderly Gulfport lawyer and state Democratic chairman who claimed that Roy Wilkins had handed Coleman "a bouquet of roses wrapped in complimentary political foil" during his speech in Jackson. During his speech Wilkins had said that Coleman "does not believe in violence as a means of settling questions which involve the two races. He is not on our side, but he wants law and order and for that we are grateful." In Mississippi in 1959, a statement like this could be extremely damaging to a white politician.[3]

"It is too early to say whether the criticism of Coleman will hurt Gartin or help him," commented Gulfport's *Daily Herald*. "If the people think Coleman has acted wisely, criticism could bring Gartin votes. It would probably cost him votes if Coleman's actions prove unpopular with the average voter." J. P. Coleman realized then that his political fortunes, those of Carroll Gartin, and "moderation" in Mississippi were in jeopardy. "Nothing but the good sense of the people of Mississippi can save us now," he said dourly. Coleman foresaw regression if Barnett won, yet the lynching and especially the FBI's investigation of it might drive people into Barnett's camp. The governor suspected that Mississippians were unwilling to adopt his mild brand of racial moderation; for Mississippians after Poplarville, even that position was too radical. Coleman explained he had been trying to save his "state from racial strife" and "was making great progress along this line until a few people like Mr. Bidwell Adam started playing selfish politics with the racial question." It was the first time the governor had mentioned the name of the cantankerous, flannel-mouthed Gulfport attorney, who had been Theodore Bilbo's lieutenant governor and had been in Poplarville on the night of the lynching at the Barnett-for-Governor meeting, since he had become a public critic of the governor six months earlier. It indicated the extent to which events worried Coleman. He felt the wound of Wilkins's compliments and the subsequent attacks by his opponents. But his protests proved ineffective. "I have never asked for compliments from the NAACP and am not doing so now." In the aftermath of the gruesome and embarrassing lynching, Coleman swore "selfish politics" were ruining the state's race relations. In the past few weeks, he complained, the situation "has grown steadily worse. I am sorry to say that I feel less hopeful about the situation today than at any time since I have been governor."[4]

The final and most devastating attack against the governor came on Tuesday, May 19, from Elmore Greaves, who was irate over his failure to obtain the arrests of Wilkins and Evers. "One might be constrained to wonder why our fearless attorney general was in Jackson at all, when surely it is obvious that his duty was in Poplarville, protecting the rights of Mississippi citizens against the arrogant 'gestapo tactics,' to use his own words, of the FBI. White citizens of Pearl River County have been subjected to

such harassment by the FBI that a number of them are hospitalized with nervous breakdowns. Yet our courageous attorney general remains in Jackson . . . perhaps the fact that our governor
begged the FBI agents to come to Poplarville explains this. It is
painfully obvious that our governor is overacting in his tooth-
some role as Mississippi's goodwill ambassador to the integrated
hinterlands."[5]

The FBI also had problems. It now faced the near certainty
that it would conclude its investigation without making any arrests. The investigation had paid off, but in a dubious way.
Agents had solved the case. They had firmly established motive
and modus operandi, secured the corpse and connected it with
the criminals. The evidence uncovered could contribute decisively in securing indictments and eventually convictions of the
mob members under Mississippi state law. But agents had failed
to identify *conclusive* violations of either the Lindbergh law or the
civil rights statutes. To be sure, strong evidence was there; the
doubt was over its ultimate durability in a court of law.[6] In spite
of the extensive investigation, agents had been unable to gather
what was felt in Washington to be conclusive proof of a federal
violation. Statements by Smith and Reyer indicated the mob had
crossed state lines, but did not provide sufficient courtroom
proof. Thus, after over three weeks of inquiry, the Justice Department returned to the basic issue of federal jurisdiction, an
issue many Southerners had been railing about since the day the
Bureau first entered the case. If agents failed to prove that the
car had crossed into Louisiana with Parker alive and still inside,
federal prosecutors could not charge the mob with violating the
Lindbergh law. Other possible federal charges concerned conspiracy to violate Parker's civil rights—something extremely difficult
to prove even to a friendly jury.[7]

Even though the Justice Department had considerable apprehension about proceeding with kidnap charges, the FBI had
developed a sound conspiracy case against several of those involved in the lynching and against several more as co-conspirators. Developing after the prayer meeting at Gumpond, the
conspiracy grew to include some of official Poplarville and
many more people in the surrounding counties. The FBI developed the conspiracy as a system of concentric circles, expanding
outward toward lesser involvement. In the Parker lynching, the
group of conspirators who actually planned and carried out the
abduction and murder occupied the innermost circle, the very

core of the conspiracy. These were the men who, with one exception, led the planning at the Davis farm, went to the jail to get Parker, and took him to the Bogalusa Bridge, where he was executed. To these general conspirators the Justice Department would later add implicated law-enforcement officers.[8]

The men who helped plan the lynching and served as lookouts around the courthouse and the lawmen who avoided the courthouse during the lynching occupied the second circle of the conspiracy. The FBI viewed many of these men as co-conspirators, leaving it up to the grand juries whether to indict them or not. In any case, these men were just a technicality away from being prime conspirators. More cooperation with the FBI on the part of local residents could easily have put some or all of these men in the first circle.[9]

People who knew of the conspiracy and approximately when the crime would occur but played no direct role in it occupied the next circle. It was here that Poplarville began to lose its claims of innocence. Some town officials and prominent men had prior knowledge of the possible conspiracy, though in most cases not intimate knowledge. Other law enforcement officers and friends and relatives of the conspirators had some knowledge of the conspiracy beforehand, as did men from Hattiesburg and other areas who had attended the meeting but had not gone to the courthouse.[10]

The FBI put those people with direct though *ex post facto* knowledge of the lynching in the fourth circle of the conspiracy. This included people who had witnessed part of the abduction but claimed not to have recognized any of the men even though several masks slipped down during the struggle with Parker. It also included several people at the Star Cafe, where some mob members met before and after the lynching.[11]

Finally, people who had only a passing knowledge of the conspiracy, of the parties involved, and of the probability that "something" was going to happen to Parker constituted the fifth circle. Many residents of Poplarville and Pearl River County belonged in this circle. In a largely rural county with about 22,400 residents, where Parker's trial was the main topic of discussion, it was difficult for people not to be aware of the possibility of a lynching and of the men forming a mob. In the realm of prior although nonspecific knowledge, Poplarville citizens assumed part of the responsibility for the lynching. Given the strong feelings in this closed community, where most of the families had lived and intermarried for generations, it would have been virtually impossible for anyone interested in the rape trial not to have had some knowledge of a possible lynching, especially considering the flamboyance and braggadocio of a J. P. Walker or a Preacher Lee. It would have taken a monumental effort to remain unaware of the pre-trial atmosphere.[12]

Almost to a man the FBI knew who had been in on the lynching. They had little or no solid evidence against several men and left them out of the conspiracy altogether, although these men were not beyond suspicion. Almost to a man as well, town officials supported the anti-Parker sentiment even if they did not express open agreement with the lynching. Although few men in official capacities had actively participated in Parker's lynching, none in positions of responsibility acted to thwart the explosive situation or to assist in the arrest and punishment of the mob after the lynching.[13] Although historically in many instances, lynchings involved the upper crust of a town or county, in many others the same people used their prestige or influence to prevent lynchings. In this case most of the lynch mob came from what in other areas would have been considered the working class. In the blurred class lines of Pearl River County, this distinction was virtually meaningless. None was wealthy by anyone's standards, but none was outside the mainstream of society. None was a habitual criminal, drifter, or outcast, all came from the rank and file. They were average citizens.[14]

In the past, the mayor had sometimes placed himself between the jail and the mob to prevent a lynching. In other cases, the mob forced its way past judges, mayors, and lawmen to enter the jail and seize its victims. In still others, the state police, highway patrol, or National Guard actively prevented lynchings through force or threat of force. On other occasions, in other places in the South, the state police virtually allowed the mob to remove a victim in their presence. Mobs often seized their victims from the local sheriff or his deputies, who usually claimed to have been unable to identify any of the mob members, whether they had been masked or not. The lynching of Mack Charles Parker, as the FBI reconstructed it, was a minor variation on this theme. At the time of the lynching, law officers were away from the courthouse. Several law enforcement officers lingered elsewhere, because they had been told by J. P. Walker or other conspirators when the lynching would take place.

When the FBI passed through the weekend of May 15–17

without making the anticipated arrests, it quickly found itself
fighting a rear guard action. The fieldwork had been completed
amid charges of brutality. The Justice Department was dragging
its feet as it agonized over the probability that it had no solid
kidnap case against members of the lynch mob even though the
FBI had successfully identified them. It was hardly the customary atmosphere in which the FBI closed an investigation. The
Bureau mourned that "it would be most desirable for the FBI to
effect arrests in this case in order to obtain the maximum public
recognition of our work." Instead, it had all the hallmarks of a
retreat, which J. Edgar Hoover felt appeared to vindicate the
people who had made allegations against the agents. Furthermore, it made J. P. Coleman appear to have backed the integra-
tionist elements on the national scene. For that, Coleman was
becoming something of a pariah in his own state. Speculation of
arrests first came when the governor's office leaked word that
arrests were close at hand. Activity around FBI headquarters in
Poplarville flourished as though the hand of justice was about to
close around the mob, but then rapidly diminished as the crisis
passed—as Wilkins was speaking in Jackson. By the following
Wednesday, May 20, nothing had happened; people wondered
what the FBI was waiting for. Had the anticipation of arrests
been speculation based more on fear than evidence? Newspaper
people and television crews filled the publicity-shy town waiting
for the final break in the case. Nothing happened.

Hoover was so upset about the charges against his agents he
had his assistant Clyde Tolson send an angry letter to Henry R.
Luce, publisher of *Life* magazine, castigating him for publishing
an article about Poplarville that spread "false charges, particularly after your representatives had checked with us as to their
validity." Tolson claimed the investigation was conducted "with
scrupulous regard for the rights of all individuals." Blaming the
charges on "a strong group of individuals" who did not want the
case solved, Tolson expressed surprise that *Life* would support
the charges. He then made a vague threat about future cooperation between the FBI and Time/Life in light of the article. "I
sincerely regret the cooperation between our headquarters office
in Washington and the office of 'Time' and 'Life' means no more
to your publication than the opportunity to deal in sensational-
ism and reporting rumors rather than a careful sifting of the
facts."[15]

While Crip Reyer remained in the Picayune hospital with his

condition unchanged and Arthur Smith languished in the Poplarville hospital still unable to speak, although his doctor had abandoned his diagnosis of cerebral hemorrhage, activity around the FBI headquarters picked up noticeably—this time on a more subdued note. The agents knew there would be no arrests. They burned four boxes of paper, preventing newsmen from photographing them as they did so. Local people, who came into contact with agents regularly, in cafes and stores, noticed a more relaxed air about them. No one in Pearl River County could decide what was going to happen. Would there be arrests or not? The question was still being decided in Washington. Reporter Cliff Sessions described the townspeople as acting like a father nervously awaiting the birth of his first child. Then the wire services picked up a report that the Justice Department could find no clear evidence of violation of any federal law. Denials by Poplarville FBI agents were useless. The word was out: no arrests. Poplarville celebrated as though the Fourth of July had come two months early. Mississippi newspapers speculated that kidnapping was no longer a viable charge. Only possible violations of the civil rights statutes—conspiracy by law officers to deprive a person of his civil rights—remained. Such a law had been unused for years.* Then Governor Coleman's office announced that Ralph Bachman and the head of the highway patrol would come to Jackson to meet with him on Friday, May 22. The subject of the meeting was the FBI's impending withdrawal. The state of Mississippi could still charge the mob members with murder or kidnap, both capital offenses, said the governor's spokesman, but no white had been convicted of such crimes against a black since 1926. Without pressure from the federal government, the mob would remain free, and everyone in Poplarville, Pearl River County, Mississippi, and the South knew it.[16]

The celebrations were premature. The Justice Department delayed Bachman's journey to Jackson because it was not ready to concede. Joseph Ryan of the Civil Rights Division had had several bitter exchanges with Malcolm Wilkey, head of the Criminal Division, over the lack of sufficient evidence to indict the sus-

---

* The very first convictions under the civil rights statutes secured against whites for violence against blacks had come in the 1943 *Screws* case in which Georgia sheriff M. Claude Screws received a sentence of three years and $1000 fine in the bludgeoning death of a black prisoner. His deputies received somewhat lighter sentences. The 1870, 1871 Reconstruction civil rights statutes had languished for almost three-quarters of a century.

pects on kidnap charges. Ryan maintained that the evidence was sufficient and their disagreement delayed the final decision.[17] In Poplarville, in the face of overwhelming public jubilation, Bachman and his men steadfastly denied they were about to end their investigation. Even though Bachman had informed Coleman that his men had completed their report, he had to await official instructions from Washington before making any public announcements. "We have issued no such report," but "that's not to say we will not abandon the investigation," Bachman hedged. "Sooner or later our probe must end, but there's been no decision on such a move yet."[18] In New York meanwhile, radio station WMCA, which had offered a $5,000 reward for information about the members of the lynch mob during its broadcast series about the lynching, sent the FBI a letter addressed to the station from a Tupelo, Mississippi, man who overheard talk on the streets of Tupelo by men he believed to be mob members, naming Jewel Alford, Crip Reyer, Jeff Lee, and Sheriff Moody as the prime conspirators and Jimmy Walters as their leader. The writer also said those five men would divulge the names of the mob members and "the jailer's wife thinks so [too, which] is why she fainted." Claiming he was "only interested in justice," the man at first refused to accept the reward. Later with his identity guarded by the FBI, he accepted the money from the radio station. The station made it known that the lynching had been planned for weeks in advance and that a police officer had shown the mob where the keys were and served as a lookout for them as they abducted Parker. The FBI quickly forwarded the letter to Bachman, who found it contained information he already knew or had considered. Alex Rosen, head of the Bureau's general investigative division, eventually reported to Hoover that "the information concerning Jeff Lee, Christopher C. Reyer, and Jewel Alford had been developed by us prior to this letter." The Bureau discounted accusations against Jimmy Walters and Sheriff Moody.[19]

J. P. Coleman also made public comments in lieu of his meeting with the FBI and highway patrol in which he once again defended his role in the lynching investigation. Accusing Reyer and Smith of being in the hospital with fake ailments, the governor stated flatly about FBI harassment, "There just isn't anything in these charges—period. It is my duty," he added, "to stand against the irresponsible. I think the time will come when all people will see the wisdom of what I have done." The widespread and harsh criticism of his order to Sheriff Moody to call in the FBI resulted from "temporary emotionalism that a few politicians have whipped up. When I asked for the governor's office four years ago, I knew it would be no ice cream party; however, I never expected to have to fool with a lynching. I have the responsibility of this office and my critics don't have that responsibility. It is my duty to stand against the irresponsible. The people of Mississippi don't condone the lynching although we've had some who have played politics with it."[20]

Coleman concluded that the Justice Department was still analyzing the results of the FBI probe. Publicly he held to the belief that arrests would follow; in a very real sense his political reputation depended upon it. "The decision [in Washington] will determine whether the mob, when arrested, will face federal or state charges." But the governor had an inkling of what might happen if the federal government pulled out of the case. "If the FBI says no federal laws have been violated, it will be due time for the state to act." The next Pearl River County grand jury was scheduled to meet in November and he pointed out with eerie prescience that if the grand jury failed to indict anyone, "that would be the end of it. The grand jury is the one tribunal in our form of government from which there is no appeal." Could it be that J. P. Coleman knew what justice in Mississippi would mean for the lynchers of M. C. Parker? "The lynching hasn't hurt Mississippi as much as I first thought it would," he claimed. "Two new industries have moved into the state since the incident. Both considered the Poplarville case but both were convinced state officials were doing all they could to apprehend the violators."[21]

Most of the sixty FBI agents had already begun leaving Mississippi, vacating their quarters in Poplarville and Bogalusa. Those agents remaining in Poplarville, waiting for the final draft of the report, lingered around the headquarters rather than conducting their notorious forays into the county. The street in front of the Main Street offices was unusually empty on Sunday the 24th. Only two cars were parked in front—Ralph Bachman's and one other agent's. During the height of the investigation as many as twenty-five cars overwhelmed the few horizontal parking spaces along the quiet, sunny street. Several agents checked out of the Magnolia Court Motel, where Bachman and fifteen other agents had stayed during the last four weeks of the investigation. As the country learned of the death of Secretary of State John Foster

Dulles, the people of Poplarville and of the South awaited a second announcement from Washington. With local papers speculating that J. Edgar Hoover was about to reveal FBI findings in the case, the fearful town tried to spend a normal, quiet Sunday . . . waiting for news.[22]

In Washington life also went on as usual. Midmorning couriers delivered a batch of memoranda and mimeographed statements from the Justice Department to various officials around the city. Dated the next day, Monday, May 25, they announced that the FBI had failed to unearth positive proof that the lynch mob had violated federal law. The Justice Department found no grounds for federal indictment. At 9:00 a.m. Monday morning, May 25th, one month after the masked, gloved mob had carried Parker, kicking and screaming, from the jail to his death on the Bogalusa Bridge, U. S. Attorney General William Rogers made the announcement Poplarville waited for. He calmly and unequivocally acknowledged that FBI investigators "clearly established that there was no violation of federal law by the persons responsible for the lynching of Mack Charles Parker at Poplarville, Mississippi." He confirmed that the FBI would turn over its files to Governor Coleman and state authorities. In the early afternoon from his home in Ackerman, Coleman telephoned the FBI in Washington to report that Ralph Bachman had hand-delivered a forty-two-page summary of the findings in the case. Coleman also asked the FBI to approve his press release about the case; he had no desire to hold a press conference.[23]

Coleman's office then announced on the governor's behalf, "Duly authorized representatives of the FBI have today delivered to me a comprehensive report on the investigation at Poplarville. The proper procedure is that I shall make this information available to the next regular session of the Pearl River County Grand Jury in November. The law requires the grand jury to keep secret for six months all testimony offered before it; therefore, pending grand jury action, I shall not under any circumstances reveal any part of the content of the FBI report. As Governor of Mississippi I want to thank the FBI for a thorough investigation and for making the results available for state action at the local level." Bachman informed Hoover that his meeting with Coleman had been cordial and that the governor told him he "saw red" when "punk politicians" in Poplarville unduly criticized the FBI. Coleman also told him he would hold onto the report for the November grand jury and not call a special grand jury to consider the case, saying the "punk politicians" could "sweat it out" until November.[24]

With the federal government officially out of the case, and with assurances from the FBI director that Bureau personnel, including scientific experts from the FBI laboratory, would be available to testify in court, the public still had no clear idea of what the FBI knew about the lynching. Hoover's own press release expressed appreciation for the cooperation given his agents by Governor Coleman, the highway patrol, "and other responsible citizens," and added only that the Bureau's investigation had discovered "just this week" that "the persons responsible for the death of Parker had not violated the federal law." What laws had they violated? In its 370-page report on the lynching, after investigating scores of people and examining "numerous items of physical evidence," the meticulous FBI clearly established the sequence of events and the parties involved, but had not obtained a signed statement from anyone who actually saw Parker murdered or the car in the act of carrying him cross state lines. Nevertheless, unknown to the public, Justice Department attorneys found evidence of a violation of, and a conspiracy to violate, the federal law against depriving a person of his or her civil rights; but Assistant Attorney General Malcolm Wilkey concluded that federal prosecution based upon the available facts would ultimately fail because it would have to rely primarily upon statements by Crip Reyer and Arthur Smith, Jr., both of whom Wilkey considered "of doubtful credibility." The Justice Department announced that the mob had not violated any federal law when in fact it had evidence to the contrary. The investigation simply failed to produce evidence that would satisfy the conservative and somewhat timid officials at Justice. Rather than admit defeat, the FBI equivocated. The department did not comment on a possible charge of conspiracy by an officer of the law to violate a person's civil rights, which left the door open for future federal prosecution along these lines.[25]

In light of the comparatively vigorous use of the civil rights statutes during the 1960s, the timidity of the federal government in this case may appear surprising. During the civil rights revolution, black protest and white reactionary violence became so intense that the government could no longer ignore its responsibilities in enforcing the law. The government could not turn a blind eye to civil rights violations after 1960. Succeeding administrations, both Democrat and Republican, since the presidency of Rutherford B. Hayes had taken a laissez-faire approach to racial problems, treating them as a local or regional issue. It was pressure from the black community that forced greater involvement by the federal government, and in 1959 this pressure was only beginning to develop; it was still too inchoate to be effective.

As the mob members breathed a collective sigh of relief, others in southern Mississippi objected to Coleman's handling of the FBI report. Sebe Dale, who would preside over the grand jury in November, argued the governor was intentionally hamstringing the court. "That report belongs to the District Attorney and the County Attorney because they have to present it in court," Dale fumed. "Suppose that these people named suspect [that] they are named in the report and leave the state between now and November 2. There's no reason for the governor to hamstring the courts in Pearl River County. I don't like it. It's just not right." District Attorney Vernon Broome questioned the governor's motives, but added that he would not try to obtain the report from him. "He can do his job as he sees fit. When court convenes in November, the people of Pearl River County will make the decisions; the grand jury has the last say."[26]

If Sebe Dale or anyone else suspected Coleman's reasons for sitting on the report, they neglected to mention them publicly. Coleman certainly feared that those cited in the report might be forewarned and allowed to flee, but more important he feared the political damage to Gartin's campaign that might result from a premature release of facts from the report, which virtually confirmed rumors of late-night, marathon interrogations of suspects. People across the nation felt otherwise. They believed Coleman kept the report to forestall calling a special grand jury, because to do so in the glare of national attention might result in indictments against the mob members.[27]

Regardless of the uncertainty over Coleman's motivation, local people rejoiced that after thirty days and $87,000 in taxpayers' money, the FBI had finally given up the case and was leaving Poplarville. Townspeople, said Mayor Pat Hyde, were relieved to see the agents leave and applauded Coleman's decision to withhold the report because they simply wanted the relief from constant publicity that a hiatus of several months would bring. Besides, Sebe Dale had made the reassuring prediction that the local grand jury would never indict the mob members without the material in the report. "If he holds that information," the crusty judge said, "I'll tell you what the grand jury will do . . .

nothing, absolutely nothing. He can't go before the grand jury, because if he did, it would throw the case out so quick it would make your head swim." Coleman was aware that even with the report, the grand jury might refuse to indict fellow citizens for lynching a black rapist.[28]

"I am not going to plan any steps in the case until something is turned over to me," said Vernon Broome. Turning Coleman's actions into grist for his political mill, Sebe Dale warned, "Suppose they thought a warrant should be issued? If he holds onto it until the grand jury meets there will be a lot of mad people in Pearl River County both ways." Dale opposed calling a special grand jury because he was busy presiding over four other counties in his district, but he remained adamant in his demand for the report. Under Mississippi law a person suspected of a capital crime was usually arrested and held without bond pending action of the next grand jury. Coleman conveniently used the law to shore up his sagging political fortune. In appearing to handcuff the investigation he handily blunted the adverse publicity that would accompany a special grand jury.[29]

Word leaked out that the FBI report given the governor contained a list of eighteen participants in the lynching. With a six-month delay in the state procedures, people outside Pearl River County worried about so many potentially guilty mob members remaining at large, not because they feared another lynching, but because they feared more damage to their state's reputation. Justice delayed, in this case, was justice denied. For the first time, average white Mississippians began to speak out against the mob. "We'll never be able to look the citizens of other states in the face again until the lynchers are caught and properly punished," said a lifelong resident of Biloxi. "We've developed a statewide inferiority complex which has destroyed our respect for ourselves and the state of Mississippi." J. B. Richmond, who later served on the federal grand jury, seldom thought about the lynching until he heard the FBI was leaving without securing indictments. Then, he claimed, he began to feel outraged "that a bunch of damn rednecks could get away with such a thing."[30]

By contrast, residents of Poplarville acted as though it were business as usual; they wanted to forget the lynching as quickly as possible. Those who objected to the crime still did so silently. Since the entire community had been damaged by the crime, they felt it was best to accept the condemnation silently. For if they disagreed with the lawless element they could face serious problems in such a small and isolated town. Meanwhile, New Orleans television station WDSU informed its viewers that the FBI had proof that eighteen persons has been involved in the lynching and every person implicated lived in the Poplarville area. Of particular interest in the broadcast, which contained several inaccuracies, was the statement "They were planning to kill Parker when the lights of an oncoming car scared the men, and they sped to the Louisiana side of the bridge and waited at a cattle inspection station." Why, WDSU asked, had the FBI been unable to prove a federal violation when a television newsman learned of it on his own?[31]

The embarrassed FBI immediately sought to counter the report by issuing information that would discredit the reporter's findings. More than eighteen people had been involved, it claimed, and agents had discovered a slip of paper with several names on it indicating the men had drawn lots to see who would go to the courthouse. The main reason for the lynching voiced at the meeting was the possibility of R. Jess Brown questioning June Walters. The men at the meeting swore they "would not stand for this." The FBI let it be known that it had "cracked" the case before leaving Poplarville and that one of the men in the mob confessed. The FBI also claimed that there had been "talk" about a possible lynching a week before the trial. It asserted further that the lynching had been poorly planned, hastily arranged during the meeting at the Davis farm shortly before two carloads of men drove into Poplarville to abduct Parker. A town official had told Bachman about plans to allow Parker to be lynched if a federal judge overturned his conviction: "We weren't going to make any further effort to try him, but we would turn him loose from the jail some dark night, about the same time this lynching occurred."[32] And the same official stated flatly that the city jailer left a key readily available and went to his home afterward. It was the first reference to Jewel Alford to appear in print, although by this time the residents of Poplarville knew of his participation in the lynching.[33]

J. P. Coleman and Joe Patterson left for Washington to testify before a subcommittee of the Senate Judiciary Committee against the civil rights bill amid public protest over the FBI withdrawal and renewed demands for a federal anti-lynching law. Letters, telegrams, and petitions protesting the absence of arrests in the case began pouring into Washington from all over the country and were equally distributed among Hoover, William Rogers, and President Eisenhower. All of the writers expressed outrage over the government's withdrawal, whether they were from a high school class in Lincoln, Nebraska, or from a black member of the Alabama State Medical Association. Each writer was answered cordially. Hoover's mail included an anonymous letter from a person who claimed to have been part of the mob. In a barely legible scrawl, the writer identified three people as having conducted the lynching. This last gesture by a person with a guilty conscience perhaps best summed up the hopelessness of the investigation. Here was someone who claimed to have participated in the abduction and murder of M. C. Parker and had aided the job by remaining silent. Only when the letter writer felt safe from indictment and reprisals from the mob did he offer a faint-hearted, anonymous confession.[34]

It was almost too happy an ending. Everyone in the mob had gotten off scot-free. With J. P. Coleman sitting on the report, there was little chance people would find out about the strength of the FBI's case. Moreover, knowing the influence of local climate on a grand jury, especially when some of the residents being investigated had vested interests in the county as property owners or businessmen, people were looking forward to thumbing their noses at their critics in November. In Poplarville, where the people protected the mob behind a scrim of silence, the prospects for justice were slim indeed.[35]

10

No Apologies

In the wake of the Justice Department's public statement that the lynch mob had violated no federal laws, congressional civil rights advocates intensified their campaign to attach an anti-lynching bill to the proposed civil rights legislation. Two civil rights bills were before Congress: an administration-backed program to speed school integration and to provide increased police power over elections, bombings, and federal court orders in the South, and a more moderate bill sponsored by Lyndon Johnson. Jacob Javits, who co-sponsored the administration's bill, felt that the withdrawal of the FBI demonstrated conclusively "the need for a Federal anti-lynch law." Three Democratic senators, Paul Douglas of Illinois, Frank J. Lausche of Ohio, and Richard L. Neuberger of Oregon, crossed party lines to back Javits. Neuberger sponsored a bill to make lynching punishable by a $10,000 fine and twenty years' imprisonment. "The accommodation which this administration has been willing to make with the leaders of the South not to press too hard for the enforcement of existing civil rights laws or for the enactment of new ones," thought Senator Douglas, "results in a most regrettable slowing down of the progress toward equal justice." Four black congressmen, Adam Clayton Powell of New York, Charles Diggs of Michigan, William L. Dawson of Illinois, and Robert Nix of Pennsylvania, initiated a write-in campaign in conjunction with the Chicago *Defender* and the NAACP to win congressional support for the Javits amendment.[1]

On May 28, Thursday morning, J. P. Coleman began his testimony before the Subcommittee on Constitutional Rights of the Senate Judiciary Committee against the pending civil rights bills. After arriving almost an hour late because his train had broken down, Coleman faced persistently sharp questions about the lynching from the angry senators. Only at the beginning and end of the two-hour session did they allow Coleman a chance to testify against the proposed bills. After reading a brief statement opposing the pending legislation, Coleman promised the packed hearing room he would deliver the secret FBI report well before the upcoming November grand jury session. When pressed by doubting senators, he refused to divulge one word of the report, which, as he was constantly reminded, an unknown source claimed contained the names of the lynchers. "I don't believe I want to shadowbox with any unidentified source," he said. "If I were to discuss it here it would be trying the case in the papers in advance of the grand jury." He refused even to disclose publicly whether the mob wore masks, and told the committee that "only a handful" of people had been involved in the affair, reminding the senators that state law forbade disclosure of evidence before a grand jury returned an indictment. The lynching resulted, he told them, from concern that Parker would have been freed because of the absence of blacks on the jury.[2]

Senator John Carroll of Colorado subjected Coleman to the most persistent questioning, asking him repeatedly if he thought William Rogers should have prosecuted the lynch mob. Coleman refused to speculate on Rogers's motives. When pressed on why he had refused to summon a special grand jury, Coleman cited the Mississippi law that prohibited calling a special grand jury to investigate one crime, and added what he had been stating publicly in Mississippi, that for one hundred years the state supreme court had been invalidating criminal indictments returned by special grand juries. Coleman told the senator he had been called upon to convene a special grand jury over a lynching in Attala County in 1950 when he was a circuit court judge. He refused. "It would be reversible error under our supreme court decision." He said emphatically that when the district attorney requested the FBI report, he would turn it over to him "in plenty of time" to prepare a case for the grand jury, but as yet neither Bill Stewart nor Vernon Broome had made such a request. Senator Carroll concluded his questioning of Coleman by asking him why the Justice Department had ignored the federal statute against conspiracy by police officers to deprive a person of his civil rights and an anti-disguise law. The governor declined to comment on that, adding only that the *Goldsby* case had caused grave concern in his state. "We look upon that case most seriously," he said. "The time of Congress could be well used to study means of regulating the use of federal writs of habeas corpus in purely state cases." This statement provoked a sharp retort from Democrat William Langer of North Dakota. In his state American Indians voted and served on juries, and he viewed complaints by Pearl River County blacks about voter and jury discrimination as justified. "I make no alibi or excuse for the Poplarville incident," Coleman told the angry senator, "but candor forces me to point out the unrest in Mississippi as a result of the previous case."[3]

Overlooking Emmett Till, Coleman told the subcommittee that the Parker lynching had been the first in twenty-five years in Mississippi. As for racial unrest in Mississippi, if "we cut out the agitation on press and radio the whole thing would disappear in 30 days." Taking over the questioning for the last minutes of the hearing, the conservative Sam Ervin of North Carolina offered Coleman the opportunity to state his arguments against the proposed civil rights legislation. Ervin, who was presiding in the absence of the regular chairman, lauded Coleman for requesting FBI assistance. "If I had been in your position I would have done the same thing," he said. He asked Coleman perfunctory questions that allowed him to castigate civil rights bills, because they "invaded the reserved rights of the state" and "assume that the congressmen should take control of the schools from the hands of the people who sent them there." The pending force bills, he thought, "utterly fail to meet the test of sound principles, upon which our republic was established," because they are "tampering with local matters, which have always belonged to the people."[4]

Testifying after the governor, Joe Patterson told the senators, "The Poplarville lynching would never have occurred" had it not been for the *Goldsby* case. He added that passage of the civil rights bills would force the closing of public schools in Mississippi. Patterson noted the lack of any clamor for a special grand

jury to try M. C. Parker, "who brutally raped a two-month pregnant woman in sight of a four-year-old child." Yet neither Coleman nor Patterson admitted what was painfully obvious to
Southerners who followed the hearings: the lynching in Poplarville could prompt passage of some sort of civil rights bill that
might otherwise not have found its way into law. Both Mississippi politicians strained to deny the need for a bill to improve
race relations that, they said, were improving on their own, and
neither was able to explain away the lynching.[5]

While the country waited to see what would happen when the
grand jury met in Poplarville in November, Sebe Dale began
attacking the federal government and J. P. Coleman for giving
the press "piecemeal leaks" from the FBI report. With his first
barrage against the governor, Dale reopened the circus world of
Mississippi politics and drew the Parker lynching back into the
arena. "If the government had turned over all its evidence to
Governor J. P. Coleman," he charged, "then it ought to stop
these piecemeal leaks and not try the case in the newspapers."
Indirectly blaming Coleman for the release of information over
the preceding weeks, Dale said, "I don't know who in government has given out this report, but I don't think it was the FBI."
Dale was unaware that the source lived in Poplarville, right
under his judicial nose. The culprit was Bill Stewart, now even
less circumspect, who told reporters, "If people here ask me if I
would prosecute this case enthusiastically, I tell them 'Hell, no.' "
And at other times, when reporters were unable to tempt Stewart with a few drinks into speaking freely, Sebe Dale often
obliged the reporters for free. As he castigated Coleman, Dale
let reporters know his own feelings whenever they asked. Because of what he felt was the brazen attitude Parker had shown
in court, he explained, he refused to condemn the mob for what
they had done.[6]

As irresponsible as Dale's veiled attacks on the governor were,
he managed to acknowledge the "merit" in Coleman's assertions
that the state supreme court often invalidated indictments returned by special grand juries. Dale himself had refused to convene a special grand jury, claiming a full docket. Dale wanted the
FBI reports ostensibly in order to enable local authorities to
make arrests to prevent the guilty men from fleeing. The simple
truth was that the prosecution of the mob was of secondary
importance; the FBI report had assumed unexpected significance. If the report lacked solid evidence against the mob mem-

bers, partisans could use it to destroy Coleman's remaining credibility with the voters, as a result of which Gartin would surely lose—or, more precisely, Ross Barnett would become the next governor. Even though, according to William Rogers, "the Justice Department clearly established" that the mob had not violated the Lindbergh law, the department had not established quite so clearly that "no other successful Federal prosecution could be maintained." Of particular interest to those who feared the fate of the case if left in the hands of white Mississippians were two other federal statutes violated by the mob. One was conspiracy to deprive a person of his or her constitutional rights (Title 18, Section 241), and the other was conspiracy "under color of law," that is, by authorities, to deprive someone of his or her rights (Title 18, Section 242). If the FBI report, which detailed the method of investigation as well as the results, revealed no grounds for future prosecution on these charges, as Coleman's critics suspected, they could use the report to discredit the governor for calling in the FBI.[7]

A reluctant President Eisenhower re-entered the public debate when, in response to the question of whether he agreed with the Justice Department's findings that the government should withdraw, he said with his usual inarticulateness, "Well, they were informed through—the Attorney General's office informed me, they felt it was necessary." Eisenhower refused to acknowledge the necessity for additional civil rights legislation. His displeasure with the *Brown* decision was well known, and when he refused to endorse the pending bills, the editor of the Poplarville *Democrat* commented, "At last, we find a Yankee who publicly admits that much of this equality propaganda is so much baloney."[8]

It may have been baloney to the editor, but two thousand miles away, Mack Charles Parker's mother found conditions extremely difficult as she struggled to restart her life. A local church group gave her a hundred dollars to provide for the two children and to send for her daughter in Bogalusa and their remaining possessions. Dolores arrived in Merced, California, three weeks after her mother to find her still despondent over the loss of her son. She sat staring into space in one of the small rooms of her sister's two-room house. She took occasional, short walks in the late afternoon, but other than that she remained alone with her misery. People came from Los Angeles, 130 miles away, and San Francisco, 275 miles away, to pay their respects to the victimized family. The local community gave her moral support, the police even offered her special protection, but nothing seemed to erase her fear of further trouble. The head of the local NAACP personally watched over Mrs. Parker. "She's been scared out of her wits," he remarked, "but she's beginning to feel assured." The local NAACP persuaded her to leave her home to speak to a meeting at the Third Street Baptist Church in San Francisco to protest the government's withdrawal from the case.[9]

In early June, even though the names of the chief suspects and the details of the lynching had become common gossip in Pearl River County, J. P. Walker announced his candidacy for sheriff and tax collector for Pearl River County, openly bragging to his friends that the lynching had garnered him additional support. "I am entering this race in good faith and with the utmost sincerity of purpose," he said in his published announcement. "My life is well-known to most of our citizenry. I, like all men, have made mistakes. I shall probably make others as it is only human for human perfection on earth has never yet been attained. However, I feel that I have conscientiously tried to make a good and useful citizen and neighbor, as I tried to make a good officer of the law while in the office of Deputy Sheriff."[10]

The statewide summer campaigns threatened to create a clash in Poplarville when Bidwell Adam, the state Democratic chairman, challenged J. P. Coleman, who would be there to speak on behalf of Carroll Gartin, to a debate. "You plan to speak in Poplarville and your subject will be the law and order in Pearl River County," taunted Adam. "Are you willing to divide your time with me? We could talk about protecting the white womanhood of the South instead of shedding so many tears over Parker." Adam said he felt sure Coleman would want to discuss attempts by "northern radical Democrats and the NAACP to melt Mississippi and the South with a blazing blowtorch." He was unable to lure Coleman into a debate during the governor's statewide speech on June 29, but he succeeded in scaring Coleman away from Poplarville. Neither Gartin nor Coleman spoke there during the campaign. From June through August, as all of Mississippi discussed the campaign, the lynching and Parker remained topics of intense debate. The August Democratic primary became a referendum on Coleman's "moderate" brand of racial politics, with many candidates for state and local offices attacking him for calling in the FBI. Not to be outdone, ardent race-baiters like Ross Barnett advocated standing up to the federal government and fighting back. Barnett wanted to put an end to the "weak-kneed" bowing to the FBI and the North that he claimed the "moderates" J. P. Coleman and Carroll Gartin represented. In Mississippi at this time, being called a racial moderate was tantamount to being called a communist, and the term "moderate" itself was extremely misleading.[11]

Barnett received crucial assistance in his election bid from Senator James Eastland. This was not necessarily because of any ideological differences between Gartin and Eastland, but because Gartin had once challenged and nearly taken Eastland's Senate seat from him, and as one of the state's bright young progressives (a label he would have eschewed), Gartin threatened Eastland's power. Eastland, who stayed in office by outmaneuvering his rivals, aided Barnett in order to keep Gartin from developing a wider political base from which he could mount a more effective challenge to Eastland. In the world of Mississippi Democratic politics, Eastland's opposition was more important than his support: he could ruin you, but not necessarily elect you. Eastland's workers began a whisper campaign throughout the state, accusing Gartin of being Coleman's man. With Eastland now joining his opponents, Gartin was in serious trouble. Posters and handbills began appearing all over the state—even in Gartin's home town of Laurel, not far from Poplarville—saying, "Remember Hungary. Remember Little Rock. Remember the Occupation of Poplarville by J. P. Coleman and the FBI. Don't forget that it was the Coleman-Gartin regime that called the FBI into Pearl River County. Vote for Ross Barnett and Preserve our Southern Way of Life." With the state in the mood it was in after the lynching, Carroll Gartin, even though he firmly supported segregation and was extremely popular throughout the state, didn't stand a chance.[12]

Amid the sweltering August heat, Mississippians trooped to the polls to select the Democratic candidate for governor and in Pearl River County to choose between Bill Owen and J. P. Walker for sheriff. Gartin and Barnett tied, eliminating two other minor candidates. Walker and Owen tied. A special, runoff election was held several weeks later in which both Barnett and Owen won by slight majorities. Gartin, who became the first progressive to be eliminated by James Eastland, carried Pearl River County, and Bill Owen carried the four precincts at Poplarville, plus the outlying rural areas. Walker won only in his home town of Picayune. Voters returned Vernon Broome to the district attorney's office, but rejected Bill Stewart, reacting negatively to his loud, expansive, "good ole boy" style. Stewart bitterly blamed his loss upon the lynching. In Ackerman in Choctaw County, the voters sent J. P. Coleman to the state legislature.[13]

Even though Coleman's tenure as the segregationist governor of Mississippi had ended on the tragic note of Parker's lynching, he judged his four years to have been largely successful. Coleman, who was considered by his opponents to be "a powerful mixture of Henry Cabot Lodge and Mortimer Snerd with the best brace of buck teeth a politician was ever blessed with," had waged a constant battle against the Citizens Councils to prevent an outbreak of violence. Yet under his guidance the state had avoided integrating its schools or even making a move in that direction. Although Gartin's defeat signaled the demise of Coleman's brand of moderation and superficial cooperation with the federal government, Mississippians now appeared genuinely sorry Coleman was leaving office.[14]

While politicians wondered if Coleman would re-enter the governor's race four years later, Coleman took a measure of revenge on Ross Barnett. He vetoed a $10,000-a-year increase in the governor's salary. During the campaign Barnett had attacked Gartin and Coleman on this issue, but once elected Barnett decided he favored the raise. Coleman was "going to try to give Barnett enough rope to hang himself," ruminated one anti-Coleman politician. "He's smart but he's vindictive sometimes. Remember, he opposed Barnett when he ran for governor and he backed Lieutenant Governor Gartin against Barnett . . . and got beat." Legislators knew Barnett could never hope to equal Coleman's accomplishment of refusing to bend on the issue of segregation while still maintaining a degree of respect in the national eye—mainly by eschewing overt violence. Coleman's national esteem was so high that in October the Eisenhower administration asked him to accept a seat on the Civil Rights Commission. He declined, preferring the Mississippi State House instead. Barnett's lieutenants feared Coleman might attempt to scuttle the new governor's programs from his position in the legislature, but Coleman made it known following the election that he considered Barnett's program to be the will of the majority and therefore he would not oppose it. After all, Coleman's policies were not so very different from Barnett's.[15]

True to his word, and well after the election, Coleman turned the FBI report over to Vernon Broome and Bill Stewart on September 9, in time for them to plan their case. Yet after spending just three days studying the detailed report that contained several confessions and descriptions of the lynching from numerous sources, Broome concluded that the report was "entirely hearsay evidence" and refused to read any part of it to the jury. He decided against using the heavily detailed report in any way at all. This meant the state of Mississippi would have no case against the lynch mob. Broome added that after hearing the testimony, the jury might then decide which witnesses it wanted to call. The trouble with this plan was that the FBI report contained all of the evidence against the mob.[16]

Broome insisted he would still present a case to the grand jury on November 2. The jury could, if it so chose, call FBI agents and other witnesses to testify. "Then it will be up to the jurors to decide what disposition to make." Thus, the grand jury had to make a preliminary decision on whether to call any witnesses on the basis of the case presented by Vernon Broome, who refused to use the FBI report and whose actions appeared to indicate that he, like Stewart and Judge Dale, felt that Parker got what he deserved.[17] Sebe Dale, who would preside over the grand jury, piously and with a hint of satisfaction refused to disclose the contents of the FBI report now in his possession, saying Coleman had sent it to Broome with instructions not to reveal its contents. "I wouldn't want to violate Coleman's unholy writ," commented Dale. He also acknowledged the possibility that if the contents were not made known to several officials in town, some of the men mentioned in the report might be called for jury duty and be in a position to hear evidence against themselves.[18]

A furious Roy Wilkins sent a long telegram to both Mississippi senators, Congressman Colmer, Governor Coleman, and District Attorney Broome. "The State of Mississippi has been grossly negligent in its protection of the rights of Negroes and evidently is unwilling to bring to justice the guilty parties," Wilkins declared. "Failure to ask court action on FBI evidence is inexcusable. We strongly urge you to reconsider your decision." Wilkins urged Coleman to "use the full authority of [his] office to assure the safety and rights of all concerned in Mississippi" and to "take all possible steps to get some action." But the NAACP had little hope for a state conviction of the mob members. All jury members would be white males. It had always been that way in Pearl River County.[19]

With opening day rapidly approaching, an eerie reticence fell over official Poplarville. From his office in Columbia, Judge Dale refused to promise anything publicly. "I don't want to be in the position of white-washing or crucifying anybody. I want to be right down the road. I can't tell what will happen," he remarked. In all my years I've found there's no telling which way a jury will go." No one in Pearl River County admitted in public what everyone now said in private: there would be no indictments.[20] The all-white voter list contained names of people who knew some of the mob members. A prosecutor pushing determinedly for indictment would face a hostile county and the possibility of reprisals. But even that seemed remote. Few in authority in Pearl River County demonstrated much desire to see the men punished for their crimes. The strongest forces pressing for indictment came from outside the state, and for the most part outside the South. National opinion constantly reminded the South that in Poplarville it was on trial before the world, yet all the while those closest to the case doubted that anyone would be punished. "I just don't think they have anything to support a conviction," remarked Sheriff Moody. "If they did, there would have been arrests when they [the FBI agents] were here."[21]

On Monday morning, November 2, Judge Sebe Dale summoned a total of sixty men from whom he would choose the fifteen- to twenty-member grand jury. The law required the vote of twelve jurors for an indictment. The county clerk selected the jury list at random from the county voter roles and Dale impaneled the first eighteen men not disqualified by health or prior commitment. After a delay of five months, the state of Mississippi was finally in a position to bring the lynch mob to justice. One Poplarville man looked up from his morning cup of coffee in the Star Cafe at the reporters flocking into town and sighed, "Here we go again."[22]

The town was defiant in its self-righteousness. It had nothing to hide. Its residents deserved no guilt or shame, and the grand jury would go to extraordinary lengths to prove it.[23] After clearing the courtroom of photographers and reasserting his ban on tape recorders, Dale reminded the jury to keep the proceedings secret for six months from the start of the proceedings. He then advised them that in order to bring a man to trial for a felony, the grand jury must first indict him. Accusations must be made in person rather than by sworn statement, he said, and should they indict someone, that person must be arrested before his name is released to the public. Judge Dale read the remainder of his four-page statement to the jury and the twenty courtroom spectators. At noon he cleared the courtroom to begin the secret proceedings that lasted until late afternoon on an unusually hot day, even for southern Mississippi.[24]

In his charge to the jury, delivered in the same building from which the masked mob had taken Parker, Dale omitted specific references to the case but warned, "We cannot be unmindful of the growing tendency to weaken our courts and to put power into the hands of those not our people. . . . Reformers have made a 'hell' for the people in some of our state, and now seem 'hell-bent' to foist the same upon us." In a slap at Governor Coleman and outsiders, particularly the Warren Court, Dale told the jury, "We should have the backbone to stand against any tyranny, whether of some individual willing to sell our birthright for a mess of political pottage, on the national level, or the reformers that would make us over, according to the mess they have made for themselves, and, yes, [even including] The Board of Sociology setting [sic] in Washington, garbed in Judicial Robes, and 'dishing out' the 'legal precedents' of Gunnar Myrdal." Dale continued like a football coach before the big game: "You are now engaged in a battle for our laws and courts for the preservation of our freedom and way of life, and for the welfare of our people. There should be no quibbling, no shirking and no cause for apology for action or place. Don't forget that 'the welfare of the people is the supreme law' " he concluded. "So like 'free men,' 'born of free men,' shoulders back, do your duty, come out like men, and keep your mouth shut."[25]

The big question was not whether the mob would go free, because this had long been a near certainty, but rather how Vernon Broome and Bill Stewart would handle the case. While many residents thought the grand jury members would be so curious to see whose names appeared in the FBI report that they would ask to see it, Vernon Broome stuck to his earlier position against reading it unless specifically asked to so. After a full afternoon, the jury recessed under strict orders to maintain silence and returned the next morning. The next day the khaki-clad farmers and paper mill workers concluded their business at 2:00 p.m., well ahead of schedule.[26] The Pearl River County grand jury handed down seventeen indictments, all unrelated to the lynching, thereby fulfilling everyone's expectations—and more.

Although the eventual outcome was hardly in doubt, even the

worst cynics thought that the case would come before the grand
jury in some form. But this was Mississippi—1959. The prosecutors subpoenaed only Sheriff Moody to testify on the county's
behalf, as they had indicated they would do. They called no
other witnesses, not even the FBI agents who participated in the
investigation and volunteered to testify without being subpoenaed. "Although none of the officials would comment on the
matter, it is known that no indictments were made in the Mack
Parker lynching case," the local newspaper crowed. "This ends
the Parker case, unless, the federal government should again
step in. Another grand jury could, possibly, look into the matter,
but it is not likely. Neither is it likely that the federal government
will again enter the case. The course of the grand jury here this
week in regard to the case was left up to the wishes of the jury.
Now that the jury has adjourned, we sincerely hope that the case
will be allowed to be forgotten. We see no reason for it to ever be
revived again. May this be the end."[27]

Despite the strict secrecy, residents did not have to wait for
those words from the *Democrat* to appear on Thursday, November 5. Word quickly spread that the mob had gotten off. Relatives of some of the grand jury members made it known that the
jury had handed down no indictments against the lynch mob.
The truth was that Broome and Stewart never even argued the
case to the jurors. As a result the jury failed to question Sheriff
Moody, who testified on all other criminal cases, or to call additional witnesses. The county had for all practical purposes ignored the lynching.[28]

The jury reconvened on Thursday for formal approval of the
indictments and to issue its final report. The following day the
first criminal case began. In its final report, which contained no
mention of the lynching, the jury concluded, Pearl River County
"compares favorably with any in the entire world from the standpoint of good citizenship and law enforcement." The panel com-
mended Sebe Dale for his "inspired charge" and "our officers,
citizens and those in authority here." The eighteen men urged
the citizenry "to continue to be alert and vigorous as to insure
morality and prosperity in our county."[29] To confirm the results
after the jury adjourned on Thursday, Sheriff Moody informed
the press rather offhandedly, "I've looked through the indictments and none of them pertains to the Parker case."[30] J. Edgar
Hoover later commented, "The grand jury met at Poplarville . . .
and ignored the case" even though his agents were "able to es-

tablish the identity of a number of members of the mob who participated in the abduction of Parker and obtained admissions from some of the participants." It appeared as though the lynchers of M. C. Parker would never be brought to justice.[31]

The grand jury action, or lack of it, was the source of considerable rancor on Capitol Hill and in various executive departments. Almost immediately Acting Attorney General Lawrence E. Walsh announced that the government would reenter the case under the provisions of the post-Civil War Ku Klux Klan Acts prohibiting conspiracy to violate a person's civil rights. The Justice Department had clearly anticipated the outcome of the Pearl River County grand jury, for less than three hours after the result was known, Walsh instructed U. S. Attorney Robert E. Hauberg in Jackson to present the FBI-gathered evidence to a south Mississippi federal grand jury.[32]

Had the federal government been holding prosecution in abeyance? No. According to Walsh, who was ignoring previous departmental announcements, departmental lawyers left it up to the state to act first, but after the state refused to indict the mob, the government felt forced to re-enter the case. Since 1957 the Justice Department had become increasingly cautious and reluctant to prosecute criminal cases under the 1870, 1871 Reconstruction laws that made conspiracy to violate someone's civil rights a federal crime. In 1958 Joseph Ryan instructed all his attorneys not to institute criminal investigations unless the Civil Rights Division received a formal complaint. This was a reversal of earlier civil rights policy, prior to the passage of the Civil Rights Act of 1957. The recent law had brought a new reluctance to the department. Additionally, this new policy under Wilson White and Ryan, who were fastidiously following William Rogers's instructions not to interfere with the FBI's close relations with local police, meant that the Civil Rights Division would not request the FBI to conduct any investigation if there was any chance the state might take action. This was why the Justice Department was all too willing to pull out of the case when the head of the Criminal Division, Malcolm Wilkey, declared that there was insufficient evidence that the mob had violated the Lindbergh law. Now, anticipating public demands for federal action, the Justice Department re-entered the case, this time with the Civil Rights Division prosecuting the mob for criminal violations of the conspiracy statutes in addition to kidnap. The attorneys felt the case was so strong against the mob, the evidence so damning, that the Justice Department had every reason to expect convictions.[33]

Vernon Broome reacted bitterly. "It seems like a strange paradox to me that when a respectable woman of Mississippi is attacked on a lonely highway, the press showed little interest in it. Then when something happens to the rapist, the press raises an endless clamor." Sebe Dale agreed. "A great deal of enmity has been directed at the people of the South. The federal authorities seem hell-bent to punish us about everything that comes up. They want to carry it to the last degree." After conferring with Broome about the outcome of the case, Dale concluded, it "could be presented to any fair jury in the South and the results would be the same." Of renewed federal involvement, he said angrily, "I'm not sure that the people kind of welcome it. I have the idea the nation may look down on Mississippi justice now. You're doggone right. But I'm not apologizing."[34] Mayor Pat Hyde also agreed with the judge's attitude. "You couldn't convict the guilty parties if you had a sound film of the lynching."[35]

Reaction to the decision by the Justice Department was swift and predictable. "As we penned our editorials of last week," wrote one local editor, "we had hoped that the so-called lynch case was being ended. Now the federal gov't is stepping back into the picture. They are determined to drain the last drop of publicity they can from the case for the benefit of the NAACP." From New York the NAACP sent a telegram to William Rogers, requesting a vigorous reentry in the interest of "national prestige and honor." The Justice Department agreed wholeheartedly and hinted that it might reopen the FBI investigation in an effort to establish other federal violations.[36]

To the nation, including more liberal Southerners, it appeared that Mississippi was incapable or unwilling to accept the responsibility for prosecuting lynchers.[37] As for federal reinvolvement, Ross Barnett grumbled, "Somebody in Washington is confused." If the federal government has no jurisdiction, he complained, it had no business re-entering the case. The governor-elect "understood federal agents had said no federal law had been violated because the lynchers never did cross the state line," yet here was the federal government back in the case again.[38]

Under these new circumstances lawyers for those under investigation warned their clients that they faced two federal violations that were relatively minor compared with earlier charges that could have led to a death sentence, and the mob members viewed them as such. They looked upon the federal grand jury as more of a nuisance and a potential embarrassment than a serious threat to their liberty. Furthermore, Pearl River County lawyers figured the mob had violated only Parker's rights under state law rather than his federal rights, which meant that the only real danger came from the lesser crime of conspiracy "under color of law" to deprive Parker of his rights.[39]

In Jackson, U. S. Attorney Robert E. Hauberg petitioned the federal district court of southern Mississippi to convene a federal grand jury in December or January at the latest and moved forward with his plans to present the federally gathered information. The federal district judge who would hear the case was Sidney Mize. The diminutive, seventy-one-year-old silver-haired native of rural Scott County, Mississippi, had graduated from Mississippi College, received his law degree from Ole Miss in 1911, and served in a number of judicial capacities in his state before Franklin D. Roosevelt elevated him to the federal bench in 1937. Mize reflected the values of his heritage; he was one of the most conservative of federal judges. His obstructionism from the bench became the standard against which the actions of other judges were measured. He went out of his way to interpret civil rights cases in a manner that would enforce the tradition of white supremacy.[40]

Mize told Hauberg he had the option of reconvening the recessed grand jury at Jackson or summoning a new one at Biloxi. The twenty-two-man Jackson jury contained one black man, but had a full docket and Mize would be unable to work the case in until late December. If the grand jury returned any indictments, the trial would take place at Biloxi. Lawrence Walsh personally telephoned his instructions to Hauberg, who told reporters on Friday, "I expect to receive additional instructions shortly, and then I will present the case as soon as practicable." He was awaiting arrival of the 370-page FBI report in order to proceed. Of his talks with Judge Mize, Hauberg said, "I get the impression he will know Wednesday or Thursday whether to recall the grand jury or empanel another."[41]

The Justice Department also undertook to justify its re-entry into the case. J. Edgar Hoover protested that the FBI made "no evaluations or determination whatsoever as to the prosecution of those cases [it] investigated." The Bureau never drew conclusions about federal violations. He defended the government's somewhat lame contention that it had bowed out of the case temporarily to allow Mississippi to prosecute the lynchers. Yet the fact remained, and it was not lost on the South, that the decision to re-enter the case marked a sharp reversal of the Justice Department's original position. After a month-long FBI investigation, the department stated unequivocally that there had been no conclusive evidence of any federal violation. Inter-departmental mail confirmed this, yet the federal government was again entering in force and with uncharacteristic alacrity.[42]

While Hoover insisted federal withdrawal was not up to the FBI, Senator Jacob Javits, who was co-sponsor of the administra-tion's civil rights bill, made it clear that the lack of action in Mississippi had created new demands for federal indictments and effective federal laws. The grand jury's negligence "certainly added proof that Congress must act early next session to make lynching a federal crime." With Senate debate set to begin on February 15, he commented, "U. S. prestige abroad suffered a very hard blow when the news broke last April that for the first time in years a Negro had been lynched in the South. It suffered again last Wednesday when a Mississippi grand jury did not do its duty; this failure was no less shocking because it had been widely predicted ever since the withdrawal of the FBI from the search for the killers and after the U. S. Attorney General deter-mined the federal government did not have jurisdiction in the case." Javits announced he would "propose and press for adop-tion of any federal anti-lynching amendment to any civil rights bill which is before Congress." To the South, he emphasized that if civil rights was a cloudy political issue, lynching was not.[43]

Sidney Mize set January 4 as the date for the new grand jury. In response to Hauberg's request, the judge made it known that the Parker case "would be given priority over routine matters. I have given the request much serious thought," Mize said. "I realize the need for early consideration of the case." He indi-cated also he had not made a final decision on calling a new grand jury in the coastal city of Biloxi, but was leaning heavily toward it. His schedule prevented him from recalling the Jack-son grand jury on December 16, despite Hauberg's specific re-quest, because of a court term in Vicksburg.[44]

Following Mize's announcement, Attorney General William Rogers offered his public comments on the renewed interest of the federal government in the case. "We are studying the need for some new criminal action in the civil rights field," he said. As the lack of action by the Pearl River County grand jury indicated, such a law was necessary because "the failure to call witnesses was as flagrant and calculated a miscarriage of justice as I know of. The harm in this case is not confined to Poplarville. The harm results to the United States and our standing before the world. We believe in a government of law, not of men. But one or two things like this make it hard for people elsewhere in the world to believe this." Rogers was particularly upset over the outcome of the case in Mississippi because of the disregarded FBI report. "The FBI report was one of the most complete I have ever seen, and we had the U. S. Attorney in the area advise local authorities the FBI agents were ready and willing to testify before the grand jury. You talk about states' rights. That's fine. I believe in states' rights also, but I also believe in state responsibility. It seems clear to me that if the states are going to disregard responsibilities to the extent of not even calling witnesses in a case like the Poplarville case, the Federal Government must consider something else." That "something else" was possibly an anti-lynching law.[45]

Rogers complained that after the expenditure of $87,150 in federal tax money and an extensive investigation, the guilty men remained free. "When the evidence is eventually adduced," he added, "I think the nation will be shocked." The evidence would become public during a trial, but there first had to be a trial. Otherwise, revelation of the evidence would violate the civil rights of the accused. Even though Rogers considered the penalties for the civil rights violations committed by the mob "not appropriate to the crime," the Justice Department concluded that its best case rested upon the cooperation that law officers, including Jewel Alford, had given the men considered the prime movers—J. P. Walker, Preacher Lee, L. C. Davis, and Herman Schulz. Pending the introduction of new evidence—perhaps a confession—the government cited Crip Reyer, Jeff Lee, and Arthur Smith as co-conspirators against whom it was not yet seeking indictments. Rogers's comments convinced people in Poplarville that the meddlesome government wanted to reap anti-Southern publicity. Yet few citizens in the county could argue that J. P. Walker, Preacher Lee, and Jeff, and Crip Reyer, were not deeply involved in the lynching.[46]

As for Jewel Alford's involvement in the lynching, the sheriff said angrily, "They don't know what they're talking about." Justice Department officials made it known that Alford's two statements to FBI agents in which he confessed to making the keys available to the mob would become the central element of the government's case. To strengthen its position further, the Justice Department dispatched two of its best trial lawyers from Washington to take over the case, Ben Brooks and William Kehoe. Brooks, an easygoing Texan with a winsome manner, was especially adept at easing the fears of cornered Southerners. Kehoe lacked the trial experience of Brooks but had taken civil rights cases all the way to the Supreme Court. Although the Justice Department had obtained convictions against law officers for conspiracy to violate a citizen's civil rights as long ago as 1943, the new posture toward civil rights dictated caution. The Eisenhower administration was extremely reluctant to step on white Southern toes, especially when some of those toes belonged to local police officers. The FBI took pride in its close association with state and local police across the country, but this relationship made it difficult for the Justice Department to prosecute law officers for criminal and civil rights offenses, lest it impinge upon J. Edgar Hoover's territory.[47]

Brooks and Kehoe subpoenaed seven witnesses to testify between January 4 and 14, including R. J. Wheat. After Ross Barnett's victory in the Democratic primary, he appointed Wheat to his staff as one of his "colonels." He was now one of the leading citizens of Poplarville.

Attorney Brooks promised to expand the FBI evidence. "This grand jury would be more of an investigating grand jury than most grand juries. This is not like an automobile theft case. We are going to have to develop it." Brooks knew it would be difficult to convince a Mississippi grand jury to indict the white men who had lynched a black man accused of raping a white woman.[48]

11

The Triumph
of Southern Justice

As the nation stirred over John F. Kennedy's announcement that he would seek his party's nomination for president, federal district judge Sidney Mize announced he would empanel the federal grand jury on Monday morning, January 4, in Biloxi's shiny new glass and marble Federal Building. A five-man team of government lawyers would represent the government's case to the twenty-three-man southern Mississippi jury. To balance the two Justice Department attorneys from Washington, U.S. Attorney Hauberg in Jackson received permission for his two assistants, Jack McDill and Ed Holmes, to participate. Leading the thirteen lawyers of the defense team were Elijah Bragg Williams of Poplarville, Bidwell Adam of Gulfport, and the able Gulfport attorney Stanford Morse, assisted closely by his two sons and grandson. As the mass of Southern legal experts crowded around the two tables in Mize's courtroom, it became apparent that there was conflict within both teams. For the worried defense, Bidwell Adam argued vehemently that they should instruct their clients to invoke the Fifth Amendment, while the cagey Elijah Bragg Williams cautioned they should obey Mize's directions as much as possible. Williams's superior preparation for the case soon made him the chief strategist. Across the aisle, Brooks and Kehoe approached their case vigorously, convinced the evidence they had was sufficient to secure indictments and convictions even in the unfriendly South, even in Biloxi with a reluctant U. S. Attorney who had limited experience in handling civil rights cases.[1]

On the eve of the hearings, *Look* magazine published an article depicting Poplarville as a "world-wide symbol of race violence." The lynching of Parker, it claimed, was a "moral problem to which the people of Poplarville have reacted with silence, self-deception, and fear." The people were trying to "fool themselves" about their responsibility. "This thing," one of Poplarville's leading citizens commented, "has caused people to turn off their emotions. That's bad for people. They'll be glad when it's over." In spite of Mayor Pat Hyde's post-lynching assessment that few people in Poplarville understood or cared about the implications of the lynching, everyone in the town and the surrounding countryside was well aware that if the grand jury indicted anyone, the trial would occur in mid-February, just as Congress was considering the new civil rights bill Southerners feared might contain an anti-lynching law. Still, people in Poplarville persisted in their refusal to acknowledge the truth of the crime, as though they were trying to fool themselves and in so doing fool the nation as well. "Why, this whole thing was a frame-up by the NAACP," one man swore on the eve of the grand jury hearing. "Most people I know think that there wasn't no rape. There wasn't no lynching. You stop to figure, now. That woman was from New York. And the night they took Parker out of jail, I saw an out-of-state car with seven, eight niggers in it. It just kept waiting there on the side of the road, then it moved off towards the jail just after midnight. Those niggers took Parker out and took him to New York. That body they found wasn't his. Why, the niggers at his home up in Lumberton knew how big he was, and they dug that grave too short for that body. They had to dig it bigger right at the funeral. The NAACP knew this was Bilbo's county, so that's why they did it here."[2]

No blacks were deceived by this sort of rationalizing. One recalled, "Right after it happened, there was a lot of rejoicing. It was like a circus in town that Saturday morning. I heard some old head say, 'That's the best news I heard in a long time.' And they were saying, 'The only good nigger's a dead nigger.' Some of 'em cut out that picture of the jail cell with Parker's shoes in it and pasted it to their windshields and drove all around. I tell you, we slept with guns by our beds. When the FBI moved in so quick and so big, that started the scared phase for white people. After they left, there was the time of wait and see. Then the grand jury met, and there was this shamming-over phase. And now they heard about this Federal grand jury gonna meet in Biloxi, they're scareder than ever. I believe they think the bottom's gonna drop out. A lot of people seem to be involved. Oh yeah, they sorry it happened now they see what happened."[3]

The jury Mize selected included one black man. The rest were white, middle-class males, mostly from the Gulfport-Biloxi area. The prosecution summoned many people from the Poplarville area to testify before the jury.[4] Forty blacks from the surrounding area crowded into the courtroom along with dozens of reporters and journalists from all over the country. Judge Mize read an hour-long charge to the jury that dealt with the lynching and the federal statutes the lynch mob may have violated. Mize's initial stern and businesslike tone indicated to the men under suspicion that this would not be another folly like the Pearl River County grand jury. They faced a determined effort by federal prosecutors to secure an indictment. At the last minute the Justice Department had decided to include kidnapping charges, and Mize discussed the Lindbergh law with the jury first. Indictment on this charge could lead to a death sentence if the person was found guilty, Mize explained, "There is a statute against kidnapping when the abducted person is carried across state lines and injured or killed. So if the evidence produced before you should indicate with sufficient definiteness to show that one or more people abducted him from the Poplarville jail and transported him across state lines and killed him, then those persons would be guilty of kidnapping. That law is known as the Lindbergh Law." But, Mize added, "it is not a violation of the Civil Rights Act if individuals conspire to seize a person from a state jail or from the sheriff and kill him. That is not violation of any federal statute. It is murder, punishable as such, only by the state.[5]

Mize counseled, "I charge you further that if individuals conspired with the sheriff or any of his deputies of Pearl River County to seize Mack Charles Parker and injure him or kill him, that was a violation of Section 242 of Title 18 of the United States Code, and all conspirators, along with the sheriff and deputy in the conspiracy, would be guilty of a crime." Mize emphasized that at least the sheriff or one or more of his deputies *had* to be involved in the conspiracy to constitute a federal violation under color of law. Such a conspiracy involving the law officers would also be a violation of the general conspiracy statutes, making it a violation of two federal laws. Mississippi ranked next to Nevada in the lowest rate of commission of crime per one thousand persons, he pointed out. "We are proud that we do not have any organized crime in Mississippi, and we do enforce the laws of the United States in Mississippi honestly and fairly. I think," he said resolutely, "that there is not a state in the Union where the relationship between the two races are [sic] as good or as highly respected as in the state of Mississippi. I am proud of that." Mize reminded the attentive jurors that Parker had been charged with a "horrible and heinous crime"; nevertheless, his crime failed to justify his lynching. If a suspect takes the Fifth Amendment, Mize told them, they cannot compel him to answer the questions. Then he instructed the jurors in the other cases they would hear and concluded by saying, "I have had only one kidnapping case before me in 23 years on the bench. In that case the defendant pleaded guilty and was given a life sentence." At the conclusion of the judge's remarks, Stanford Morse rose to ask the judge to inform the jurors that they did not have to follow the orders or advice of the U. S. attorneys; if they chose, they could request outside counsel. Mize acknowledged the correctness of Morse's statement and so instructed the jury, saying he felt it unnecessary, since a Mississippi grand jury had never requested outside aid in the past. After the chief clerk swore in the jury, it adjourned to the small hearing room.[6]

Many courtroom observers found the early action by the attorney, who like each of his fellow lawyers would not name his client, unusual, since no indictments had been returned and no suspects had been named publicly. But Morse knew what was at stake in the hearing and resorted to every device possible to forestall indictments. After recessing for lunch, the jury began its proceedings, calling June Walters as its first witness. Immediately sides within the grand jury appeared. Some members of the jury seemed genuinely concerned to identify and indict members of the mob, but others seemed more interested in the more grisly details of the rape.

June Walters recounted the night of the rape for the jurors. She insisted she was not absolutely positive that Parker had been the man and emphasized that he looked too young and his voice was higher than the rapist's. The jurors were more interested in asking questions about the attack than in the possibility of Parker's innocence. Walters described how her assailant broke into her car and, after dragging her from it, told her to get in the front seat of his, take her pants off, and spread her legs. "You mean you let that nigger fuck you?" cried one incredulous juror. Mrs. Walters protested that she had no choice. The jurors badgered the woman with similar challenges until she fled the hearing room in tears. One solid fact emerged from the rough session—June Walters had never been positive that Mack Charles Parker was the rapist. A timid and harassed Jimmy Walters followed his wife to the stand. The next question was, "You mean to tell me that after that nigger fucked your wife you still lived with her?" Walters responded that his family had been under such intense pressure that they had finally moved to Bogalusa.[7] Walters maintained he had been approached by two men from Poplarville but had refused to go with them to the lynching. The first day of questioning ended with the strong indication that Parker might well have been found not guilty of raping June Walters.[8]

As the jurors filed out of the court building, they joked casually with photographers waiting on the sidewalk. The foreman, Charles Long, a fifty-eight-year-old insurance salesman from Biloxi's twin city of Gulfport, refused to answer any questions about the proceedings although all the men including the lone black juror, Freddie Woodward, who walked shyly behind the white men, were in obvious good humor. The number of reporters at the hearing far exceeded the number in attendance at the grand jury hearing in November in Poplarville. News teams from television stations from all over the South crowded into the Federal Building to cover the most spectacular story of the day, even in this election year. Of the reporters who had covered the post lynching events in Poplarville, only Cliff Sessions of UPI, Claude Sitton of the New York *Times,* Charles Kuralt of CBS with his cameraman Reggie Smith, and Bill Minor of the New Orleans *Times-Picayune* came to Biloxi. All major Southern newspapers and the wire services sent reporters. The sizable number of Southern journalists indicated the South realized that it as well as the suspects was on trial in Biloxi.[9]

The grand jury began its second day of deliberations at 9:00 the next morning. Reduced to twenty-one men because of illness, five above the quorum level of sixteen, it went into secret session to hear testimony from Jeff Lee. The surly Lee, who underwent four hours of intensive grilling, frequently requested permission to consult with his lawyer, Ed Williams, son of Elijah Bragg Williams, from Poplarville. Lee left the hearing room so many times to ask his lawyer questions that Mize took the unprecedented and illegal measure of allowing Williams to enter the grand jury room to advise his client. This highly improper action evoked considerable protest from attorneys Brooks and Kehoe, but without result. According to grand jury member J. B. Richmond, a thirty-four-year-old vice-president of the Jefferson Davis Insurance Company, most of the jurors were unaware that defense attorneys could not legally enter the grand jury room, so this had little effect on the course of the questioning.[10]

On the advice of his attorney, Jeff Lee continually invoked the Fifth Amendment. Many jurors, unacquainted with this famous amendment, became openly agitated when Lee invoked it. They complained to Mize about it after the lunch break. Jewel Alford, Tullie Dunn, and later Crip Reyer testified during the long afternoon session. Each of the Pearl River County men gave testimony that followed closely the information they had given the FBI. Jeff Lee gave his name and maintained he had had nothing whatsoever to do with the lynching. Dunn acknowledged being at the meeting, but denied going to Hattiesburg to see Jimmy Walters and denied taking part in the lynching. Crip Reyer told the jury that unidentified men had asked to use his car for the lynching, but he himself had been at Rester's truck stop when Parker was lynched. Jewel Alford underwent the most intensive questioning by the prosecutors. Alford refused in his slow, deliberate drawl to discuss how the mob had approached him on that Friday night, but on advice from his lawyer, he finally relented and described his trip to the courthouse for the keys, admitting nothing more about his role in the abduction of Parker. He maintained steadfastly that he knew none of the men in Reyer's car who confronted him. Alford sadly told the entranced jury he feared for his life if he gave evidence against the men who came to his house.[11]

Ralph Bachman and two of his assistants, in testimony that lasted the remainder of the day, summarized the FBI's findings incorporated in the much discussed report. The three FBI agents showed film clips of the removal of Parker's body from the Pearl River and distributed eight-by-ten-inch photographs as they narrated a detailed account of the lynching. At the end of the first two days of testimony, J. B. Richmond thought the jury "had enough on those guys to send them up for years." Richmond was convinced after only two days that the grand jury could have voted indictments against eight men. Jewel Alford left the federal courthouse that afternoon tired and drawn. He had invoked the right to remain silent when asked about his prior knowledge of the lynching. Fear of an indictment placed him under considerable strain, and he had been making frequent visits to his minister to seek guidance. Alford dreaded returning the next day; he looked forward to going home and being with his wife. Jeff Lee, on the other hand, was the picture of confidence when he left. Released from further testimony at the end of the day, he joked to reporters as they questioned him about the grand jury, "I think they liked my company." Lee had returned to the courthouse after lunch but did not return to the small, third-floor hearing room in the rear of the Federal Building and did not testify further.[12]

As the proceedings entered the third day, open rancor developed not only between the defense and the prosecution but also between Judge Mize and the attorneys from Washington. Invocation of the Fifth Amendment increased, and the prosecution wanted Mize to direct the witnesses to answer more of the questions. Mize reluctantly agreed over the vociferous objections of the huge team of defense lawyers. Bidwell Adam wanted to instruct all witnesses to give their names and nothing more, to offer the grand jury absolutely no help as a clear statement that Mississippians would not stand for federal involvement in their affairs, especially in a case of interracial rape when the black rapist had received justice at the hands of a loyal Southern lynch mob. Urging caution and the ruse of ostensible cooperation, Elijah Williams persuaded the lawyers to ignore Adam and counsel their clients to cooperate as much as possible without incriminating themselves or anyone else. In this way, Williams argued, the witnesses reduced the risk of offending Mize, the jury, and the Southern faction of the prosecuting team. Williams also insisted they had a capable ally on the bench. Sidney Mize, a lifelong conservative Southern jurist and a Senator Eastland ally, would not allow the jury to indict anyone in this case if he could possibly avoid it. As though to confirm Williams's assurances to his fellow attorneys, on Wednesday, the third day of the hearings, Mize began, through his rulings on the Fifth Amendment, to limit the scope of the investigation.[13]

While J. P. Coleman gave his farewell address to the Missis-

sippi legislature in Jackson, pointing to his achievements in pre-
serving school segregation through his "moderate" approach,
Judge Mize was demonstrating the continued strength of the
more traditional Southern approach.[14]

As Coleman departed the Governor's Mansion, as if on cue,
events began to swing toward the accused in Biloxi. Judge Mize
began to flex his judicial muscles. Five witnesses appeared before
the grand jury in the third-floor hearing room on Wednesday,
but after Mrs. Odell Loveless's brief opening testimony about
what the nurse heard from the hospital on the night of Parker's
abduction, the jury spent more time in the second-floor courtroom listening to Mize's rulings on the Fifth Amendment. Sheriff
Moody was the only witness to go before the jury in the afternoon.
At the end of the day the grand jury released only Nurse Loveless.
Moody, R. J. Wheat, Petey Carver, and John Reyer all had to
return on Thursday. Judge Mize now stated that kidnapping was
a federal violation only if it could be proven that the men transported their victim across state lines for personal benefit or gain.
Brooks and Kehoe strenuously objected without success to this
interpretation of the Lindbergh law. Mize also made it clear that
government prosecutors could not compel a witness to answer
questions if the witness claimed constitutional protection. "Should
a witness invoke the Fifth Amendment, that witness cannot be
compelled to answer the question or questions," he said. But he
added quickly that the witness could be compelled to answer "if it
was apparent that the answer would not tend to incriminate the
witness." According to J. B. Richmond, Mize's new instructions on
the Lindbergh law so confused the grand jury that they virtually
assured there would be no indictments for kidnapping. They also
signaled a strange turn of events.[15]

On Wednesday morning, while the grand jury was in session,
Judge Sebe Dale had appeared at the U. S. Marshal's office in
the Federal Building. He claimed he was there on a personal
visit with the marshal that had nothing to do with the lynching
investigation, but he also spoke to at least one juror, Lamar
Scarborough of Pascagoula, and even allowed himself to be photographed with this man on the elevator in the building. Later,
after lunch, he conferred briefly with Judge Mize in the judge's
chambers. It was during the afternoon session that Mize changed
his stance on the Lindbergh law and narrowed the focus of the
conspiracy statutes.[16]

After lunch, with spectators barred from the courtroom, the

judge questioned individual witnesses to determine which questions they had the right to refrain from answering. Mize warned the witnesses not to bring up substantive matters in open court, but to reserve them for the hearing room. Reporters present felt that Dale was trying to learn how the hearings were progressing. Dale's encounter with one of the jurors may well have been accidental, but it clearly violated legal decorum and could have had an adverse effect upon that juror's opinions. It was well known to the jurors that Dale had presided over the hearings in the Parker case.[17]

On Thursday, for the second day, the grand jury spent more time in Mize's courtroom receiving explanations on various points of law than in the hearing room. For a total of three and a half hours in a closed session before Judge Mize, the grand jury asked questions about the Lindbergh law and its relevance to the lynching. The judge read to them from the 1936 U. S. Supreme Court decision *Gooch v. United States,* which said that the kidnappers must transport their victim across state lines to secure personal benefit such as ransom. For the second time, U. S. attorneys argued that such a narrow interpretation might mislead the jury into thinking that the transportation of Parker across state lines might not have violated the Lindbergh law, which it clearly did if it could be proven, as Mize had pointed out in his opening-day charge. The questions the jurors posed to Mize indicated they were trying to find a *personal* motive in the kidnapping of Parker. Mize reiterated, "Unless the one who kidnaps another and crosses a state line does so for some personal gain or benefit to himself, then there is no crime of kidnapping under the Lindbergh law."[18]

An intense argument also developed once again between the prosecution and the defense over the number of times four of the five witnesses coming before the grand jury that day had invoked the Fifth Amendment, refusing to answer questions about the identity of some of the mob members. After receiving detailed instructions from Mize in which he repeated the conditions necessary for him to compel a witness to answer a question, the jurors filed out of the courtroom and up the steps to their hearing room, where all the witnesses from the day reappeared and retracted their testimony. By the close of the day the government's case had started to crumble. "Mize turned the key that locked the door," said J. B. Richmond. "As the government built up the case, Mize began to tear it down." It was "one arm of the government versus the other." What particularly angered Richmond was that Mize supported the right of the witnesses to alter their own testimony.[19]

There were problems within the prosecution team as well. Robert Hauberg had not objected to Brooks and Kehoe superseding him in the case. It was traditional for the Justice Department to send attorneys from Washington for special cases, and in 1960 civil rights was special. The Civil Rights Division, still in its infancy, lacked seasoned trial lawyers. Since Hauberg was a resident Southerner, Washington leadership was allowing him to blame any potential conviction on outsiders and thereby deflect local anger. But he and his assistants provided little support and cooperation, which left Brooks and Kehoe working in virtual isolation. Brooks telephoned A. B. Caldwell, the head of the trial section of the Civil Rights Division, in Washington to send another attorney to Biloxi to aid them. But Caldwell's superior, St. John Barrett, blocked this peremptorily, saying, "We cannot afford the luxury of assigning more than two men to any one case." This denial shocked and angered the zealous Caldwell, who protested that the government was damaging its own case. "Slim" Barrett, however, sensed the reluctance of his superiors to press the case too far beyond established procedure and went along.[20]

In the midst of the intense pressure on Brooks and Kehoe, trouble flared up with Barrett on another matter. Again, sensing the outlook of his superiors, he took a decidedly more conservative stance than Brooks and Kehoe. As they developed their case before the jury, Brooks and Kehoe wanted to seek indictments under Title 18, Sections 241 and 242, but Barrett demurred, reasserting that they could not prove intent, that the mob had lynched Parker to prevent him from exercising his civil rights or because he had already exercised them. Thus they would use 242 and the more general conspiracy statute 371, which carried a maximum penalty of five years and a $10,000 fine. Barrett maintained all along that Parker was lynched for raping June Walters, not to prevent him from receiving a fair trial. Brooks and Kehoe wanted to seek indictments under Section 241, the more severe of the conspiracy statutes, which could conceivably result in ten years imprisonment for members of the mob. In forcing his trial lawyers to toe the line, Barrett reflected the unwillingness of the Rogers Justice Department to challenge old standards. Barrett's intransigence seriously crippled the already weakened federal attack.[21]

As a result of Barrett's positions, the prosecution team fell into considerable disarray. Opposition existed in Biloxi, and this had been anticipated by both Joseph Ryan and A. B. Caldwell in the Civil Rights Division. But the Justice Department hobbled its own case by blocking Caldwell's plea for reinforcements and by not demanding total cooperation from its own attorneys in the field, Hauberg and his two assistants. Caldwell and others at Justice had been convinced at the outset that the federal government would secure indictments against some or all of the lynch mob. Now, in light of the government's reluctance to act decisively, they no longer felt that way.[22]

News of a major leak in the case broke in Thursday night's news reports of the hearings. UPI reporter Cliff Sessions and CBS newsman Charles Kuralt obtained the FBI report, which listed twenty-three "known and suspected participants" in the lynching. During his summer-long stay in Poplarville, Sessions had become friendly with County Prosecutor Bill Stewart, who, like Sheriff Moody, left office on January 19. Sessions described Stewart as a "good ole boy" who wanted to be liked by everyone in spite of his well-known views on the lynching. He gave a copy of the FBI report to Sessions, and while Kuralt's cameraman took Stewart out for a drink, Sessions and Kuralt dashed back to their hotel, where they poured over the report, furiously scribbling notes on the statements by Jewel Alford, Crip Reyer, and Arthur Smith.[23] Of particular interest was Alford's statement that he knew the mob members "wouldn't hesitate" to do him or his family harm if he had refused to furnish the keys. He feared he "would have to leave the Poplarville area permanently in order to avoid possible violence to himself or his family." Sessions also incorporated into his story Arthur Smith's accounts of the meeting at the Davis farm, the scene at the courthouse, the crossing into Louisiana, and his arrival on the bridge after other mob members had dumped the body into the water. He included Crip Reyer's statement that his car had been used, that he had attended the pre-lynching meeting, and that "several men" had volunteered to go to the jail to get Parker. Sessions also reported that two men had traveled to Hattiesburg to enlist Walters, but that Walters had told them, "My wife was not sure and had not identified Parker as the man who raped her." Sessions's stories and Kuralt's filmed report frightened and angered the defense lawyers. More important, the two reporters made public a large and important part of the government's evidence.

The stories indicated to everyone who cared to notice just how strong a case the government had against the lynch mob.[24]

The next morning during a break in the hearing, encouraged by the information he had gleaned from the FBI report the day before, the enterprising Sessions sneaked into the grand jury hearing room and emptied the contents of the wastebasket into his briefcase. Again Sessions raced back to his hotel, this time alone. He dumped his briefcase onto his bed and excitedly began to assemble the bits of paper. To his delight he had retrieved voting slips the jury had used and discarded as they tried to arrive at indictments. Sessions found as he tallied the slips of paper that the jury had come extremely close to indicting seven men for conspiracy to violate Parker's civil rights under the color of law. The government had fallen one ballot short.[25]

Also on Friday, Mize made rulings that permanently crippled the government's case. He informed the jury in one of its many sessions before him that they must indict all the conspirators or no one for conspiracy under color of law. Although several members of the jury openly sided with the mob, there was a general feeling that they should indict some of the men on at least two of the charges. Mize's rulings effectively prevented that. According to juror Sam Allman, they were anxious "to show the nation that Mississippi law was just." After Friday, little hope remained for achieving any semblance of justice. The jury was told to vote true bills on all or none. This left the jury unable to reach any indictments. Said J. B. Richmond, "I was so disappointed at the travesty of justice I was sick."[26]

The number of people released at the close of hearings on Friday indicated that the jury was leaning away from indictments. Had the opposite been true, it would have kept Jewel Alford and Crip Reyer around for more testimony. At 3:30 that afternoon, the jury concluded its first week of work. Neither the prosecution nor the defense would comment on the progress of the case, but Stanford Morse and Bidwell Adam, chagrined by the UPI stories, indicated at the close of business that if the grand jury returned a true bill against some or all of the suspects, they and other top lawyers in Mississippi would defend the men at trial. More than fifteen of the witnesses who went before the grand jury during the week had secured legal representation—and while their clients testified, the attorneys paced nervously in front of the grand jury room, waited in the courtroom, or strolled the halls with the phalanx of newsmen awaiting word of a break in the hearings.

No one expected the hearings, scheduled for up to two weeks, to last beyond Thursday, January 14. Only the statements by Adam and Morse indicated that the jury might possibly decide against the suspects. All other indications—Dale's mysterious visit, the rulings by Mize, the release of part of the FBI report, which people viewed at the time as a desperate move by someone on the prosecution to rally forces for an indictment—hinted that the hearings were going well for the suspects.[27]

Judge Mize made it known over the seemingly endless weekend that he had a heavy court docket at Jackson the following week and if the grand jury could not finish that week, he would call a recess until mid-February, when the regular term of federal district court convened at Biloxi. Mize considered allowing the grand jury to continue its deliberations without him, but decided against after conferring with U. S. Attorney Robert Hauberg, who promised he would urge the jurors to complete their business within the next five days. Mize had the power to delay the opening date of the grand jury, but was unwilling to delay the Jackson jury to allow the Biloxi jury more time to complete its work.

There was other activity over the weekend. Authorities escorted three prisoners who had been in the Poplarville jail when Parker was kidnapped to the jail at Biloxi. Marshals placed them in the Hinds County jail in Jackson on Saturday and on Sunday transferred them to Biloxi. The three men who had witnessed the abduction of Parker had cooperated with the FBI extensively during the investigation in Pearl River County. But their testimony had little impact on the case.[28]

On Monday the grand jury worked through lunch and recessed at 2:00 p.m. At the end of the day, Mize dismissed more witnesses, and on Tuesday he informed the jury, the press, and spectators that he would call a recess until February if the jury failed to finish by Friday. The jury took his warning to heart; on Tuesday it summarily canceled the appearance of all further witnesses. Jurors indicated they had heard sufficient testimony from the thirty-two men and women who had appeared before them. Prosecutors announced the jury would take its final vote Wednesday morning.[29] Judge Mize's efforts to end the deliberations by Friday had succeeded. J. P. Walker never appeared before the grand jury. He was one of fifteen witnesses whose appearance was canceled.

The grand jury reconvened Wednesday morning promptly at

nine and immediately went into executive session. No witnesses remained in the building: its halls were unusually quiet as reporters huddled together, trying to glean last-minute facts from one another as they waited for a decision. The tension was palpable among the spectators assembled in the courtroom. Many of them talked quietly among themselves while they waited. Publicly, the spectators avoided speculating on the outcome; privately, few interested parties felt the jury would return any indictments because it had peremptorily dismissed the remaining witnesses. The rumor was that the lawyers from Washington had been unable to make a case against the lynchers. In the small, third-floor hearing room, prosecutors walked the jurors through the testimony, trying to persuade them to recall the remaining witnesses. At one point the jurors summoned Judge Mize to explain a point in his charge, but before he could respond, a messenger met him in the hall and told him the point had been clarified. At noon the jury recessed without a word, leaving newsmen standing in the halls, wondering what had happened. The jurors filed into the elevators, determined to remain silent about the morning's proceedings.

Reporters were especially vexed by the silence in the courtroom. Mississippi law forbids the press from mentioning the name of a rape victim unless the rapist has been indicted and the indictments made public. June Walters's name was known, of course. Many reporters had interviewed her after the lynching and after her testimony in Biloxi. But they were unable to name her in their stories.[30]

On Thursday morning at 10:35 the long-awaited news floated down from the hearing room: no indictments. "We were unable to arrive at any true bill," the foreman Charles Long reported to Judge Mize before the hushed courtroom. In a statement he wrote himself, Long told the judge that after listening to the testimony of thirty-two witnesses, some of whom had a great deal to say, others of whom offered little, the jury felt it could "never arrive at a true bill on the evidence that was presented." As reporters and spectators rustled in their seats at the incredible news, Judge Mize rapped his gavel and sternly cautioned the people to restrain themselves. He warned photographers against taking pictures. "This is a court of law where legal procedures are involved. It is not a show." Long informed Mize that a jury had reviewed the evidence late Tuesday afternoon and all day Wednesday. Late on Wednesday it took its first vote based on all the evidence. The results had been extremely close on the violations of the civil rights laws, but the jurors voted heavily against indictment for kidnapping. Not in any instance did the jurors attain the necessary twelve votes for indictment, he told the judge. They even went over the evidence one last time before coming down to him this morning, Long continued, but they found no grounds for indictment. Taking the sensational news calmly without a hint of the emotion that had clouded the affair, Mize thanked Long for his supervision of the jury and congratulated the jurors for conducting themselves "diligently and fairly." The divided prosecution sat silently at its table in stark contrast to the self-congratulatory smiles of the thirteen defense lawyers, who had expected indictments against some of their clients. The prosecutors merely nodded when Mize thanked them for their efforts on behalf of the government. Mize then recessed the jury until its regularly scheduled meeting date of February 23.[31]

The lynching was over, finally, and everyone in the courtroom knew it. The prosecutors packed up their documents and left without comment. "Southern Justice has triumphed," proclaimed Stanford Morse. "Thank God," bellowed Bidwell Adam, "justice was served." As the defense team marched down the hall to the elevators, Ed Williams told reporters gathered around him, "We had five names of persons" against whom action had been expected. Defense attorneys, who had no idea just how close the grand jury had come to indicting some of their clients, had already made arrangements for bail with a bondsman in case the jury indicted these men.[32]

Even with the detailed FBI report, the prosecution had been unable to obtain indictments. This stirred considerable anger throughout the country. The mob had gotten away with murder. Aided and abetted by fellow Southerners, it had laughed at justice. "Our own correspondent," said the New York *Times,* "reports that 'details of the lynching and the names of those involved were common knowledge' in the area. What to do about it? Unfortunately there isn't much that can be done."[33]

Senators Jacob Javits and Philip Hart, lonely voices in the hostile or indifferent Senate chamber, resumed their pleas for an anti-lynching provision in the upcoming civil rights bill, citing the lack of action in Biloxi as "conclusive evidence" that the nation urgently needed an anti-lynching law. Hart wrote to the chairman of the Senate Subcommittee on Constitutional Rights, urging prompt approval of his anti-lynching bills. And in an action that revealed the NAACP's attitude toward the entire affair, Roy Wilkins dispatched an angry telegram to William Rogers, urging him to release the FBI report to the public "so that the world may know who the suspects are and be able to appraise the quality of justice administered in the state of Mississippi." Wilkins should have known better. Throughout its campaign to have Parker's murderers brought to justice, the NAACP acted perfunctorily in issuing the usual telegrams and lobbying the usual agencies and individuals. Wilkins and the entire organization had reacted more strongly to the lynching of Emmett Till just four years earlier. But Till's innocence had never been at issue, whereas the presumption of Parker's guilt hung heavily over the NAACP and hindered its activities. The thoughtlessly worded telegram revealed an uncharacteristic ineptitude that forced the usually sympathetic ACLU to issue a prompt response. A release of the FBI report, argued the ACLU head, violated both the Fifth and Sixth Amendments. "Despite our strong feeling about the Parker case, we do not believe that a vital civil liberties principle should be vitiated in the understandable desire to seek stronger action in the Parker case." The chastened Wilkins responded apologetically. "I suppose we knew all along that Rogers should not release this, but we were so outraged at the turn of events that we yelled for something that we felt certain would ease some of our pain."[34]

In response to the outrage expressed by concerned people throughout the country, Joseph Ryan announced that the case "has not been closed." Rather, the Justice Department was considering submitting the case to another federal grand jury, a common practice when the government thinks it has strong evidence against the defendants. The Justice Department thus kept the case open without intending either to pursue it seriously or to allow it to die. In an election year it remained too critical an issue for the administration to appear to be giving up on it. Critical black and liberal support had become inextricably linked to the willingness of the administration to push for new civil rights legislation. One week later Rogers announced his decision against releasing the FBI report. Despite his previous statement that the public would be shocked by what the report revealed and his belief that the reluctance of two grand juries to indict the mob represented a "serious injustice," he defended his decision to withhold the report in this "flagrant case. If an injustice exists,

I don't think the case should be dropped, but it doesn't justify releasing the report." American jurisprudence taught that a man was innocent until proved guilty in a court of law, and even though the mob had denied Parker this basic right, Rogers refused to forgo this principle and violate the rights of the members of the lynch mob by releasing the report. Rogers thought, and correctly so, that it would be a "dangerous precedent for a law enforcement officer to release evidence when he is dissatisfied with grand jury action."[35]

The proud J. Edgar Hoover reflected the embarrassment and outrage his Bureau felt after having conducted a massive and largely successful investigation only to have it lead to nothing. Testifying before a House Appropriations Subcommittee, Hoover remarked, "We were able to establish the identity of a number of members of the mob who participated in the abduction of Parker and obtained admissions from some of the participants." The FBI withdrew and turned its evidence over to state and local authorities. Then, "the Pearl River County grand jury met at Poplarville in November of 1959 and ignored the case. A Federal grand jury met at Biloxi, Mississippi, in January of 1960 and considered the case but returned no true bill. The case is still pending in the Department of Justice." When asked about the status of the case in light of the director's testimony, William Rogers replied, "We do not have it closed, but we do not have anything pending on it. We presented it to the grand jury and they voted no bill."[36]

Epilogue

Ross Barnett entered the Governor's Mansion, proclaiming, "The people of Mississippi will soon find out that I am not one who will meddle in local affairs." He soon learned that countless others were willing to meddle. Within another year the NAACP launched Operation Mississippi, a voter registration drive led by Medgar Evers under the auspices of the new Civil Rights Act of 1960, which provided a measure of federal support to voter registration efforts. The NAACP hoped to increase the number of black voters from the low figure of 4 percent of those eligible. In addition to the voter registration campaign, the NAACP intended Operation Mississippi to be "an all-out and continuous drive to eliminate discrimination in Mississippi." In May 1961 the courageous Freedom Riders arrived in the state to challenge white supremacy on its home ground. The Freedom Riders called national attention to the unparalleled degree of discrimination in the state, setting the stage for the violence-filled Mississippi Freedom Summer of 1964. By the time Barnett left office, Mississippi had become public enemy number one on racial matters.[1]

Because of its isolation and size, Poplarville largely escaped the civil rights revolution. Racial practices and attitudes in the small town did not change much after 1959. Not until 1972 were blacks allowed to sit on the main floor of the courtroom, and not until the following year was the school integrated. The Klan firmly established itself and conducted yearly parades down Main Street. Most of the mob members remained in Pearl River County; others died; one moved away. J. P. Walker was elected sheriff in 1963. Four years later his wife was elected and appointed him deputy. In 1971 the voters again elected him sheriff, and he continued his illustrious career as the county's chief lawman. Residents still talk about an incident in 1971 when Walker's deputies planted marijuana on a rock group called the American Indians, while serving as special guards at their concert in Picayune. After the concert the deputies arrested the performers and shaved their heads. The fiery Walker tried to drive his cruiser over newsmen and cameramen from New Orleans who sought to interview him about the incident. In 1976, after the county voided the law prohibiting the sheriff from succeeding himself, Walker ran again, but his brother-in-law defeated him. Walker died soon afterward. Herman Schulz became a county constable in the early 1960s. Eventually he moved away and lost contact even with Jewel Alford. Petey Carver remained a police officer through the 1970s and into the 1980s. Sebe Dale conducted a speaking tour through the North in 1963 on behalf of the State Sovereignty Commission, "the watchdog of segregation." During one speech in Connecticut, when asked if he thought the lynchers would ever be apprehended, Dale thought for a moment and allowed as how they wouldn't. "Besides," he quipped, "three of them are already dead." Dale himself died in 1968.[2]

The Parker family stayed in California and eventually disappeared from view as they dispersed into America's black underclass. Mack Parker's ex-wife moved with her mother to Chicago, where they continue to live, returning yearly to Lumberton to visit friends and relatives. Curt Underwood, Parker's closest friend and brother-in-law, lives in New Orleans, haunted by the memory of the lynching and the death of his friend.

On the other side of the racial fence, separated from their black counterparts by hundreds of years of history and prejudice, are the Walters family, who reside in the Hattiesburg area. The Komp Equipment Company dismissed Jimmy four months after the lynching, and shortly after that his tenuous marriage dissolved in bitterness and rancor. The very people who sought to defend June's honor by lynching Mack Charles Parker turned on this woman they once called "the flower of Southern womanhood" with disparaging epithets when they learned she still refused to make a positive identification of Parker as the rapist. June eventually remarried and then divorced her second husband. Jimmy lives with his brother Eddie in their late mother's house. They are the only whites left in the neighborhood. Not far away is the public-assisted apartment project where June lives with her youngest children. Jimmy continues to sit in for other musicians at the American Legion on Saturday nights. He and his brother talk infrequently about the lynching because it is still a sore point between them. Eddie never admitted to his brother his role in the affair, although Jimmy has suspected all along that his brother was involved. Jimmy has been unable to hold down a job for more than several months at a time and is left only with bitter memories. Most of their time is spent in front of a small, black-and-white portable TV set.[3]

J. P. Coleman, who became a federal judge on the Fifth Circuit Court of Appeals, where he continued to uphold Southern conservatism, faced another racial crisis when he ran for governor in 1963. The controversy over James Meredith's enrollment at Ole Miss so inflamed the white public that Paul ("Stand Tall with Paul") Johnson, whom even the State Sovereignty Commission considered an extremist, defeated the "moderate" Coleman by almost as great a margin as Coleman had defeated Johnson in 1955.[4]

As for Poplarville, the town scarcely grew after 1960. By 1980 its total population had risen only by a few hundred whites, while the percentage of blacks in the county dropped. In August 1969 Hurricane Camille destroyed what remained of the tung nut industry, and although the advent of the NASA facility below Picayune provided jobs for many citizens and attracted new residents, the end of the moon program brought a cut in NASA funding that prompted an exodus Poplarville has not recovered from. As late as August 1977, a former newspaper editor worried about the "huge number of people in this county who are unemployed." The new editor of the Poplarville *Democrat*, William M. Posey, consoled his readers that "growth for the City of Poplarville is just a matter of time. But how much time depends on how we present our city to others who are interested in locating elsewhere." Ironically, the town, which had once laughed about lynching, worried openly about its image, so seriously damaged by a moment of blind hatred in April 1959. "The old saying goes, that a town is only as good as its people," wrote Posey, "and there is no doubt that Poplarville has the best people you'll find anywhere."[5]

The lynching of Mack Charles Parker, which had stunned and sickened the nation, disappeared quickly from America's memory, as though it had never happened. As with most lynchings, the country pushed it from its mind. The specifics of Mack Charles Parker's gruesome and unnecessary death also slipped from the pages of history, unlike the civil rights murders, the slaying of Medgar Evers, the bombing of the black church in Birmingham, the murder of Viola Liuzzo, and other violent events in the violence-fraught history of the civil rights movement.

For the citizens of Poplarville, on the other hand, Parker's death persisted like a recurring nightmare. According to Arthur Smith's brother Cecil, "We don't talk about it no more. We're still tryin' to forget it." Even so, as William Posey reluctantly admitted, it remained the first thing a new resident heard about upon moving into the county. True to the Jackson *Clarion-Ledger*'s observation that "national publicity on the Mack C. Parker case is meager when compared with the headline attention given the Emmett Till case of 1955," the case faded quickly and quietly, and has never been mentioned in accounts of the civil rights campaigns in the South. Yet Poplarville deserves a place in history along with other towns in the deep South made infamous by racial violence—Montgomery and Selma, Alabama; Little Rock, Arkansas; Philadelphia and Jackson, Mississippi. "Although this isn't to invite attention to the Parker case," the *Clarion-Ledger* reflected, "that case does—from a standpoint of principle—deserve more attention than the Till case, for Parker was in the hands of the law." The nation wanted as desperately as the citizens of Poplarville to forget the lynching. In 1959 white America was not yet ready to confront its deep-seated racism. The lynching was just too barbaric and cast too horrid a shadow across the land, a shadow twisted and bent by racism and its contempt for colorblind justice.[6]

During the turbulent years that followed, interracial violence increased; nevertheless, mindful of the grim lesson learned in Poplarville, angry Southern whites, in the words of Erle Johnston, "knew [they] had to adjust in some way." Reflecting on the incident in Poplarville, Johnston said, the "Parker lynching brought such bad publicity to Mississippi, people knew they couldn't continue to lynch." We "found out pretty quick those things were not good for the state." Authorities, he maintained, wanted to attract new industry and investment and so they arrived, rather belatedly and rather painfully, at "a mutual agreement to stop lynching." The murder of Medgar Evers in 1963 and the civil rights murders in 1964 indicated that their perpetrators feared the strong arm of the FBI enough to alter their form of racial retaliation.*

The men who lynched Emmett Till wore no masks and acted with a brazen disregard for the law when they kidnapped him late at night, executed him, and went about their business as though nothing very extraordinary had happened. And indeed, it would not have been unusual for a lynching *in the 1890s*. But this was the 1950s, and the men who lynched Mack Charles Parker saw fit to hide their faces. In this the lynching departed from the historical norm.

Racial violence continued into the 1960s. In fact, it increased. But methods changed. The public spectacle of a lynching bee in which the participants flouted the law, their identities known to everyone, disappeared until 1981, when the Klan lynched a young black man chosen at random in Mobile, Alabama, and townspeople in Skidmore, Missouri, lynched the white town bully. In the 1960s and 1970s, the lynching was replaced by assassination, bombing, beating, and race riot. Although gruesome and terrifying, these acts were not quite the same as the "classic" type of lynching whose very existence emphasized to blacks or any other oppressed group that whites were operating relatively free from legal or moral restraint.

The case itself remained open—it was never officially closed—and records of it remained in J. Edgar Hoover's personal files in his office until his death, when they were transferred to permanent storage. Hoover never took kindly to cases that reflected poorly on the Bureau. And this one did so on two counts. The perpetrators, although essentially "caught," got off scot-free.

---

* Since the 1938 lynching at Duck Hill, Mississippians had considered lynchings in which newspapers announced the lynching, special trains brought in spectators, and the torture of the victim went on for hours to be a thing of the past. In 1953 the Asheville *Citizen* said, "Education, respect for the law—these things have prevailed." The Duck Hill lynching was the lynching most Mississippians remembered as being the last time an angry mob stormed a jail after a black man. Quoted in the New York *Times,* May 3, 1959. Prior to Poplarville, the last time a mob removed a man from jail was in May 1949 in Irwinton, Georgia, when an irate mob seized a man from his cell, beat him, and shot him to death. New Orleans *Times-Picayune,* April 26, 1959.

And the charges of agent harassment of the local citizens soiled the Bureau's unblemished image. The Justice Department debated resuming action in the case in 1961, 1971, and in 1972, but concluded that the possibilities of a successful prosecution would be remote and worried that such actions would be an affront to the U. S. district judge in Mississippi because federal action had failed already.

After 1959 rural whites became less likely to vent their frustration and anger on blacks by lynching them, not so much because these passions decreased, but because it became increasingly difficult to get away with vigilante-style violence. Nonviolent black protesters—placing their lives on the line to expose the moral hypocrisy and cowardice of white mobs and thugs—the FBI, the news media, and an increasingly self-conscious white Southern leadership saw to that. The lynching in Poplarville became the last—denatured—gasp of a bygone era when unrestrained recourse to violence had been a way of life, expected of all white men who took pride in themselves, their state, and their race. That Parker's death evoked the response it did, and that the nation so quickly forgot about it, served as a painful reminder that human civilization had not progressed so far that baser instincts could not surface at unexpected moments.[7]

Appendix A

Conclusions of the Justice Department about
Violations of Federal Law by Lynch Mobs
(contained in letter from Malcolm R. Wilkey
to William Rogers, May 25, 1959)

On the basis of the facts disclosed by the investigation, it would appear that there is some evidence of violence and a conspiracy to violate Section 1201 of Title 18, United States Code, relating to the transportation in interstate commerce of any person who has been unlawfully abducted and held for ransom or reward or otherwise. This evidence indicates that pursuant to a prearranged plan, Parker was taken from the jail by force and against his will, placed in Reyer's Oldsmobile, which was observed to leave the scene of the abduction and later was seen proceeding on Highway 26, across the Pearl River Bridge [Bogalusa Bridge], presumably into the State of Louisiana.

Examination of the facts developed to date reveals that any federal criminal prosecution would encounter serious difficulties. In this regard your attention is invited to the following:

1. There is no direct evidence that Parker was actually in Reyer's car at the exact time that it allegedly crossed into Louisiana.
2. Though the evidence indicates that Reyer's car reached the Louisiana side of the Pearl River Bridge, it has not been conclusively shown that the car actually crossed the boundary line between Louisiana and Mississippi.
3. There is no evidence concerning the time and place of the murder; it is impossible to determine, therefore, whether or not Parker was alive at the time of the alleged interstate transportation. If Parker was fatally shot prior to such transportation, then it

206

would appear that Section 1201 is inapplicable since the section refers to "any person," and the weight of authority seems to indicate that a corpse cannot be classified as a "person." We are aware of no cases construing Section 1201 wherein this point has been decided.

4. Investigation has revealed that known witnesses are of doubtful credibility in view of prior inconsistent statements to agents of the Federal Bureau of Investigation.

Accordingly, it is the opinion of the Criminal Division that a federal criminal prosecution based upon the facts available would not be successful.

Appendix B

Judge Sebe Dale's Charge to the Pearl River County
Grand Jury (Poplarville *Democrat,* Nov. 5, 1959)
Nov. 5, 1959, Judge Sebe Dale Delivers
Strong Charge to Grand Jury
without Mentioning Specific Cases

Gentlemen of the Jury: It has seemed well that my charge on this occasion should be written, and read as written, for a wise man of old said "that writing makes an exact man" and there are times when we should be careful, if not exact.

You are called upon to perform one of the most serious and important duties that is the part of a citizen to perform. Many of you have worn the uniform of the armed services, and before doing so you took a solemn oath. But I doubt that such duty in the armed forces was more sacred and more important than that which you are now called on to perform, and in registering to vote, thereby qualifying for jury duty, you took an oath that was just as solemn as was the oath upon entering the armed forces, for in each instance you closed with "and will bear true faith and allegiance to the same. So Help Me God." So it seems that you are no less soldiers today, guarding and protecting the welfare of your people, requiring much courage. May we truly understand and believe.

Section 1781, Mississippi Code, reads in part; "The judge shall charge the grand jury concerning its duties and expound the law to it as he shall deem proper; and he shall particularly give it in charge the statutes against gambling, bucket shops and the unlawful selling of intoxicating liquors, those relating to gambling minors, and the giving or selling them tobacco or liquors; those providing for assessment, collection and disbursement of the public revenues, state and county; those defining the duties of public officers; and especially those relating to collection and payment over fines and forfeitures those against gambling with public funds, nepotism, drunkenness and other misdemeanors in public office," with certain sections thereafter mentioning "burning of woods, election laws": and then reverting to an opening phrase, "and such others as he shall deem proper."

I do not propose to insult your intelligence by any detailed discussions of laws and offences, deeming it more important to discuss the qualities called for in the statutory requirement for jurors, for Section 1786, Miss. Code, reads in part "that the supervisors shall select and list the names of qualified persons of good intelligence, sound judgment and fair character" and your supervisors believing you possess those qualities, coming from every nook and corner of your county, you are certain to know more about acts and conduct bordering on law violations than I can possibly know. And, too, having the assistance and counsel of the DA and County Attorney all the time you are ready to determine whether such acts and conduct violates your laws.

Believing you to be men of "good intelligence", sound judgment, and fair character, and coming from parts of your county, you are particularly charged to "diligently inquire into" and "true presentment make" of all such matters and things as may be given you in charge or otherwise coming to your knowledge. Therefore, if questionable matters come to your knowledge, present such to the whole jury, in session, duly investigate and pass upon same, as men of good intelligence, sound judgment, and fair character.

Qualities needed as jurors can be known from your oath, namely: "You shall diligently inquire into and true presentment make of all such matters and things as may be given you in charge or otherwise coming to your knowledge, touching your present service. The counsel of the state, your fellows and your own you will keep secret; you shall not present any person through fear, favor or affection, or for any regard, hope or promise thereof: but in all your presentments you shall present the truth, the whole truth, and nothing but the truth, to the best of your skill and understanding. So Help You God," from which it is readily seen that any with weak knees and no backbone are lacking necessary qualifications.

Permit me to discuss briefly those duties; "you will diligently inquire into all matters given you or you otherwise know," "you will keep secret the proceedings of the grand jury," and this you should sacredly keep; "you shall not indict any person through malice, hatred or ill will," so I beg that you divest yourself of such, if there be any: "nor shall you leave any person unpresented through fear, favor or affection," thereby calling for courage, character and intelligence in abundance, needed, perhaps today, as never before, when mass thinking and mass action are making distressing demands on our people tending to make us a mere cog in the wheel of mass movement.

Let me suggest, also, that it calls for individual action, for each should make his own decision, and having made it should have the courage and conviction to stand by it, so long as he believes he is right, regardless of the person or group that opposes. Should you lack the courage of your conviction it is likely you will fail to meet the prime need of citizenship, for it seems, as said of old, "these are the times that try men's souls," and we know that "the summer soldier and sunshine patriot will not long stand" and it is further true that "he that stands it now, deserves the love and thanks of man and woman," and I fain would suggest that if there is one that does not have the courage to stand up and be counted now in the problems facing us, his room could well be used by a man.

One of the greatest of English judges, Francis Bacon, in instructing other judges as to their duties, reminded them of a fundamental truth of law, "Salus populi suprema lex," from the latin, meaning "the welfare of the people is the supreme law" and may we, as jurors and judge, ever be mindful of this truth, for truly "the welfare of the people is the supreme law" as we of this county and state face the duty of maintaining our precious rights and liberties, under the laws and courts of our state, and we should have the backbone to stand against any tyranny, whether of some individual willing to sell our birthright for a mess of political pottage, on the national level, or the reformers that would make us over, according to the mess they have made for themselves, and, yes, The Board of Sociology setting [sic] in Washington, garbed in Judicial Robes, and "dishing out" the "legal precedents" of Gunnar Myrdal.

From a great man of other days, we find these stirring truths: "The germ of the best patriotism is in the love that a man has for the home he inhabits, for the soil that he tills, for the trees that give him shade, and the hills that stand in his pathway—exalt the citizen. As the state is the unit of the government, he is the unit of the state. Teach him that his home is his castle, and his sovereignty rests beneath his hat. Make him self-respecting, self-reliant and responsible. Let him lean on the state for nothing that his own arm can do, and on the government for nothing that his state can do. Let him cultivate independence to the point of sacrifice, and learn that humble things with unbartered liberty are better than splendors brought with its price. Let him neither surrender his individuality to the government nor merge it with the mob. Let him ever stand upright and fearless, a free man born of free men, sturdy in their own strength, dowering his family in the sweat of his brow, loving to his state, loyal to his republic, earnest in his allegiance wherever it rests, but building his altar in the midst of his household gods, and shrining in his own heart the uttermost temple of its liberties," which of course you recognize as coming from Henry W. Grady as the South fought its way back from a terrible defeat, to become, as it is now, the Promised Land of the World, and the envy of all people.

The price they paid was manhood, when it seemed helpless, for then, as now, there is no substitute, while with manhood there is ample provisions in the laws and courts of the state for "the welfare of the people" to be the supreme law, for our system of courts and jurisprudence, within our state, comes as near being perfect as any that a man has ever devised. Of course, there are failures, because of the human elements, but the answer is not to surrender our laws and weaken our courts, but rather to maintain them by and through the manhood of our people. This we must not forget.

It is related that in days of old, when it was the practice for one country to raid, conquer and enslave the people of another, that such a raid and enslaving took place on the freest people then living, with a number of choice young men being carried away as slaves. But there was one that always walked with his shoulders back, his chest out, and his chin up, regardless of abuse and punishment. Years passed, when a prominent visitor noticing the manly stance and posture of this particular slave made inquiry and was told: 'he has never forgotten that he is the son of a free man, and was born a free man.' Nor must we ever forget that we are a free people, or a sovereign state, that the "welfare of the people is the supreme law," that "our sovereignty rests beneath our hat" and that the dignity of the individual and the rights of our people, county and state, under the laws and courts of our state, must be maintained at all costs.

We cannot be unmindful of the growing tendency to weaken our courts, and to put power in the hands of those not our people, and it occurs to me that if this tendency increases, with results proportionate, that is the beginning of the end of free people in our country, and by all the power of the righteousness of free people we must oppose it. Again I say there is no substitute for man-hood given us under our laws and courts, with the most important part being our jury system of which you are the greatest. Reformers have made a "hell" for the people in some of our state, and now seem "hell-bent" to foist the same upon us. Perhaps I should be ashamed for the telling, but this little story seems apropos; it is related that a young man pressed his suit very ardently upon a young lady whose father had been a regular "devil" with always the answer being, *no*. Finally, after an appeal more loving and ardent than ever before the young lady replied rather sharply, "go to father." He stood amazed, then the light dawned, whereupon he was heard to muse, "She knew that I knew that her father was dead, she knew that I knew what a life he had led, she knew that I knew what she meant when she said *go to father*," and without being disloyal to constitutional made law, the welfare of the people of our country and state demand that we have no part in the efforts to destroy our individual rights and sovereignty.

While composed of individual citizens, neither of whom must ever surrender his honest opinion simply to please someone or to harmonize any proceedings, whether individual or mass, you are a self-governing body, independent of any officer, group, or power, free from pressure from every source, except conscience under the constitution and laws of our state, and I don't believe any of you have heard of a soldier coming from battle, in which he had stood like a man, faced the fire, suffered wounds and agony, apologizing for having done so. You are now engaged in a battle for our laws and courts for the preservation of our freedom and way of life, and for the welfare of our people. There should be no quibbling, no shirking and no cause for apology for action or place.

Don't forget that "the welfare of the people is the supreme law," and that you are on guard for the people of our country and state, so like "free men," "born of free men," shoulders back, do your duty, come out like men, and keep your mouth shut.

Notes

Introduction

1. Arthur Raper, *The Tragedy of Lynching* (Chapel Hill, 1933), 293.

2. Interview with Erle Johnston, June 30, 1978; Walter Prescott Webb, "Afterword," in Walter Van Tilburg Clark, *The Ox-Bow Incident* (New York, 1960), 223.

3. Interview with William Posey, Aug. 25, 1977; interview with Keith Glatzer, Aug. 27, 1980.

Chapter 1. "Just Joe-Jacking Around"

1. Interview with James H. Walters, Sept. 11, 1980; interview with Edward William Walters, Sept. 11, 1980; interview with Virginia June (Walters) Pace, Sept. 11, 1980; Jackson *Clarion-Ledger*, Feb. 25, 1959.

2. Interview with James H. Walters, Sept. 11, 1980; interview with Edward William Walters, Sept. 11, 1980; Jackson *Clarion-Ledger*, Feb. 25, 28, 1959; New York *Times*, April 28, 1959; *The Abduction of Mack Charles Parker from the Pearl River County Jail, Poplarville, Mississippi, April 24–25, 1959* (hereafter cited as FBI Report), 1; memorandum, Malcolm R. Wilkey to William P. Rogers, May 25, 1959.

3. Poplarville *Democrat*, Feb. 26, 1959; Jackson *Daily News*, May 13, 1959, Tuskegee lynching records, file 27h (1); interview with James H. Walters, Sept. 11, 1980; William Bradford Huie, "Rape-Lynch That Shocked America," *Cavalier* 10 (May 1960), 15.

4. Interview with Lee Curtis Underwood, Aug. 25, 1980; interview with James H. Walters, Sept. 11, 1980; Jackson *Clarion-Ledger*, Feb. 25, 26, March 1, April 29, 1959; Huie, "Rape-Lynch," 61.

5. Jackson *Daily News,* May 13, 1959, Tuskegee lynching records, file 27h (1).

6. Huie, "Rape-Lynch," 61; FBI memorandum, A. Rose to J. Edgar Hoover, April 28, 1959. R. Jess Brown told FBI agents that both Underwood and Grant confirmed these events. Underwood changed his story several times, but told Brown and later Huie the same version, confirmed by Grant.

7. Interview with Lee Curtis Underwood, Aug. 25, 1980; interview with James H. Walters, Sept. 11, 1980; Huie, "Rape-Lynch," 61.

8. Gulfport *Daily Herald,* Feb. 24, 1959; Chicago *Defender,* May 9, 1959.

9. Interview with Lee Curtis Underwood, Aug. 25, 1980; Huie, "Rape-Lynch," 15, 61.

10. Huie, "Rape-Lynch," 61; Gulfport *Daily Herald,* Feb. 24, 1959; Chicago *Defender,* May 9, 1959.

11. Jackson *Clarion-Ledger,* March 5, 1959; interview with Lee Curtis Underwood, Aug. 25, 1980; interview with James H. Walters, Sept. 11, 1980.

12. Interview with James H. Walters, Sept. 11, 1980; Huie, "Rape-Lynch," 61.

13. Interview with Virginia June (Walters) Pace, Sept. 11, 1980; Jackson *Daily News,* May 13, 1959, Tuskegee lynching records, file 27h (1); Picayune *Item,* Feb. 26, 1959; Poplarville *Democrat,* Feb. 26, 1959; Gulfport *Daily Herald,* Feb. 24, 1959; Jackson *Clarion-Ledger,* Feb. 25, 26, 27, 28, March 5, 1959.

14. Huie, "Rape-Lynch," 61.

15. Interview with Virginia June (Walters) Pace, Sept. 11, 1980; interview with James H. Walters, Sept. 11, 1980; Jackson *Daily News,* May 13, 1959, Tuskegee lynching records, file 27h (1); Jackson *Clarion-Ledger,* Feb. 25, 26, 27, 28, March 5, 1959.

16. Interview with Virginia June (Walters) Pace, Sept. 11, 1980; interview with James H. Walters, Sept. 11, 1980.

17. Jackson *Daily News,* May 13, 1959; Tuskegee lynching records, file 27h (1); interview with Virginia June (Walters) Pace, Sept. 11, 1980; Gulfport *Daily Herald,* Feb. 14, 1959.

18. Jackson *Daily News,* March 13, 1959; Tuskegee lynching records, file 27h (1); interview with J. B. Richmond, June 21, 1978; interview with James H. Walters, Sept. 11, 1980.

19. Jackson *Daily News,* March 13, 1959; Tuskegee lynching records, file 27h (1).

20. Interview with Virginia June (Walters) Pace, Sept. 11, 1980; interview with James H. Walters, Sept. 11, 1980.

21. Huie, "Rape-Lynch," 62.

22. Interview with Virginia June (Walters) Pace, Sept. 11, 1980; interview with James H. Walters, Sept. 11, 1980.

23. Ibid.; Jackson *Clarion-Ledger,* Jan. 31, March 5, 1959.

24. Picayune *Item,* Feb. 26, 1959; Poplarville *Democrat,* Feb. 26, 1959; Chicago *Tribune,* Feb. 25, 1959, Tuskegee lynching records, file 27h (1).

25. Jackson *Clarion-Ledger,* Feb. 25, 26, 1959; Gulfport *Daily Herald,* Feb. 25, 26, 1959.

26. Poplarville *Democrat,* Feb. 26, 1959; Jackson *Clarion-Ledger,* Feb. 26, 28, 1959; FBI Report, 1; Huie, "Rape-Lynch," 62.

27. Letter from St. John Barrett to Ben Brooks and William Kehoe, Dec. 21, 1959; interview with Tony Rhoden, July 24, 1980.

28. Huie, "Rape-Lynch," 62; interview with James H. Walters, Sept. 11, 1980.

29. Interview with James H. Walters, Sept. 11, 1980; interview with Virginia June (Walters) Pace, Sept. 11, 1980.

30. See note 29.

31. Ibid.

32. Ibid.

33. Huie, "Rape-Lynch," 62.

34. Poplarville *Democrat,* March 5, 1959; New Orleans *Times-Picayune,* April 26, 1959; Jackson *Clarion-Ledger,* April 28, 1959; Jackson *Daily News,* Feb. 25, 1959, and Memphis *Commercial Appeal,* Feb. 27, 1959, Tuskegee lynching records, file 27h (1); interview with James H. Walters, Sept. 11, 1980; interview with Virginia June (Walters) Pace, Sept. 11, 1980.

35. Jackson *Clarion-Ledger,* Feb. 26, 1959; Chicago *Defender,* May 9, 1959.

36. Chicago *Defender,* May 9, 1959; Jackson *Clarion-Ledger,* March 5, 1959; interview with Lou Palmer, Jan. 3, 1980.

37. Chicago *Defender,* May 9, 1959; Jackson *Clarion-Ledger,* March 5, 1959; interview with Lee Curtis Underwood, Aug. 25, 1980. Underwood said that they saw the Walters car and stopped, but he denied that Parker raped June Walters.

38. Jackson *Clarion-Ledger,* Feb. 27, 28, 1959.

39. Jackson *Clarion-Ledger,* Feb. 27, 28, 1959; New Orleans *Times-Picayune,* April 26, 1959; Jackson *Daily News,* Feb. 27, 1959, and Memphis *Commercial Appeal,* Feb. 26, 1959, Tuskegee lynching records, file 27h (1).

40. Poplarville *Democrat,* March 5, 1959; Picayune *Item,* March 5, 1959.

41. Chicago *Defender,* March 5, 1959; interview with Tony Rhoden, July 24, 1980; interview with Ruthamay Sanford, Sept. 1, 1980; interview with Lou Palmer, Jan. 3, 1980; interview with Ruth Underwood, Aug. 12, 1980.

42. New Orleans *Times-Picayune,* April 27, 1959; Chicago *Defender,* May 9, 26, 1959; interview with R. Jess Brown, Aug. 30, 1977; Jackson *Clarion-Ledger,* April 28, 1959. The NAACP largely stayed out of the affair except to mail telegrams to various parties; see NAACP papers, Group III, Boxes B-80, B-327, B-412, B-383, B-188, B-20, B-191.

43. Interview with William M. Posey, Aug. 25, 1977; interview with George Rester, Jr., Feb. 27, 1979; interview with Joshua Morse, June 21, 1979; interview with Mrs. J. M. Howard, Aug. 26, 1977.

44. Jackson *Clarion-Ledger,* April 28, 1959; New Orleans *Times-Picayune,* April 26, 27, 1959; Chicago *Defender,* May 2, 1959; Gulfport *Daily Herald,* May 19, 1959.

45. Chicago *Defender,* May 2, 1959; interview with Ruth Underwood, Aug. 12, 1980.

46. New Orleans *Times-Picayune,* Nov. 7, 1959; interview with R. Jess Brown, Aug. 30, 1977; interview with Bill Minor, June 19, 1979; interview with Erle Johnston, July 30, 1979; interview with Joshua Morse, Jr., June 21, 1979.

47. New Orleans *Times-Picayune,* Nov. 7, 1959; interview with Joshua Morse, Jr., June 21, 1979; interview with Bill Minor, June 19, 1979; interview with Erle Johnston, July 30, 1979.

48. Interview with Erle Johnston, July 30, 1979; New Orleans *Times-Picayune,* Nov. 7, 1959.

49. Letter from St. John Barrett to Ben Brooks and William Kehoe, Dec. 21, 1959; Memphis *Commercial Appeal*, April 14, 1959; Tuskegee lynching records, file 27h (1); Gulfport *Daily Herald*, April 20, 1959; Poplarville *Democrat*, April 16, 23, 1959; interview with R. Jess Brown, Aug. 30, 1977.

50. Memphis *Commercial Appeal*, April 14, 1959; Tuskegee lynching records, file 27e (2); Poplarville *Democrat*, April 16, 23, 1959; Jackson *Clarion-Ledger*, April 23, 1959; New Orleans *Times-Picayune*, April 26, 1959; interview with R. Jess Brown, Aug. 30, 1977.

51. As in the *Goldsby* case, had Brown's ploy been successful, and it would have been, Parker would not have been released necessarily. Goldsby was not. Parker's case would have been remanded to the district court for retrial. See the hearings of the Senate Subcommittee on Constitutional Rights, May 28, 1959, testimony of J. P. Coleman.

52. Poplarville *Democrat*, April 23, 1959; Gulfport *Daily Herald*, April 20, 1959; Jackson *Clarion-Ledger*, April 26, 1959.

53. FBI interview report, May 13, 1959, pp. 28–29.

Chapter 2. Some Proud Southern Whites

1. Poplarville *Democrat*, Aug. 11, 1977; New York *Times*, April 27, 1959; Mississippi *County Business Patterns*, 26-10, 26-13, 26-16, furnished by Congressman Trent Lott's office; interview with William M. Posey, Aug. 25, 1977; interview with Arthur L. Smith, Feb. 26, 1979.

2. Jackson *Clarion-Ledger*, March 8, 1959.

3. U.S. Bureau of the Census, *1960 . . . Mississippi*, 26-198, 26-199, 26-171; "Mississippi Community Data," furnished by Congressman Trent Lott; Poplarville *Democrat*, April 30, 1959; Chicago *Defender*, May 9, 1959.

4. Poplarville *Democrat*, May 7, 1959.

5. V. O. Key, Jr., *Southern Politics in State and Nation* (New York, 1949), 229–47.

6. Daniel T. Williams, Introduction to *The Lynching Records at Tuskegee Institute* (Tuskegee, 1969), 6–7.

7. Charles S. Johnson, *Growing Up in the Black Belt: Negro Youth in the Rural South* (New York, 1941), 317–18.

8. Key, *Southern Politics* 230–50; Paul Lewinson, *Race, Class and Party* (New York, 1932), 190–91; Charles N. Fortenberry and F. Glenn Abney, "Mississippi: Unreconstructed and Unredeemed," in William C. Havard, ed., *The Changing Politics of the South* (Baton Rouge, 1972), 473, 480 (hereafter cited as Fortenberry and Abney).

9. Key, *Southern Politics*, 229; Fortenberry and Abney, 485, 506–7.

10. "Mississippi Community Data."

11. Interview with George Vaught Moody, Feb. 26, 1979; interview with Joshua Morse, June 21, 1979.

12. Ibid.; U.S. Bureau of the Census, *1960 . . . Mississippi*, 26-70; see also James W. Silver, *Mississippi: The Closed Society* (New York, 1966).

13. Interview with George Vaught Moody, Feb. 26, 1979.

14. Jackson *Clarion-Ledger*, April 26, 1959.

15. FBI Report, 27-28; interview with George Vaught Moody, Feb. 26, 1979.

16. Florence Mars, *Witness in Philadelphia* (Baton Rouge, 1977), 65-69.

17. A considerable amount of rivalry existed between Picayune (population 7,034) and Poplarville over which town should serve as county seat. Senator Theodore Bilbo had long ago moved the county seat from Picayune to Poplarville. Residents of Picayune always grumbled about getting it back.

18. FBI Report, 49; interview with Erle Johnston, July 30, 1979.

19. Interview with Eddie Ladner, Sept. 22, 1978, March 1, 5, 1979; interview with Joshua Morse, Jr., June 21, 1979.

20. FBI Report, 242–43, 340; interview with R. Jess Brown, Aug. 30, 1977.

21. Washington *Post*, May 26, 1959; interview with Joshua Morse, Jr., June 21, 1979.

22. FBI Report, 255–56.

23. FBI Report, 256; Washington *Post*, May 26, 1959.

24. FBI Report, 242; Jackson *Clarion-Ledger*, May 14, 1959; interview with Jewel Alford, Sept. 13, 1978; interview with George Vaught Moody, Feb. 26, 1979; interview with Eddie Ladner, Sept. 22, 1978, March 1, 5, 1979.

25. Jackson *Clarion-Ledger*, May 14, 1959; Washington *Post*, May 14, 1959; interview with Arthur L. Smith, Feb. 26, 1979; interview with Cecil Smith, March 9, 1979; interview with Bill Minor, June 19, 1979; interview with Erle Johnston, July 30, 1979.

26. Jackson *Clarion-Ledger*, May 14, 1959; Washington *Post*, May 14, 1959; interview with Arthur L. Smith, Feb. 26, 1979; interview with Cecil Smith, March 9, 1979; interview with Bill Minor, June 19, 1979; interview with Joshua Morse, Jr., June 21, 1979; interview with Erle Johnston, July 30, 1979; interview with Keith Glatzer, Aug. 27, 1980; FBI Report, 233; Atlanta *World*, May 14, 1959, and Jackson *Times-Union*, May 14, 1959, Tuskegee lynching records, file 27a.

27. Gulfport *Daily Herald*, May 19, 1959; *Down South* 7 (July 1959), 17; interview with Joshua Morse, Jr., June 21, 1979.

28. Interview with George Vaught Moody, Feb. 26, 1979; interview with Eddie Ladner, Sept. 22, 1978.

29. Picayune *Item*, April 23, 1959.

30. Justice Department memorandum, Joseph M. F. Ryan, Jr., to W. Wilson White, July 1, 1959, 3.

31. FBI Report, 338–40; Jackson *Clarion-Ledger*, May 17, 1959.

32. FBI Report, 338, 340–41, 352; Ryan to Murphy, p. 3.

33. Interview with James H. Walters, Sept. 11, 1980; interview with Virginia June (Walters) Pace, Sept. 11, 1980; with Edward William Walters, Sept. 11, 1980; FBI Special Agent's Report, May 19, 1959, c.

34. Huie, "Rape-Lynch," 14–5; interview with James H. Walters, Sept. 11, 1980; interview with Edward William Walters, Sept. 11, 1980; interview with Jimmy Swann, Sept. 2, 1980.

35. Interview with James H. Walters, Sept. 11, 1980; interview with Edward William Walters, Sept. 11, 1980; interview with Paul Phillips, Sept. 3, 1980; interview with Jimmy Swann, Sept. 2, 1980; interview with Elliott Chaize, Aug. 26, 1980.

36. Washington *Post*, May 14, 1959; FBI Report, 233; *Life* 42 (June 1, 1959), 24–25; interview with Joshua Morse, Jr., June 21, 1979; interview with Bill

Minor, June 19, 1979; Talladega *Daily Home,* April 23, 1959, Tuskegee lynching records, file 27a.

37. FBI Report, 186; interview with Cecil Smith, March 9, 1979.

38. Wilkey to Rogers, May 25, 1959; interview with Richard Angelico, Sept. 26, 1977; *Life* 42 (June 1, 1959), 24–25; Anthony Lewis, *Portrait of a Decade* (New York, 1964), 212.

39. Interview with Jewel Alford, Sept. 13, 1978; Wilkey to Rogers, May 25, 1959; FBI Report, 188; interview with Eddie Ladner, Sept. 22, 1978; interview with Joshua Morse, Jr., June 21, 1979; interview with Bill Minor, June 19, 1979.

40. FBI Report, 27–28, 214–15.

41. Justice Department memorandum, Joseph Ryan to W. Wilson White, July 1, 1959, 4–6; FBI Report, 214–15.

42. Wilkey to Rogers, May 28, 1959; FBI Report, 188; FBI memorandum, May 25, 1959, p. 24.

43. FBI Report, 29–30, 24, 203–4, 211, 232; Ryan to White, July 1, 1959, p. 8.

44. FBI Report, 20204; Ryan to White, July 1, 1959, pp. 8–9.

45. FBI memorandum, Jackson Branch, Feb. 16, 1971; anonymous letter from a Poplarville resident to FBI, received May 25, 1959; interview with Jewel Alford, Sept. 13, 1978; Jackson *Clarion-Ledger,* May 28, 1959; interview with Joshua Morse, Jr., June 21, 1979; Rosen to Hoover, May 20, 1959.

Chapter 3. A Quiet Friday Evening

1. FBI memoranda, May 25, 1959, p. 24; FBI interview report, May 17, 1959, pp. 2–3.

2. FBI Report, 70–71, 73, 220; Ryan to White, July 1, 1959.

3. FBI Report, 220–22; Ryan to White, July 1, 1959.

4. FBI Report, 23, 221–22; Washington *Post,* April 25, 1959; interview with Jewel Alford, Sept. 13, 1978.

5. FBI Report, 80–84; interview with Eddie Ladner, Sept. 22, 1978.

6. FBI Report, 80–84, 124–25; *Time* 13 (May 4, 1959), 16; Picayune *Item,* April 30, 1959; Ryan to White, July 1, 1959, p. 5.

7. New Orleans *Times-Picayune,* April 26, 1959.

8. FBI Report, 84, 117–18, 124–25; Ryan to White, July 1, 1959, p. 5; Jackson *Clarion-Ledger,* April 26, Nov. 1, 1959; Washington *Post,* April 25, 1959; New York *Times,* April 26, 1959; Chicago *Defender,* May 2, 1959; Picayune *Item,* April 30, 1959.

9. FBI Report, 124–25.

10. Ibid.

11. Ryan to White, July 1, 1959, 6; Chicago *Defender,* May 7, 1959; New Orleans *Times-Picayune,* April 26, 1959; FBI Report, 85; Jackson *Clarion-Ledger,* April 26, 1959; *Time* 73 (May 4, 1959), 16.

12. Washington *Post,* April 25, 1959; FBI Report, 85, 125; Jackson *Clarion-Ledger,* April 26, 1959; *Time* 73 (May 4, 1959), 16.

13. Ryan to White, July 1, 1959, 6.

14. FBI Report, 86; Picayune *Item,* April 30, 1959; New Orleans *Times-Picayune,* April 26, 1959.

15. *Life* 46 (May 4, 1959), 44.

16. Jackson *Clarion-Ledger,* April 26, 1959; Gulfport *Daily Herald,* April 25, 1959; New York *Times,* April 26, 1959.

17. Interview with Dimple (Burge) Shill, Nov. 25, 1979.

18. Interview with George Vaught Moody, Feb. 26, 1979; interview with Mrs. J. M. Howard, Aug. 25, 1977.

19. Interview with Dimple (Burge) Shill, Nov. 25, 1979; interview with Liz Sandlin, Dec. 2, 1979; Chicago *Defender,* May 2, 1959; FBI Report, 23, 221–22; interview with Jewel Alford, Sept. 3, 1978.

20. Ryan to White, July 1, 1959, 6; Jackson *Clarion-Ledger,* April 27, 28, 1959.

21. FBI Report, 87; Jackson *Clarion-Ledger,* April 27, 28, 1959; Picayune *Item,* April 30, 1959; Poplarville *Democrat,* April 30, 1959; interview with Alvin Gipson, June 11, 1979.

22. Although the FBI unearthed strong evidence that the car carrying Parker crossed the Pearl River into Louisiana (confirmed by Arthur Smith's statement), neither the grand juries nor the Justice Department found it sufficient, which prevented a federal indictment for kidnapping against the mob members. See Appendix A.

23. Interview with Keith Glatzer, Aug. 27, 1980; interview with Richard Angelico, Sept. 26, 1977; Rose to Hoover, Dec. 24, 1959, Bachman to Hoover, Nov. 11, 1959. That J. P. Walker was the man who actually murdered M. C. Parker was common gossip in Poplarville, and continued to be at the time of the interviews for this book, but Walker never admitted to having anything to do with the actual lynching.

24. Ryan to White, July 2, 1959; interview with Edward William Walters, Sept. 11, 1980.

25. FBI Report, 203–4, 232; interview with Mrs. J. M. Howard, Aug. 25, 1977; Ryan to White, July 1, 1959, p. 7.

26. Interview with Joshua Morse, Jr., June 21, 1979; FBI Report, 30, 35, 40. Orr later told FBI agents in a statement he refused to sign that had he known of an attempt to abduct Parker, he would not have attempted to prevent it, since it was a matter for the sheriff to handle and no concern of his. Petey Carver admitted later that had Parker gotten off in court, he personally would have favored "drastic action" to punish him. Neither man signed any statements to the FBI.

27. FBI Report, 31, 35.

Chapter 4. The Morning After the Night Before

1. Interview with George Vaught Moody, Feb. 26, 1979; FBI Report, 21.

2. Interview with George Vaught Moody, Feb. 26, 1979; interview with Eddie Ladner, Sept. 22, 1978; FBI Report, 21–22; Ryan to White, July 7, 1959, 13.

3. FBI Report, 21–23; interview with Bill Minor, June 19, 1979.

4. FBI Report, 23–24, 42, 122.

5. Ibid; U.S. Congress, Senate, Subcommittee on Constitutional Rights, Judiciary Committee, *Civil Rights,* Hearings, 57th Congress, 2d Session, May 28, 1959, 1303–4; interview with Joseph M. F. Ryan, Aug. 21, 1980.

6. FBI Report, 24–25; interview with Ralph W. Bachman, June 11, 1979.

7. FBI Report, 29–30, 34, 203–4, 212, 232.

8. FBI Report, 36.

9. FBI Report, 39–40.

10. FBI Report, 27–28, 43, 70–71, 73; Ryan to White, July 1, 1959.

11. Interview with Keith Glatzer, Aug. 27, 1980.

12. FBI Report, 44; New York *Times,* April 26, 1959; Washington *Post,* April 26, 1959; Los Angeles *Times,* April 26, 1959; New Orleans *Times-Picayune,* April 26, 1959; Poplarville *Democrat,* April 30, 1959; Picayune *Item,* April 30, 1959.

13. Gulfport *Daily Herald,* April 25, 1959.

14. FBI Report, 44; Jackson *Clarion-Ledger,* April 26, 1959; Gulfport *Daily Herald,* April 25, 1959; interview with Mrs. J. M. Howard, Aug. 25, 26, 1977; interview with George Vaught Moody, Feb. 26, 1979; New Orleans *Times-Picayune,* April 27, 1959.

15. FBI Report, 180–81; Hoover to Rogers, May 25, 1959; interview with Eddie Ladner, March 5, 1979; interview with Edward William Walters, Sept. 11, 1980; interview with James H. Walters, Sept. 11, 1980.

16. Interview with George Vaught Moody, Feb. 26, 1979; interview with Bill Minor, June 19, 1979; Silver, *Mississippi: The Closed Society,* 8.

17. Picayune *Item,* April 30, 1959; Jackson *Clarion-Ledger,* April 26, 1959.

18. Jackson *Clarion-Ledger,* May 30, 1959; New York *Times,* May 30, 1959.

19. Hodding Carter III, *The South Strikes Back* (New York, 1959), 62–63.

20. Ibid., 51.

21. Ibid., 15. Violence had gradually fallen into disrepute among the white Southerners as a means of enforcing white supremacy after World War II. Especially after Emmett Till, according to Hodding Carter III, "lynch law was no longer practiced or condoned by the mass of southern whites as it had once been, but there were still Negroes who found that the doors of their jails were conveniently open when the mob came" (p. 15). After 1954, whites organized themselves for massive resistance against what they felt was Communist infiltration led by the NAACP and the "pinkish" Supreme Court. The creation of the white Citizens Councils in Mississippi brought about the decline of Southern liberalism, or moderation on racial matters. The propaganda effort was massive. And when the legislature created the State Sovereignty Commission, this solidified the ranks of whites.

22. Ibid., 18–20.

23. New Orleans *Times-Picayune,* April 26, 1959; Jackson *Clarion-Ledger,* April 26, 1959; Gulfport *Daily Herald,* April 25, 1959; Brown vacillated on his request for a change of venue. Local papers reported he had requested it. On Saturday after the lynching he denied he had, adding that he had been treated "as any other attorney." But in an interview on Aug. 30, 1977, he claimed that he was convinced at the time "something would have happened if not that weekend, then in court, Monday."

24. Gulfport *Daily Herald,* April 25, 1959, Jan. 16, 1960; Jackson *Clarion-Ledger,* April 26, 1959; interview with Cliff Sessions, June 12, 1979; Coleman neglected to mention during his press conference the 1955 lynching of Emmett Till or the January 1950 lynching in which he himself as a district court judge presided over the trial of the lynchers in which two men received life sentences and a third, ten years. See the testimony by Coleman before the Senate Subcommittee on Constitutional Rights, May 28, 1959, 1303–4.

25. Gulfport *Daily Herald,* April 25, 1959; Jackson *Clarion-Ledger,* April 26, 1959; interview with Donald G. Burkhalter, June 28, 1977.

26. New York *Times,* April 26, 1959; New Orleans *Times-Picayune,* April 26, May 28, Nov. 6, 1959; Jackson *Clarion-Ledger,* April 26, 1959; Jackson *Daily News,* May 22, 1959, clipping in FOIA material from Justice Department; interview with Ralph Bachman, June 11, 1979. In 1959 the New Orleans headquarters controlled regional offices in southern Mississippi.

27. Justice Department memorandum, J. Edgar Hoover to William Rogers, May 25, 1959; interview with Cliff Sessions, June 12, 1979; interview with Ralph Bachman, June 11, 1979; interview with Claude Sitton, June 19, 1979.

Chapter 5. *A Small Town in Mississippi*

1. Carver's mother was a sister of Orr's mother.

2. Interview with Eddie Ladner, Sept. 22, 1978; FBI Report, 220–22. See Wilbur J. Cash, *The Mind of the South* (New York, 1941), 65–66, 90–91.

3. Interview with Mrs. Pat Hyde, Sept. 30, 1979.

4. Interview with George Vaught Moody, Feb. 26, 1979; interview with Bill Minor, June 19, 1979; Gulfport *Daily Herald,* Jan. 16, 1960.

5. New York *Times,* April 26, 1959; New Orleans *Times-Picayune,* April 26, 1959; interview with R. Jess Brown, Aug. 30, 1977.

6. Jackson *Clarion-Ledger,* April 26, 27, 1959.

7. New York *Times,* April 26, 1959; Gulfport *Daily Herald,* April 25, 1959.

8. New York *Times,* April 26, 1959; New Orleans *Times-Picayune,* April 26, 1959.

9. Washington *Post,* April 26, 1959.

10. New York *Times,* April 26, 1959; New Orleans *Times-Picayune,* April 26, 1959; interview with Will D. Campbell, June 19, 1978; testimony of Joe Patterson before House, U.S. Congress, Judiciary Subcommittee, April 23, 1959.

11. NAACP press release, April 30, 1959, NAACP papers, Group III, Box B-80, LC; Jackson *Clarion-Ledger,* April 26, 1959.

12. Washington *Post,* April 27, 1959.

13. New Orleans *Times-Picayune,* April 27, 1959; interview with Keith Glatzer, Aug. 27, 1980.

14. Chicago *Defender,* May 2, 9, 1959.

15. Interview with R. Jess Brown, Aug. 30, 1977.

16. Chicago *Defender,* May 2, 9, 1959; Jackson *Clarion-Ledger,* April 26, 1959; New York *Times,* April 27, 1959; New Orleans *Times-Picayune,* April 27, 1959.

17. Interview with Tony Rhoden, July 24, 1980.

18. *Look* 24 (Jan. 18, 1960), 82–83.

19. Interview with Erle Johston, July 30, 1979; interview with Mrs. Pat Hyde, Sept. 30, 1979.

20. New York *Times,* April 27, 1959.

21. Ibid.

22. Interview with George Vaught Moody, Feb. 26, 1979; interview with George Rester, Jr., Feb. 27, 1979; interview with Mrs. Osborne Moody, Feb. 26, 1979; Jackson *Clarion-Ledger,* April 26, 1959; interview with Eddie Ladner, March 5, 1979.

23. Interview with Claude Sitton, June 19, 1979; interview with Cliff Sessions, June 12, 1978; interview with Bill Minor, June 19, 1979.

24. *Look* 24 (Jan. 19, 1960), 82–83.

25. Interview with Mrs. J. M. Howard, Aug. 25, 1977; interview with William Posey, Aug. 25, 1977. Posey thought he could name some of the participants. When asked to do so, he quickly changed the subject. Interview with Lawrence Halladay, Aug. 25, 1977. Halladay said that under no circumstances would it be advisable to ask locals about the lynching because of some of the "hotheads" in the area; at the time Jeff Lee was one of his deputies. Interview with Brad Williams, Aug. 25, 1977; interview with Sam Hopkins, Aug. 25, 1977; interview with Eddie Ladner, Sept. 22, 1978; New York *Times,* Jan. 4, 1960; interview with Joshua Morse, Jr., June 21, 1979. Alvin Gipson was still worried in an interview twenty years after the lynching that his phone was tapped by people friendly to the mob. Interview, June 11, 1979.

26. Poplarville *Democrat,* April 30, May 28, June 4, 1959.

27. New York *Times,* Jan. 4, 1960.

28. Poplarville *Democrat,* May 7, 1959.

29. Jackson *Clarion-Ledger,* April 27, 1959; Gulfport *Daily Herald,* April 27, 1959; *Look* 24 (Jan. 19, 1960), 82–83; Chicago *Defender,* May 9, 1959.

30. Interview with Cliff Sessions, June 11, 1979; interview with Claude Sitton, June 19, 1979; interview with Bill Minor, June 19, 1979. Newsmen reported the same friendly atmosphere following Emmett Till's lynching.

31. *Look* 24 (Jan. 19, 1960), 82–83.

32. Poplarville *Democrat,* Jan. 10, 1960.

33. *Look* 24 (Jan. 19, 1960), 82–83. Chicago *Defender,* May 9, 1959.

34. Washington *Post,* April 27, 1959.

35. Jackson *Clarion-Ledger,* April 27, 1959; New Orleans *Times-Picayune,* April 27, 1959.

36. When discovered, Parker's body wore only an undershirt and underpants. His Ivy League-style pants were never recovered. New Orleans *Times-Picayune,* April 27, 1959; New York *Times,* April 27, 1959.

37. New Orleans *Times-Picayune,* April 27, 1959; interview with Cliff Sessions, June 11, 1979.

38. Washington *Post,* April 27, 1959; interview with Eddie Ladner, Sept. 22, 1978; New Orleans *Times-Picayune,* April 27, 1959; interview with Cliff Sessions, June 11, 1979.

39. Gulfport *Daily Herald,* April 27, 1959; Jackson *Clarion-Ledger,* April 27, 28, 1959.

40. New Orleans *Times-Picayune,* April 28, 1959; New York *Times,* April 28, 1959; Washington *Post,* April 28, 1959; interview with Bill Minor, June 19, 1979. Joshua Morse claimed that before the lynching and immediately afterward Sebe Dale comported himself with dignity and courtesy in court. Only later, Morse claimed, when tempers flared did Dale act like the typical Bilbo protégé. Interview, June 21, 1979.

41. Jackson *Clarion-Ledger,* April 28, 1959; New Orleans *Times-Picayune,* April 28, 1959; Picayune *Item,* April 30, 1959. The Mississippi legislature agreed with Dale and passed a law that allowed nonvoting residents to serve on juries. Interview with Joshua Morse, Jr., June 21, 1979.

42. A. Rosen to J. Edgar Hoover, April 28, 1959; interview with R. Jess Brown, Aug. 30, 1977; interview with Lee Curtis Underwood, Aug. 21, 1980.

Chapter 6. "The Floodgates of Hate and Hell"

1. Gulfport *Daily Herald,* May 14, 1959; Poplarville *Democrat,* May 14, 28, 1959; Jackson *Clarion-Ledger,* May 19, 1959; interview with Mrs. Pat Hyde, Sept. 30, 1979; interview with Mrs. Osborne Moody, Feb. 26, 1979; Picayune *Item,* May 21, 1959; New Orleans *Times-Picayune,* Nov. 7, 1959.

2. Jackson *Clarion-Ledger,* April 28, 1959. Eddie Ladner claimed in an interview that most townspeople still believed the mob beat up Moody for the keys. Interview, Sept. 22, 1978. FBI Report, 64–68, 214.

3. Governor Coleman held daily press briefings about the lynching until he went to Washington to testify on May 28. Gulfport *Daily Herald,* April 28, 1959; New Orleans *Times-Picayune,* April 28, 1959; Jackson *Clarion-Ledger,* April 28, 1959; Atlanta *Journal,* April 28, 1959, Tuskegee lynching records file 27a.

4. New Orleans *Times-Picayune,* April 28, 1959; Gulfport *Daily Herald,* April 28, 1959; New York *Times,* April 28, 1959.

5. Memo, the Attorney General to the Director, FBI, Dec. 28, 1959.

6. Atlanta *Journal,* April 28, 1959; Tuskegee lynching records, file 27a; interview with Cliff Sessions, June 12, 1979.

7. Gulfport *Daily Herald,* April 28, 1979; New Orleans *Times-Picayune,* April 28, 1959.

8. Interview with Mrs. Pat Hyde, Sept. 30, 1979; interview with Erle Johnston, July 30, 1979; Gulfport *Daily Herald,* April 28, 1959.

9. Interviews with Virginia June (Walters) Pace and James H. Walters, Sept. 11, 1980.

10. Memorandum, J. P. Mohr to Clyde Tolson, Nov. 17, 1959; Gulfport *Daily Herald,* April 28, 1959; New Orleans *Times-Picayune,* April 28, 1959; FBI Report, 337–55; interview with Virginia June (Walters) Pace, Sept. 11, 1980; interview with James H. Walters, Sept. 11, 1980; Montgomery *Advertiser,* May 7, 1959, Tuskegee lynching records, file 27a; Picayune *Item,* April 30, 1959; New York *Times,* April 28, 1959, Jan. 6, 1960; Gulfport *Daily Herald,* April 28, 1959; A. Jones to DeLoach, April 15, 1969, 2.

11. New York *Times,* April 28, 1959; Montgomery *Advertiser,* May 7, 1959, Tuskegee lynching records, file 27a; Gulfport *Daily Herald,* April 28, 1959; NAACP press release, April 30, 1959; telegram, Wilkins to members of Senate and House committees, April 27, 1959, NAACP papers, Group III, Box B-80, LC.

12. New York *Times,* April 28, 1959; Gulfport *Daily Herald,* April 29, 1959; Washington *Post,* April 28, 1959; New Orleans *Times-Picayune,* April 29, 1959.

13. Gulfport *Daily Herald,* April 29, 1959; New York *Times,* April 29, 1959; Washington *Post,* April 29, 1959.

14. New Orleans *Times-Picayune,* April 29, 1959; Jackson *State-Times,* April 28, 1959; Memphis *Commercial Appeal,* April 29, 1959; Tuskegee lynching records, file 27a.

15. All editorials quoted in Montgomery *Advertiser,* April 30, 1959, Tuskegee lynching records, file 27a.

16. Chicago *Defender,* May 9, 1959; Birmingham *Post-Herald,* May 1, 1959, Tuskegee lynching records, file 27a; *The Nation* 188 (May 9, 1959), 418; *Commonweal* 70 (May 8, 1959), 140–41.

17. Washington *Post,* April 29, 1959.

18. Jackson *Clarion-Ledger*, April 29, 1959; New York *Times*, April 29, 1959; Poplarville *Democrat*, June 28, 1959; interview with Elliott Chaize, Aug. 26, 1980

19. Interview with Lou Palmer, Jan. 3, 1980; Chicago *Defender*, May 9, 1959.

20. Interview with Lou Palmer, Jan. 3, 1980.

21. Ibid.; Chicago *Defender*, May 9, 1959.

22. Ibid.; New Orleans *Times-Picayune*, April 30, 1959.

23. Chicago *Defender*, May 9, 1959; Memphis *Commercial Appeal*, May 3, 1959, Tuskegee lynching records, file 27a; interview with Lou Palmer, Jan. 3, 1980.

24. Chicago *Defender*, May 9, 1959; interview with Lou Palmer, Jan. 3, 1980.

25. Jackson *Clarion-Ledger*, April 30, 1959.

26. Gulfport *Daily Herald*, April 30, 1959; Birmingham *Post-Herald*, May 1, 1959, Tuskegee lynching records, file 27a.

27. New Orleans *Times-Picayune*, April 30, 1959; Washington *Post*, April 30, 1959; Chicago *Defender*, May 9, 1949. Curiously, after its first account of Underwood's new version of his activity on the night of the rape (in the May 9 edition), the paper never mentioned it or Underwood again. While the paper continued to run follow-up stories about the investigation, this crucial story disappeared. All papers, black and white, simply dropped it. Such carelessness left unanswered important questions about the charges Mississippi lodged against Parker.

28. Interview with Nathan Straus, Jr., May 12, 1980; Poplarville *Democrat*, May 7, 1959; Gulfport *Daily Herald*, April 30, 1959; telegram, Roy Wilkins to President Eisenhower, April 27, 1959, NAACP papers, Group III, Box B-80, LC.

29. Birmingham *Post-Herald*, May 1, 1959, Tuskegee lynching records, file 27a.

30. New Orleans *Times-Picayune*, May 5, 1959.

31. Wilkins to Morsell, Moon, Odom, DeVore, Cater, April 27, 1959; Wilkins to Herman Gorodesky, June 4, 1959, NAACP papers, Group III, Box B-80, LC. The lame actions Wilkins took were an embarrassment to the NAACP. "On the Poplarville lynching we have done the following":

1. Sent a telegram to all members of the House and Senate Judiciary Committees.

2. Sent a mimeographed letter to all Congressmen except those in a few Deep South states. This consisted mostly of quoting to them the telegrams sent to members of the Judiciary Committee.

3. Sent telegram to the presidents of 100 branches asking them to write Senators, get others to do so, etc.

4. Sent a letter directly to members of the executive committee of the branches asking them to write letters and to get others to do so.

5. We have in process a letter to all Senators (individually typed) urging support for strong civil rights bill, etc.

Wilkins to Clarence Mitchell, May 1, 1959, NAACP papers, Group III, Box B-80, LC.

32. Poplarville *Democrat*, May 7, 1959; Gulfport *Daily Herald*, April 30, 1959; Memphis *Commercial Appeal*, May 5, 1959, Tuskegee lynching records, file 27a.

33. Poplarville *Democrat,* April 30, 1959; interview with Eddie Ladner, Sept. 22, 1978, March 1, 5, 1979; FBI Report, 79–139; Washington *Post,* May 1, 1959; interview with Joshua Morse, Jr., June 21, 1979; Rosen to Hoover, May 4, 1959.

34. New Orleans *Times-Picayune,* May 1, 1959; interview with Ralph Bachman, June 11, 1979.

35. Washington *Post,* May 4, 1959; Jackson *Clarion-Ledger,* May 4, 1959; interview with A. B. Caldwell, Aug. 15, 1980.

36. Jackson *Clarion-Ledger,* May 3, 1959; Washington *Post,* May 3, 1959.

37. Washington *Post,* May 3, 1959; New Orleans *Times-Picayune,* May 5, 1959. Brown refused to attend when informed of Mrs. Parker's departure. Washington *Post,* May 3, 1959; Chicago *Defender,* June 6, 1959.

Chapter 7. *"Don't Let Them Kill Me"*

1. FBI Report, 166; Jackson *Clarion-Ledger,* May 5, 1959; Birmingham *News,* May 5, 1959, Tuskegee lynching records, file 27a; interview with Keith Glatzer, Aug. 27, 1980.

2. Washington *Post,* May 5, 1959; Jackson *Clarion-Ledger,* May 5, 1959; FBI Report, 166; New Orleans *Times-Picayune,* May 5, 1959.

3. New York *Times,* May 5, 1959; FBI Report, 166; Memphis *Commercial Appeal,* May 5, 1959, Charleston *News and Courier,* May 5, 1959, Talladega *Daily Home,* May 5, 1959, Tuskegee lynching records, file 27a.

4. FBI Report, 167; Jackson *Clarion-Ledger,* May 8, 1959; New Orleans *Times-Picayune,* May 5, 1959; Gulfport *Daily Herald,* May 5, 1959.

5. Gulfport *Daily Herald,* May 5, 1959; New York *Times,* May 25, 1959; FBI Report, 167–70.

6. Interview with Tony Rhoden, July 24, 1980; interview with Lou Palmer, Jan. 3, 1980; interview with Ruth Underwood, Aug. 12, 1980.

7. Interview with Tony Rhoden, July 24, 1980; interview with Lou Palmer, Jan. 3, 1980.

8. Interview with Tony Rhoden, July 24, 1980.

9. Ibid.

10. Ibid.

11. Ibid.

12. Ibid.

13. Ibid.

14. Ibid.

15. Ibid.

16. Ibid.

17. Ibid.

18. New Orleans *Times-Picayune,* May 6, 1959; Gulfport *Daily Herald,* May 5, 1959; Washington *Post,* May 6, 1959; Montgomery *Advertiser,* May 6, 1959, Tuskegee lynching records, file 27a.

19. New Orleans *Times-Picayune,* May 5, 6, 1959; Chicago *Defender,* May 16, 1959; Washington *Post,* May 5, 6, 1959; Gulfport *Daily Herald,* May 9, 1959; Jackson *Clarion-Ledger,* May 6, 1959; Montgomery *Advertiser,* May 6, 1959, Tuskegee lynching records, file 27a; interview with Tony Rhoden, July 24, 1980.

20. Chicago *Defender*, May 16, 23, 1959; interview with Tony Rhoden, July 24, 1980.

21. Chicago *Defender*, May 16, 1959; Washington *Post*, May 9, 1959; Gulfport *Daily Herald*, May 9, 1959.

22. Jackson *Clarion-Ledger*, May 9, 1959; Gulfport *Daily Herald*, May 9, 1959.

23. Interview with Mrs. Pat Hyde, Sept. 30, 1979; interview with Eddie Ladner, Sept. 22, 1978. The funeral director, E. T. Hall, later admitted he had had no idea who was going to pay his fee. The state finally did. Poplarville *Democrat*, April 30, May 7, 1959; Picayune *Item*, May 7, 1959; Alabama *Journal*, May 14, 1959, Tuskegee lynching records, file 27a.

24. Jackson *Clarion-Ledger*, May 6, 1959; interview with James H. Walters, Sept. 11, 1980.

25. Jackson *Clarion-Ledger*, May 6, 1959.

26. Interview with George Vaught Moody, Feb. 26, 1979.

27. Poplarville *Democrat*, May 7, 1959.

28. Gulfport *Daily Herald*, May 6, 1959; Chicago *Crusader*, May 2, 1959, Tuskegee lynching records, file 27a.

29. Jackson *Clarion-Ledger*, May 6, 1959; New York *Times*, May 6, 1959; Washington *Post*, May 6, 1959.

30. New Orleans *Times-Picayune*, May 6, 1959; Chicago *Defender*, May 16, 1959.

31. Poplarville *Democrat*, May 14, 1959; Picayune *Item*, May 14, 1959; Jackson *Daily News*, May 12, 1959, Tuskegee lynching records, file 27a.

32. Jackson *Clarion-Ledger*, May 13, 1959, Tuskegee lynching records, file 27a.

33. Gulfport *Daily Herald*, May 14, 1959; Picayune *Item*, May 14, 1959.

34. Interview with Mrs. Osborne Moody, Feb. 26, 1979; Jackson *Daily News*, May 13, 1959, Tuskegee lynching records, file 27a.

Chapter 8. *The FBI in Peace and War in Mississippi*

1. Jackson *Clarion-Ledger*, May 7, 1959; Montgomery *Advertiser*, May 7, 1959, Tuskegee lynching records, file 27a.

2. FBI Report, 38; Ryan to Murphy, July 1, 1959, p. 14.

3. Jackson *Clarion-Ledger*, May 10, 1959; Chicago *Defender*, May 16, 1959. The government's response to anti-lynching petitions and letters changed dramatically after the horrible lynching of Claude Neal in 1934.

4. Chicago *Defender*, May 16, 1959; New York *Times*, May 7, 1959.

5. Chicago *Defender*, May 26, 1959; interview with Tony Rhoden, July 24, 1980; interview with Lou Palmer, January 3, 1980. The Walters did not become estranged until after the lynching. When they separated, it was because of post-lynching pressure. Pittsburgh *Courier*, May 30, 1959, Tuskegee lynching records, file 27a.

6. Jackson *Clarion-Ledger*, May 10, 1959.

7. Jackson *Clarion-Ledger*, May 13, 1959, Tuskegee lynching records, file 27a (1); interview with Joshua Morse, Jr., June 21, 1979.

8. Interview with Virginia June (Walters) Pace, Sept. 11, 1980; interview with James H. Walters, Sept. 11, 1980.

9. J. P. Mohr to Clyde Tolson, Nov. 17, 1959; interview with Keith Glatzer, Aug. 27, 1980.

10. Jackson *Clarion-Ledger*, May 19, 1959; Silver, *Mississippi: The Closed Society*, 44.

11. New York *Times*, May 11, 1959; Silver, *Mississippi: The Closed Society*, 44.

12. Interview with Joshua Morse, Jr., June 21, 1979; Ryan to White, July 7, 1959, pp. 10–12, 15; Washington *Post*, May 12, 1959; *Time* 73 (June 1, 1959), 18–19; interview with Eddie Ladner, March 5, 1979. Atlanta *World*, May 13, 1959, Tuskegee lynching records, file 27a. Houston Amacker committed suicide by drinking sulfuric acid the following year.

13. Washington *Post*, May 12, 1959; Gulfport *Daily Herald*, May 11, 1959; Atlanta *World*, May 13, 1959, Tuskegee lynching records, file 27a; FBI Report, 214–22.

14. FBI Report 185–86; Ryan to Murphy, July 1, 1959.

15. FBI Report, 195–214; interview with Joshua Morse, Jr., June 21, 1979.

16. FBI Report, 221–22.

17. Washington *Post*, May 12, 1959; FBI Report, 178–79; Jackson *Clarion-Ledger*, May 17, 1959; Jackson *Daily News*, May 15, 1959, Tuskegee lynching records, file 27a; interview with Eddie Ladner, March 27, 1979; interview with Brad Williams, Aug. 25, 1977.

18. Chicago *Defender*, May 23, 1959; Washington *Post*, May 14, 1959; New Orleans *Times-Picayune*, May 14, 1959; FBI Report, 242–44; Birmingham *News*, May 14, 1959, and Jackson *Daily News*, May 14, 1959, Tuskegee lynching records, file 27a.

19. Washington *Post*, May 17, 1959; FBI Report, 178–79; Rosen to Hoover, Dec. 13, 1959.

20. FBI Report, 180–82.

21. FBI Report, 182–95; Jackson *Clarion-Ledger*, May 19, 1959.

22. Interview with Eddie Ladner, March 5, 1959; Jackson *Clarion-Ledger*, May 13, 1959; interview with Joshua Morse, Jr., June 21, 1979; interview with Bill Minor, June 19, 1979.

23. FBI note no. 44-1018, cover page L1.

24. Interview with Eddie Ladner, March 5, 1979; Jackson *Clarion-Ledger*, May 13, 1959; interview with Alvin Gipson, June 11, 1979; Jackson *Daily News*, May 13, 1959, Tuskegee lynching records, file 27a; interview with Joshua Morse, Jr., June 21, 1979; interview with George Vaught Moody, Feb. 26, 1979; Washington *Post*, May 14, 1959.

25. Jackson *Clarion-Ledger*, May 17, 1959.

26. Ibid.; Chicago *Defender*, May 23, 1959; Jackson *Daily News*, May 13, 15, 1959, Tuskegee lynching records, file 27a; *Life* 46 (June 1, 1959), 24–25; Atlanta *World*, May 14, 1959, and Jacksonville *Times-Union*, May 14, 1959, Tuskegee lynching records, file 27a. Over 2000 pages of FBI records released under the FOIA revealed no such wounding of an agent. Chicago *Defender*, May 23, 1959; Wilkey to Rogers, May 25, 1959; Hoover to Rogers, May 25, 1959.

27. Chicago *Defender*, May 23, 1959; FBI Report, 236–37.

28. Washington *Post*, May 16, 1959; FBI Report, 250–51; Picayune *Item*, May 21, 1959; New Orleans *Times-Picayune*, May 10, 1959; Jackson *Daily News*, May 16, 1959, Tuskegee lynching records, file 27a.

29. Jackson *Clarion-Ledger,* May 14, 15, 16, 17, 1959; New Orleans *Times-Pic-ayune,* May 16, 1959; Washington *Post,* May 17, 1959; Gulfport *Daily Herald,* May 16, 1959.

30. Jackson *Clarion-Ledger,* May 18, 1959; Washington *Post,* May 18, 1959.

31. FBI Report, 195; Picayune *Item,* May 21, 1959.

32. Washington *Post,* May 18, 1959; Gulfport *Daily Herald,* May 18, 1959; Memphis *Commercial Appeal,* May 18, 1959, Tuskegee lynching records, file 27a.

33. New Orleans *Times-Picayune,* May 18, 1959; Washington *Post,* May 18, 1959; Picayune *Item,* May 21, 1959; Jackson *Daily News,* May 18, 1959, Montgomery *Advertiser,* May 18, 1959, Tuskegee lynching records, file 27a.

34. Jackson *Clarion-Ledger,* May 19, 1959; Louisville *Courier-Journal,* May 18, 1959; Jackson *Daily News,* May 18, 1959, Tuskegee lynching records, file 27a.

35. Jackson *Clarion-Ledger,* May 19, 1959; interview with Charles McCracken, Sept. 16, 1977. Reflecting on FBI activity in Poplarville nearly twenty years later, Erle Johnston agreed that agents had in fact harassed some of the men they questioned, but he pointed out a reason why local whites regarded the FBI with such a jaundiced eye. People in Mississippi, he claimed, were "not used to FBI methods, not used to the fact that they could go to jail for lying to the FBI." The FBI worked diligently to explore every angle, he explained, while the people in the highly isolated state of Mississippi even as late as 1959 were used to the "small-town sheriff" who investigated casually with a low-keyed approach that reflected more concern for the next election than for justice. As Johnston characterized it, " 'John, you didn't have nuthin' to do with that crime, did ya?' 'Nope,' responded John. 'Okay, I'll be seein' ya.' " The people, Johnston asserted, were unaccustomed to a law officer who refused to take "nope" for an answer. It frightened and angered them. Interview, July 30, 1979.

36. Jackson *Clarion-Ledger,* May 19, 1959; Jackson *Daily News,* May 18, 1959, Tuskegee lynching records, file 27a.

37. Picayune *Item,* May 21, 1959; interview with Brad Williams, Aug. 25, 1977; interview with Keith Glatzer, Aug. 27, 1980.

38. Jackson *Clarion-Ledger,* May 19, 1959; New York *Times,* May 19, 1959.

39. Jackson *Clarion-Ledger,* May 19, 1959; Gulfport *Daily Herald,* May 18, 19, 1959; Jackson *Daily News,* May 16, 1959; Tuskegee lynching records, file 27a.

40. Jackson *Clarion-Ledger,* May 19, 1959; Gulfport *Daily Herald,* May 17, 18, 19, 1959; Jackson *Daily News,* May 16, 1959. Tuskegee lynching records, file 27a.

41. DeLoach to Tolson, June 1, 1959.

42. Gulfport *Daily Herald,* May 14, 20, 1959; Clyde Tolson to J. Edgar Hoover, May 21, 1959; Jackson *Clarion-Ledger,* May 20, 1959; New York *Times,* May 20, 1959.

43. J. Edgar Hoover to William Rogers, May 21, 1959.

44. Jackson *Clarion-Ledger,* May 20, 1959; New Orleans *Times-Picayune,* May 21, 1959.

45. *Life* 46 (June 1, 1959), 24–25; Rosen to Hoover, June 6, 1959.

46. *Life* 46 (June 1, 1959), 24–25.

47. Gulfport *Daily Herald,* May 20, 1959.

48. J. Edgar Hoover to John A. Hannah, May 22, 1959; Gordon Tiffany to William Colmer, May 20, 1959; Hoover to William Rogers, May 20, 22, 1959; Washington *Post,* May 21, 1959; Jackson *Clarion-Ledger,* May 21, 1959.

According to Smith's brother, Arthur was unable to speak for several weeks afterward and had a long, slow convalescence. The entire Smith family had to chip in to pay the medical expenses. Interview with Cecil Smith, March 9, 1979.

49. Jackson *Clarion-Ledger*, May 19, 1959; Van Landingham to Hoover, May 20, 1959.

50. Hoover to Hannah, May 22, 1959; Gulfport *Daily Herald*, May 21, 23, 1959; New Orleans *Times-Picayune*, May 21, 1959.

51. Washington *Daily News*, May 22, 1959. Of the score of articles on the FBI in Poplarville, the FBI clipped and saved only two for their files—both of which were favorable to the Bureau, and both of which Hoover sent to Rogers and several congressmen.

Chapter 9. Bad News from Bilboville

1. New Orleans *Times-Picayune*, May 18, 1959; Memphis *Commercial Appeal*, May 18, 1959, Tuskegee lynching records, file 27a.

2. New Orleans *Times-Picayune*, May 18, 19, 1959; Chicago *Defender*, May 30, 1959.

3. New Orleans *Times-Picayune*, May 19, 1959.

4. Ibid.; Gulfport *Daily Herald*, May 23, 1959.

5. Jackson *Daily News*, May 19, 1959, clipping in NAACP papers, Group II, Box B-188, LC.

6. New Orleans *Times-Picayune*, May 21, 1959; Gulfport *Daily Herald*, May 21, 1959; Poplarville *Democrat*, May 21, 1959; Montgomery *Journal*, May 21, 1959, Tuskegee lynching records, file 27a.

7. Tolson to Hoover, May 21, 1959; Wilkey to Rogers, May 25, 1959.

8. Interview with Charles McCracken, Sept. 16, 1977; Justice Department draft of criminal indictments (18 U.S.C. Section 242). Justice Department draft of criminal indictments (18 U.S.C. Section 371).

9. Interview with Charles McCracken, Sept. 16, 1977; Justice Department draft of criminal indictments; Ryan to White, July 7, 1959, pp. 10–17.

10. Interview with Charles McCracken, Sept. 16, 1977; interview with Joshua Morse, Jr., June 21, 1979; interview with Mrs. Pat Hyde, Sept. 30, 1979.

11. Interview with Charles McCracken, Sept. 16, 1977; interview with George Vaught Moody, Feb. 26, 1979.

12. Interview with Charles McCracken, Sept. 16, 1977; interview with George Vaught Moody, Feb. 26, 1979.

13. Interview with George Vaught Moody, Feb. 26, 1979; interview with Bill Minor, June 19, 1979; FBI document, Section F, "Local Opposition to FBI Investigation," F-8; Ryan to Murphy, 13–14.

14. Interview with Joshua Morse, Jr., June 21, 1979.

15. Jackson *Clarion-Ledger*, May 21, 1959; Jackson *Daily News*, May 14, 16, 1959; Washington *Post*, May 17, 1959, Tuskegee lynching records, file 27a.

16. Gulfport *Daily Herald*, May 19, 1959; interview with Cliff Sessions, June 12, 1979; Jackson *Clarion-Ledger*, May 21, 22, 1959. In 1926 the guilty man was judged temporarily insane, treated, and released the next year.

17. Interview with Joseph M. F. Ryan, Aug. 21, 1980; Wilkey to Rogers, May 28, 1959.

18. Memphis *Commercial Appeal*, May 22, 1959, Tuskegee lynching records, 27a; Jackson *Clarion-Ledger*, May 22, 23, 1959; Gulfport *Daily Herald*, May 22, 23, 1959.

19. Nathan Straus to J. Edgar Hoover, May 22, 1959; interview with Nathan Straus, Jr., May 12, 1980; New York *Times*, May 23, 1959; New Orleans *Times-Picayune*, May 23, 1959; Rosen to Hoover, May 25, 1959.

20. Jackson *Clarion-Ledger*, May 23, 1959; Washington *Post*, May 23, 1959; Chicago *Defender*, May 30, 1959; New Orleans *Times-Picayune*, May 23, 1959.

21. Washington *Post*, May 23, 1959; New Orleans *Times-Picayune*, May 23, 1959; Chicago *Defender*, May 30, 1959.

22. Jackson *Clarion-Ledger*, May 25, 1959.

23. J. Edgar Hoover to William Rogers, and James C. Hagerty, May 25, 1959; FBI press release, May 25, 1959; FBI interdepartmental memo, May 25, 1959; Hoover to Rogers, May 25, 1959; Ralph Bachman to J. P. Coleman, May 25, 1959.

24. Hoover to Rogers, May 25, 1959; Montgomery *Advertiser*, May 26, 1959, Tuskegee lynching records, file 27a.

25. FBI press release, May 25, 1959; Wilkey to Rogers, May 25, 1959. See Appendix A for the Justice Department's conclusion on federal violations by the lynch mob. Birmingham *News*, May 25, 1959, Tuskegee lynching records, file 27a; interview with A. B. Caldwell, Aug. 15, 1980.

26. Poplarville *Democrat*, May 28, 1959; Picayune *Item*, May 28, 1959, June 4, 1959.

27. Gulfport *Daily Herald*, May 26, 1959.

28. New Orleans *Times-Picayune*, May 26, 1959; J. P. Mohr to Clyde Tolson, Nov. 12, 1959.

29. Jackson *Clarion-Ledger*, May 26, 1959; Picayune *Item*, May 21, 18, 1959; Gulfport *Daily Herald*, May 26, 1959.

30. The FBI Report listed 24 known and suspected participants. Washington *Post*, May 26, 1959; interview with J. B. Richmond, June 21, 1979.

31. Interview with George Vaught Moody, Feb. 26, 1979; interview with Eddie Ladner, Sept. 22, 1978; interview with Mrs. Pat Hyde, Sept. 30, 1979; Jackson *Clarion-Ledger*, May 27, 1959; interview with Richard Angelico, Sept. 26, 1977; Gulfport *Daily Herald*, May 26, 1959; Pittsburgh *Courier*, June 20, 1959, and New Orleans *Weekly*, July 4, 1959, Tuskegee lynching records, file 27a.

32. New Orleans *Times-Picayune*, May 28, 1959, p. 18.

33. Chicago *Tribune*, May 27, 1959; Jackson *Clarion-Ledger*, May 28, 1959; interview with Charles McCracken, Sept. 16, 1977; New Orleans *Times-Picayune*, May 28, 1959; Chicago *Defender*, June 6, 1959; Washington *Post*, May 28, 1959; Gulfport *Daily Herald*, May 27, 1959.

34. Chicago *Defender*, June 6, 1959; New York *Times*, May 26, 1959; New Orleans *Times-Picayune*, May 17, 1959; Wilkins to Coleman, May 26, 1959, NAACP papers, Group III, Box B-80, LC; Wilkins to Paul Douglas, June 17, 1959, NAACP papers, Group III, Box B-80, LC; New York *Times*, May 28, 1959; *The Nation* 188 (June 6, 1959), 20; *The Christian Century* 76 (June 10, 1959), 691; *New Republic* 140 (June 15, 1959), 2; Gerald W. Johnson, "The Superficial Aspect," *New Republic* 140 (June 15, 1959), 14; Gulfport *Daily Herald*, May 26, 1959; Picayune *Item*, May 28, 1959; anonymous telegram to Wil-

liam Rogers, May 25, 1959; anonymous letter to J. Edgar Hoover, n.d. (May 25, 1959).

35. Jackson *Clarion-Ledger*, May 31, 1959.

Chapter 10. No Apologies

1. Washington *Post*, May 27, 1959; Chicago *Defender*, June 13, 27, 1959. Earlier efforts by the NAACP to try large-scale write-in campaigns to secure passage of an anti-lynching bill had failed twice before—in 1922 and 1937. This latest effort proved halfhearted. New York *Times*, May 30, 1959; Pittsburgh *Courier*, Aug. 1, 1959, Tuskegee lynching records, file 27a; Wilkins to Herman Gorodesky, June 4, 1959, NAACP papers, Group III, Box B-80, LC.

2. U.S. Congress, Senate, Subcommittee on Constitutional Rights, Judiciary Committee, *Civil Rights*, Hearings, 87th Congress, 2d Session, May 28, 1959, 1303–4; Jackson *Clarion-Ledger*, May 19, 1959; New York *Times*, May 29, 1959; New Orleans *Times-Picayune*, May 29, 1959; Washington *Post*, May 29, 1959.

3. Gulfport *Daily Herald*, May 28, 29, 1959.

4. Coleman was probably referring to the 1938 Duck Hill lynching. Poplarville *Democrat*, June 4, 1959; Senate hearings, May 28, 1959, 1303–4.

5. Senate hearings, May 28, 1959, 1303–4; Jackson *Clarion-Ledger*, May 29, 1959; New York *Times*, May 29, 1959; Washington *Post*, May 29, 1959; Gulfport *Daily Herald*, May 29, 1959.

6. Senate hearings, May 28, 1959, 1303–4; Jackson *Clarion-Ledger*, May 29, 1959; New York *Times*, May 29, 1959; Washington *Post*, May 29, 1959; Gulfport *Daily Herald*, May 29, 1959.

7. New York *Times*, May 30, 31, 1959. In fact, some members of the mob violated both laws. New Orleans *Times-Picayune*, Nov. 2, 1959.

8. New York *Times*, June 4, 1959; Poplarville *Democrat*, June 11, 1959.

9. Chicago *Defender*, June 6, 1959; Atlanta *World*, June 21, 1959, Tuskegee lynching records, file 27a.

10. Anthony Lewis, *Portrait of a Decade* (New York, 1964), 211; Picayune *Item*, June 11, 1959.

11. Montgomery *Advertiser*, June 22, 1959, and Jackson *News Advocate*, May 23, 1959, Tuskegee lynching records, file 27a; interview with Bill Minor, June 19, 1979.

12. Interview with Ed Jussley, Aug. 27, 1980; interview with Keith Glatzer, Aug. 27, 1980; Huie, "Rape-Lynch," 62.

13. Picayune *Item*, July 2, Aug. 6, 27, 1959; interview with Joshua Morse, Jr., June 21, 1979; Jackson *Daily News*, Oct. 31, 1959, Tuskegee lynching records, file 27a.

14. Montgomery *Advertiser*, June 22, 1959, Tuskegee lynching records, file 27a.

15. J. P. Coleman ran for governor in 1963 and lost to Paul Johnson. Voters judged Coleman too "moderate." Gulfport *Daily Herald*, Oct. 16, 1959, Ja... 16, 1960; interview with Joshua Morse, Jr., June 21, 1979.

16. Jackson *Clarion-Ledger*, Sept. 12, 13, 1959.

17. Jackson *Clarion-Ledger*, Sept. 12, 1959.

18. Washington *Post*, Sept. 13, 1959.

19. Telegram, Roy Wilkins to Vernon Broome, Sept. 11, 1959, NAACP

papers, Group III, Box B-80, LC; *Crisis* 9 (Nov. 1959); Jackson *Clarion-Ledger*, Nov. 1, 1959; Jackson *Daily News*, Oct. 31, 1959, Tuskegee lynching records, file 27a.

20. Gulfport *Daily Herald*, Oct. 31, 1959.

21. Jackson *Clarion-Ledger*, Sept. 13, 1959.

22. New Orleans *Times-Picayune*, Nov. 2, 1959; Montgomery *Advertiser*, Nov. 1, 1959, Tuskegee lynching records, file 27a; Jackson *Clarion-Ledger*, Nov. 2, 1959; Gulfport *Daily Herald*, Oct. 31, 1959.

23. Poplarville *Democrat*, Oct. 29, 1959.

24. Gulfport *Daily Herald*, Nov. 2, 3, 1959; Jackson *Clarion-Ledger*, Nov. 3, 1959.

25. Jackson *Clarion-Ledger*, Nov. 3, 1959; Poplarville *Democrat*, Nov. 5, 1959. For Dale's complete charge to the jury, see Appendix B.

26. Poplarville *Democrat*, Nov. 5, 1959; New Orleans *Times-Picayune*, Nov. 3, 4, 1959; Washington *Post*, Nov. 3, 4, 1959.

27. Lewis, *Portrait of a Decade*, 213; Jackson *Clarion-Ledger*, Nov. 4, 5, 1959; Poplarville *Democrat*, Nov. 5, 1959.

28. Interview with Joshua Morse, Jr., June 21, 1979; interview with Joseph M. F. Ryan, Aug. 21, 1980; Picayune *Item*, Nov. 5, 1959.

29. Picayune *Item*, Nov. 5, 1959.

30. New Orleans *Times-Picayune*, Nov. 6, 1959.

31. *Time* 74 (Nov. 16, 1959), 33; New York *Times*, April 2, 1960.

32. New York *Herald Tribune*, Nov. 6, 1959, Tuskegee lynching records, file 27a; New Orleans *Times-Picayune*, Nov. 6, 1959; criminal complaint and proceedings record for Southern Mississippi Federal District 43, Jan. 1960.

33. John Elliff, "Aspects of Federal Civil Rights Enforcement: The Justice Department and the FBI, 1939–1964," in Donald Fleming and Bernard Bailyn, eds., *Perspectives in American History* (Cambridge, 1971), 603–50; interview with A. B. Caldwell, Aug. 15, 1980.

34. New Orleans *Times-Picayune*, Nov. 6, 7, 1959.

35. New York *Times*, Jan. 4, 1960.

36. Poplarville *Democrat*, Nov. 12, 1959; telegrams, Wilkins to Rogers, Nov. 4, 6, 1959, NAACP papers, Group III, Box B-80, LC; New Orleans *Times-Picayune*, Nov. 6, 1959; New York *Times*, Nov. 8, 1959; Washington *Post*, Nov. 6, 1959.

37. *The Nation* 189 (Nov. 28, 1959), 390; *Time* 74 (Nov. 16, 1959), 33; Greenville *Delta Democrat-Times*, Nov. 7, 1959.

38. Jackson *Clarion-Ledger*, Nov. 6, 1959.

39. New Orleans *Times-Picayune*, Nov. 7, 1959; Gulfport *Daily Herald*, Nov. 5, 1959; Washington *Post*, Nov. 7, 1959, Tuskegee lynching records, file 27a.

40. New Orleans *Times-Picayune*, Nov. 7. 1959; Washington *Post*, April, 1, 27, Sept. 25, 1965; New York *Times*, Nov. 6, 7, 1959; Jackson *Daily News*, Nov. 6, 1959, Tuskegee lynching records, file 27a; Jack Bass and Walter DeVries, *The Transformation of Southern Politics* (New York, 1976), 198–99; Jack Bass, *Unlikely Heroes* (New York, 1981), passim; Charles V. Hamilton, *The Bench and the Ballot* (New York, 1973), 121–22. During the 1960s Mize and Ben Cameron of the Fifth Circuit Court of Appeals would become two of the most obstructionist of all Southern federal judges, having their recalcitrant decisions repeatedly reversed or overruled.

41. New Orleans *Times-Picayune*, Nov. 7, 1959; New York *Times*, Nov. 6, 7, 1959; Jackson *Daily News*, Nov. 6, 1959, Tuskegee lynching records, file 27a.

42. Washington *Post*, Nov. 7, 1959; Talladega *Daily Home*, Nov. 7, 1959, Tuskegee lynching records, file 27a; see Appendix A.

43. Jackson *Clarion-Ledger*, Nov. 8, 1959; New York *Times*, Nov. 8, 1959.

44. Robert Hauberg to Sidney Mize, Nov. 7, 1959; Gulfport *Daily Herald*, Nov. 6, 11, 12, 1959; Jackson *Clarion-Ledger*, Nov. 12, 1959; Washington *Post*, Nov. 12, 1959; New York *Times*, Nov. 12, 1959.

45. Washington *Post*, Nov. 18, 1959; Jackson *Clarion-Ledger*, Nov. 18, 1959; Charleston *News and Courier*, Nov. 18, 1959, Tuskegee lynching records, file 27a.

46. Washington *Post*, Nov. 18, 1959; Chicago *Defender*, Nov. 14, 21, 1959; Ryan to White, July 7, 1959. Twenty years after the lynching, the names of Walker, Preacher and Jeff Lee, and Crip Reyer still came up in conversation about the lynching. Gulfport *Daily Herald*, Nov. 18, 1959; New York *Times*, Nov. 18, 20, 1959.

47. Interview with A. B. Caldwell, Aug. 15, 1980; interview with St. John Barrett, Aug. 19, 1980.

48. Poplarville *Democrat*, Nov. 26, 1959; Chicago *Defender*, Nov. 18, 1959, Dec. 5, 1959; Gulfport *Daily Herald*, Nov. 24, 27, Dec. 30, 1959; New York *Times*, Dec. 7, 31, 1959; New Orleans *Times-Picayune*, Dec. 30, 1959; Picayune *Item*, Dec. 3, 1959; interview with A. B. Caldwell, Aug. 15, 1980.

Chapter 11. The Triumph of Southern Justice

1. Gulfport *Daily Herald*, Jan. 2, 4, 7, 1960; New Orleans *Times-Picayune*, Jan. 3, 1960; interview with Joshua Morse, Jr., June 21, 1979; interview with Eddie Ladner, Sept. 22, 1978; *Newsweek* 55 (Jan. 18, 1960), 23–24; interview with Joseph M. F. Ryan, Aug. 21, 1980.

2. Gulfport *Daily Herald*, Jan. 4, 1960; *Look* 24 (Jan. 2, 1960), 82–83; New York *Times*, Jan. 4, 1960.

3. *Look* 24 (Jan. 2, 1960), 82–83.

4. Jackson *Clarion-Ledger*, Jan. 3, 1960; Poplarville *Democrat*, Jan. 7, 1960.

5. Gulfport *Daily Herald*, Jan. 4, 1969; New Orleans *Times-Picayune*, Jan. 5, 1960.

6. Ibid.

7. New York *Times*, Jan. 4, 5, 1960; New Orleans *Times-Picayune*, Jan. 5, 1960; see Lewis, *Portrait of a Decade*, 211; interview with J. B. Richmond, June 21, 1979.

8. Interview with Bill Minor, June 19, 1979; interview with Joshua Morse, Jr., June 21, 1979; interview with Sam Allman III, June 21, 1979.

9. Jackson *Clarion-Ledger*, Jan. 5, 1960; New York *Times*, Jan. 5, 1960; Gulfport *Daily Herald*, Jan. 5, 1960.

10. Gulfport *Daily Herald*, Jan. 5, 1960; New York *Times*, Jan. 5, 1960; Gulfport *Daily Herald*, Jan. 5, 1960.

11. New York *Times*, Jan. 6, 1960; interview with J. B. Richmond, June 21, 1979.

12. Interview with J. B. Richmond, June 21, 1979; interview with Jewel Alford, Sept. 13, 1978; interview with George Vaught Moody, Feb. 26, 1979; Jackson *Clarion-Ledger*, Jan. 6, 1960.

13. Interview with Joshua Morse, Jr., June 21, 1979; interview with J. B. Richmond, June 21, 1979.

14. Gulfport *Daily Herald*, Jan. 6, 1960.

15. New Orleans *Times-Picayune,* Jan. 7, 8, 1960; Gulfport *Daily Herald,* Jan. 7, 1960; interview with J. B. Richmond, June 21, 1979.

16. According to Joshua Morse, Sebe Dale had a habit of showing up at any gathering in his district at any time. Interview with Joshua Morse, Jr., June 21, 1979; interview with Sam Allman III, June 21, 1979.

17. New Orleans *Times-Picayune,* Jan. 8, 1960.

18. Gulfport *Daily Herald,* Jan. 8, 1960; Jackson *Clarion-Ledger,* Jan. 8, 10, 1960.

19. Interview with J. B. Richmond, June 21, 1979; interview with Sam Allman III, June 21, 1979.

20. Interview with A. B. Caldwell, Aug. 15, 1980; interview with St. John Barrett, Aug. 19, 1980; interview with Joseph M. F. Ryan, Aug. 21, 1980.

21. Ibid.; Interview with Joseph M. F. Ryan, Aug. 21, 1980; interview with John L. Murphy, Aug. 19, 1980; St. John Barrett to Brooks and Kehoe, Dec. 20, 1959, 6–7; Barrett to Ryan, Dec. 30, 1959.

22. Interview with A. B. Caldwell, Aug. 15, 1980.

23. Interview with Cliff Sessions, June 1, 1979; Cliff Sessions maintains that he is still not certain what prompted Stewart to give him the report.

24. New Orleans *Times-Picayune,* Jan. 9, 1960; Jackson *Clarion-Ledger,* Jan. 9, 1960; Washington *Post,* Jan. 9, 1960.

25. Interview with Cliff Sessions, June 1, 1979; interview with Joseph M. F. Ryan, Aug. 21, 1980.

26. Interview with Sam Allman III, June 21, 1979; interview with J. B. Richmond, June 21, 1979.

27. New Orleans *Times-Picayune,* Jan. 9, 1960; Gulfport *Daily Herald,* Jan. 9, 1960.

28. Gulfport *Daily Herald,* Jan. 11, 1960; New Orleans *Times-Picayune,* Jan. 12, 1960.

29. Gulfport *Daily Herald,* Jan. 11, 12, 1960; New Orleans *Times-Picayune,* Jan. 12, 1960; Jackson *Clarion-Ledger,* Jan. 13, 1960.

30. Jackson *Clarion-Ledger,* Jan. 13, 14, 1960; New Orleans *Times-Picayune,* Jan. 13, 14, 1960; Gulfport *Daily Herald,* Jan. 13, 1960.

31. Gulfport *Daily Herald,* Jan. 14, 1960; New Orleans *Times–Picayune,* Jan 15, 1960; Jackson *Clarion-Ledger,* Jan. 15, 1960; Poplarville *Democrat,* Jan. 14, 1960.

32. New York *Times,* Jan. 15, 1960; Chicago *Defender,* Jan. 23, 1960.

33. New Orleans *Times-Picayune,* Jan. 15, 1960; New York *Times,* Jan. 15, 17, 1960.

34. New York *Times,* Feb. 16, 1960; Wilkins to Rogers, Jan. 14, 1960; NAACP press release, Jan. 14, 1960; Patrick Murphy to Wilkins, Jan. 25, 1960; Wilkins to Malin, Jan. 27, 1960; Malin to Rogers, Jan. 25, 1960; all letters contained in NAACP papers, Group III, Box B-327, LC.

35. Poplarville *Democrat,* Jan. 14, 1960; Chicago *Defender,* Jan. 30, 1960; Gulfport *Daily Herald,* Jan. 29, 1960; *Look* 24 (Jan. 2, 1960), 82–83; *Commonweal* 71 (Jan. 15, 1960), 434; Jackson *Clarion-Ledger,* Jan. 13, 19, 21, 27, 1960; New Orleans *Times-Picayune,* Jan. 21, 27, 1960. In the 1955 lynching of Emmett Till in Greenwood, Mississippi, several courageous journalists made the facts in the case known and the town ostracized the guilty men.

36. New York *Times,* April 2, 1960.

Epilogue

1. "M is for Mississippi and Murder," pamphlet, NAACP papers, Group III, Box 190, LC; "Operation Mississippi," pamphlet, NAACP papers, Group III, Box 383, LC.

2. Interview with Richard Angelico, Oct. 3, 1977. Dale quoted in Silver, *Mississippi: The Closed Society*, 8, 240. Bill Minor, who supplied Silver with this famous quotation, claims that Dale said that only two mob members had died. Interview with Bill Minor, June 11, 1979.

3. Interview with Ruth Underwood, Aug. 12, 1980; interview with Ruthamay Sanford, Sept. 1, 1980; interview with Lee Curtis Underwood, Aug. 25, 1980; interview with James H. Walters, Sept. 11, 1980; interview with Virginia June (Walters) Pace, Sept. 11, 1980; interview with Paul Phillips, Sept. 3, 1980.

4. Coleman to author, Aug. 16, 1977; interview with Erle Johnston, July 30, 1978; Silver, *Mississippi: The Closed Society*, 355.

5. "Mississippi Community Data"; Poplarville *Democrat*, Aug. 11, 1977.

6. Interview with Cecil Smith, May 9, 1979; interview with William Posey, Aug. 25, 1977; Jackson *Clarion-Ledger*, Nov. 11, 1959.

7. Interview with Erle Johnston, July 30, 1979.

Bibliography

Archival Sources

A considerable amount of the research material came from the Justice Department through the Freedom of Information Act (FOIA). Some of this material will not be available to the general public for several years, unless specifically requested through the FOIA. The most important single document from the Justice Department was the FBI's final report on the lynching, *The Abduction of Mack Charles Parker from the Pearl River County Jail, Poplarville, Mississippi, April 24–25, 1959* (cited as FBI Report). This comprehensive 370-page report details the FBI's investigation of the lynching. The Civil Rights Division, the Criminal Division, and the Executive Office for United States Attorneys, all within the Justice Department, also furnished information through the FOIA. The Criminal Division supplied FBI correspondence, letters, telegrams, and memos or reports about the lynching. In this study any letter, memo, press release, or report not otherwise identified came from the FOIA material from the Justice Department.

Record Group 60 in the National Archives contains the Justice Department's Criminal Division records through World War II. Within these files are letters, memos, newspaper clippings, and telegrams concerning almost every lynching since 1900. This material proved to be invaluable for developing a thorough background of lynching in twentieth-century America. It was through these records that the Parker lynching first came into consideration. The best known and most complete repository of lynching records is located in the Tuskegee Institute Archives. The Tuskegee lynching records contain press reports on virtually every lynching in America since 1888, when the records came into existence. The newspapers clipped generally were Southern, at least for the

Parker lynching, but provided a wide coverage of press opinion. They proved to be invaluable.

Alabama *Journal*	Jackson *News-Advocate*
Atlanta *Journal*	Jacksonville *Times-Union*
Atlanta *World*	Louisville *Courier-Journal*
Baltimore *Afro-American*	Memphis *Commercial Appeal*
Birmingham *News*	Montgomery *Advertiser*
Birmingham *Post-Herald*	Montgomery *Journal*
Charleston *News and Courier*	New Orleans *Weekly*
Chicago *Crusader*	New York *Herald-Tribune*
Chicago *Tribune*	Pittsburgh *Courier*
Jackson *Daily News*	Talladega *Daily Home*

The NAACP papers at the Library of Congress, Division of Manuscripts, proved to be a disappointing source of information. Perhaps reflecting that organization's lack of involvement in this lynching, the NAACP papers, Group III, have one slender file on the lynching, containing letters to and from Roy Wilkins. The legal files contain a tremendous amount of material on past lynchings and the two federal anti-lynching laws and provided excellent background.

Interviews

On any topic as contemporary as the lynching of Mack Charles Parker, interviews are among the most valuable sources. Although several members of the lynch mob are still living, only two agreed to an interview. Many other citizens of Poplarville and southern Mississippi as well as several of the reporters who covered the lynching agreed to lengthy interviews. The following persons were interviewed:

Jewel Alford, Sept. 13, 1978
Sam Allman III, June 21, 1978
Richard Angelico, Sept. 26, Oct. 3, 1977
Ralph Bachman, June 11, 1979
St. John Barrett, Aug. 19, 1980
R. Jess Brown, Aug. 30, 1977
Donald G. Burkhalter, June 28, 1977
A. B. Caldwell, Aug. 15, 25, 1980
Will D. Campbell, June 18, 1978
Elliott Chaize, Aug. 26, 1980
John Elliff, Aug. 19, 1980
Alvin Gipson, June 11, 1979
Keith Glatzer, Aug. 27, 1980
Lawrence Halladay, Aug. 25, 1977
Robert Hauberg, Aug. 20, 1980
Sam Hopkins, Aug. 25, 1977
Mrs. J. M. Howard, Aug. 25, 26, 1977
Maceo Hubbard, July 27, Aug. 12, 1980
Mrs. Pat Hyde, Sept. 30, 1979
Erle Johnston, July 30, 1979
Ed Jussley, Aug. 27, 1980

Eddie Ladner, Sept. 21, 22, 1978, March 1, 5, 27, 1979
Charles McCracken, Sept. 15, 16, 1977
Bill Minor, June 19, 1979
George Vaught Moody, Feb. 26, 1979
Mrs. Osborne Moody, Feb. 26, 1979
Joshua Morse, Jr., June 21, 1979
John L. Murphy, Aug. 19, 1980
Regal Napier, April 17, 1981
Virginia June (Walters) Pace, Sept. 11, 1980
Lou Palmer, January 3, 1980
Paul Phillips, Sept. 3, 1980
William M. Posey, Aug. 25, 1977
Henry Putzell, Aug. 18, 1980
George Rester, Jr., Feb. 27, 1979
Tony Rhoden, July 24, 1980
J. B. Richmond, June 21, 1979
Joseph M. F. Ryan, Aug. 21, 1980
Liz Sandlin, Dec. 2, 1979
Ruthamay Sanford, Sept. 1, 1980

Cliff Sessions, June 12, 1979
Dimple (Burge) Shill, Nov. 25, 1979
Claude Sitten, June 19, 1979
Arthur L. Smith, Feb. 26, 1979
Cecil Smith, March 9, 1979
Nathan Straus, Jr., May 12, 1980
Jimmy Swann, Sept. 2, 1980

Lee Curtis Underwood, Aug. 25, 1980
Ruth Underwood, Aug. 12, 1980
Edward William Walters, Sept. 11, 1980
James H. Walters, Sept. 11, 1980
Malcolm R. Wilkey, Aug. 22, 1980
Brad Williams, Aug. 25, 1977

Newspapers

Chicago *Defender*
Greenville *Delta Democrat-Times*
Gulfport *Daily Herald*
Jackson *Clarion-Ledger*
Jackson *State-Times*
Los Angeles *Times*
Memphis *Commercial Appeal*
New Orleans *Times-Picayune*

New York *Times*
Picayune *Item*
Poplarville *Democrat*
St. Louis *Post-Dispatch*
Washington *Daily News*
Washington *Post*
Washington *Star*

News Magazines and Other Periodicals

Christian Century, The, 1959
Commonweal, 1959–60
Crisis, 1959–61
Down South, 1959
Gallery, 1960
Life, 1959

Look, 1960
Nation, The, 1959
New Republic, 1959
New South, 1951–55
Newsweek, 1960
Time, 1959

Books and Pamphlets

Ames, Jessie Daniel. "The Changing Character of Lynching" (Atlanta, 1942).

Baker, Ray Stannard. *Following the Color Line* (New York, 1973).

Bass, Jack. *Unlikely Heroes* (New York, 1981).

Bass, Jack, and Walter DeVries. *The Transformation of Southern Politics* (New York, 1976).

Brown, Richard Maxwell. *Strain of Violence* (New York, 1975).

Carter, Hodding, III. *The South Strikes Back* (New York, 1959).

Cash, Wilbur J. *The Mind of the South* (New York, 1941).

Chadburn, James H. *Lynching and the Law* (Chapel Hill, 1933).

Cutler, James. *Lynch-Law* (New York, 1905).

Dinnerstein, Leonard. *The Leo Frank Case* (New York, 1968).

Hamilton, Charles V. *The Bench and the Ballot* (New York, 1973).

Hofstadter, Richard, and Michael Wallace. *American Violence: A Documentary History* (New York, 1970).

Johnson, Charles S. *Growing Up in the Black Belt: Negro Youth in the Rural South* (New York, 1941).

Key, V. O., Jr. *Southern Politics in State and Nation* (New York, 1949).

Lewinson, Paul. *Race, Class and Party* (New York, 1932).

Lewis, Anthony. *Portrait of a Decade* (New York, 1964).

Lord, Walter H. *The Past That Would Not Die* (New York, 1965).

Lowen, James W., and Charles Sallis, eds. *Mississippi: Conflict and Change* (New York, 1974).

Mars, Florence. *Witness in Philadelphia* (Baton Rouge, 1977).

McGovern, James R. *Anatomy of a Lynching: The Killing of Claude Neal* (Baton Rouge, 1982).

Pierce, Neal R. *The Southern States of America* (New York, 1972).

Quarles, Benjamin. *The Negro in the Making of America* (New York, 1964).

Raper, Arthur. *The Tragedy of Lynching* (New York, 1933).

Robertson, William J. *The Changing South* (New York, 1927).

Silver, James W. *Mississippi: The Closed Society* (New York, 1966).

Southern Commission on the Study of Lynching. "Lynchings and What They Mean" (Atlanta, 1932).

Tannenbaum, Frank. *Darker Phases of the South* (New York, 1924).

Tindall, George B. *The Emergence of the New South* (Baton Rouge, 1967).

Wells-Barnett, Ida B. *On Lynchings* (New York, 1969).

White, Walter F. *Rope and Faggot* (New York, 1929).

Williams, Daniel T. "The Lynching Records at Tuskegee." In Daniel Williams, ed., *Eight Negro Bibliographies* (New York, 1970).

Zangrando, Robert L. *The NAACP Crusade Against Lynching, 1909–1950* (Philadelphia, 1980).

Articles

Elliff, John T. "Aspects of Federal Civil Rights Enforcement: The Justice Department and the FBI, 1939–1964." In Donald Fleming and Bernard Bailyn, eds., *Perspectives in American History* (Cambridge, Mass., 1971).

Fleming, Harold C. "The Till Case." *New South* 10 (Sept. 1955).

Fortenberry, Charles V., and F. Glenn Abney. "Mississippi: Unreconstructed and Unredeemed." In William C. Havard, ed., *The Changing Politics of the South* (Baton Rouge, 1972).

Hackney, Sheldon. "Southern Violence." In Hugh Davis Graham and Ted Robert Gurr, eds., *The History of Violence in America* (New York, 1969).

Huie, William Bradford. "Rape-Lynch That Shocked America," *Cavalier* 10 (May 1960).

Webb, Walter Prescott. "Afterword." In Walter Van Tilburg Clark, *The Ox-Bow Incident* (New York, 1960).

Young, Earle F. "The Relation of Lynching to the Size of Political Area." *Sociology and Social Research* 7 (March-April 1928).

Congressional Hearings

U. S. Congress, House, Subcommittee number 5, Judiciary Committee, *Civil Rights,* Hearings, 87th Congress, 2d Session, April 23, 1959.

U. S. Congress, Senate, Subcommittee on Constitutional Rights, Judiciary Committee, *Civil Rights,* Hearings, 87th Congress, 2d Session, May 28, 1959.

Census-Related Material

"Mississippi Community Data," furnished by Congressman Trent Lott to constituents.

"Mississippi County Business Patterns: Pearl River County," furnished by
Congressman Trent Lott to constituents.

U. S. Bureau of the Census, *1960 Census of Population, Mississippi: General Social
and Economic Characteristics.*

U. S. Bureau of the Census, *1970 Census of Population, Mississippi: Number of
Inhabitants.*

Dissertations

Abney, F. Glenn. "The Mississippi Voter: A Study of Voting Behavior in a
One-Party Multifactional System" (Ph.D. dissertation, Tulane University,
1968).

Grant, Donald L. "The Development of the Anti-Lynching Reform Movement
in the United States, 1883–1932" (Ph.D. dissertation, University of Missouri,
Columbia, 1972).

Index